To Bru~
for the earth

Jim Wallman

WHY WE GARDEN

WHY WE GARDEN

Cultivating a Sense of Place

Jim Nollman

A JOHN MACRAE BOOK

Henry Holt and Company
New York

To the Seventh Generation

Henry Holt and Company, Inc.
Publishers since 1866
115 West 18th Street
New York, New York 10011

Henry Holt® is a registered
trademark of Henry Holt and Company, Inc.

Published in Canada by Fitzhenry & Whiteside Ltd.,
195 Allstate Parkway, Markham, Ontario L3R 4T8.

Library of Congress Cataloging-in-Publication Data
Nollman, Jim.
Why we garden: cultivating a sense of place/Jim Nollman.
—1st ed.
p.   cm.
"A John Macrae book."
Includes bibliographical references and index.
1. Gardening—Philosophy.   I. Title.
SB454.3.P45N64   1994   93-41563
635—dc20   CIP

ISBN 0-8050-2719-X
ISBN 0-8050-4561-9 (An Owl Book: pbk.)

Henry Holt books are available for special promotions
and premiums. For details contact: Director, Special Markets.

First published in hardcover in 1994 by
Henry Holt and Company, Inc.

First Owl Book Edition—1996

Designed by Betty Lew

Printed in the United States of America
All first editions are printed on acid-free paper.∞

1   3   5   7   9   10   8   6   4   2
1   3   5   7   9   10   8   6   4   2   (pbk.)

Contents

Introduction: The Local Garden

People often turn to gardening to re-create a bit of paradise within an imperfect world. The gardener's vision of paradise is both simple and organic. It offers none of the fantastic cities, techno-gadgetry, and whimsical social plans articulated by so many Utopian idealists, futurists, and science-fiction writers throughout history. The reasons are obvious. Gardens are real places. They exist right now. They have little to do with historical notions of progress. Gardens are usually the creation of a single individual and rarely correspond to a grand social blueprint.

Nor does the gardener's vision of paradise necessarily promise much in the way of a larger-than-life hedonism. Gardening is hard work; it doesn't make life any easier, although it often makes it more fulfilling. An individual seeking the gardener's brand of paradise has to knuckle under to some very strict *natural* rules. Buck these rules, and be assured of failing miserably.

Unlike other visions of paradise, which look to the future, gardening is already a well-established institution. A National Gardening Association poll tells us there are at least seventy million gardens in the United States alone. That same poll concludes that a significant percentage of the people who garden value their avocation as the most creative act in their lives. That may explain why gardens flourish just about everywhere we look—why the people who garden believe they are immersed in something downright inspiring rather than merely worthwhile.

A garden is the place millions of people go to touch the earth, to smell flowers—to use some of that fabled human brainpower in the cause of better participating with natural processes in the place they call home. It serves as an art project, an organic produce market, a spiritual practice, a pharmacy. It offers ongoing lessons in ecology, biology, chemistry, geology, meteorology. Gardening imparts an organic perspective on the passage of time. It bestows on its practitioners a genuine sense of admiration for the plants, the soil, the sun, the water.

In its organic form, gardening makes a powerful social and economic statement. It offers, perhaps, *the* basic tool for those hoping to wean themselves from an overly consumptive lifestyle. Growing our own food weakens the cord that binds us to the centralized food distribution system with its unsustainable reliance on fossil fuels, chemical additives, excessive packaging, and unwelcome advertising. Homegrown food is less expensive. And much fresher, which potentially annuls our need to participate in the food supplement business. Organic gardening also annuls our complicit collaboration with the herbicide and pesticide industry and the havoc its products wreak upon the environment and upon human health. Even the fitness industry is affected. Gardens provide us with exercise in the cause of feeding ourselves.

Gardening encourages a hands-on complicity with local nature. I call the perceptions that inform this participation *a sense of place*. Unfortunately, like certain other ideas basic to human life—for instance, love, home, and even living—the concrete meaning of *a sense of place* is only dimly present in our consciousness and can be difficult to articulate plainly. How much easier to define it poetically as the perception of the human soul singing with nature. Or politically, as the measure of our stewardship of the land. Let us value it spiritually as a sacred link connecting home life to planet. Or let us know it educationally as the process of shifting our awareness of natural processes to the very center of our lives.

If these shades of meaning hint that the word *place* is here used as a neologism, the new meaning is hardly my own. Over the past few years, *place* has emerged—especially within the ecology movement—to stand as much for a *relationship* to the land as for the land itself. It reflects an ecological longing by people everywhere to recognize themselves as an integral component of the ecosystem they happen to inhabit. Notice that in every one of these new shades of meaning, *place* suggests an intense participation with the local. We might couch this new meaning in the form of a question. Unless we figure out how to heal the Earth from the place we already live, is there any real hope of healing it anywhere else?

The idea of a *sense* of place also begs clarification. Is this a sense like smelling, seeing, hearing? For instance, is it asking gardeners to revitalize the old technique of tasting the soil to measure acidity? A sense of place develops as we hone our five senses to participate more fully with the relationship called *place*. The fact that we *develop* this sense implies that we are not born with it. A sense of place evolves as we live, experience, grow, touch and perhaps taste soil, learn to predict weather, garden. It begins to evolve only after a person starts to perceive himself or herself participating—in a positive manner—with the natural processes of place.

The ideas referred to by the phrase *a sense of place* might also seem to be served by a synonymous phrase: *an attitude of place*. But whereas an attitude is a thought process—an offspring of the human brain—a sense emanates from every part of the body. In other words, a sense of place includes attitudes. And perceptions. And a touch of spirituality: a sensitivity to dreams, perceptions, and visions. And gut feelings—like the gut feeling that is currently prompting so many of us to put down roots as the best hope of ever achieving an ecological lifestyle.

A sense of place also provides an ethic. It signifies a respectful, cooperative, and occasionally compliant relationship with the landscape we inhabit. In this regard, a sense of place has recently emerged as a favorite subject of nature writers; the best known among them are Barry Lopez, Annie Dillard, Wendell Berry, and Gary Snyder. Each of these writers urges us, in one way or another, to consider *a sense of place* as a discipline—a lifestyle discipline—that teaches people to become ecologically literate. Some writers go so far as to promote this discipline as our best hope for ever solving the environmental crisis. It instructs us in how to reconnect with nature for the benefit of nature.

Who could deny that there is a great need for reconnecting? I myself have written elsewhere that "the environmental crisis is largely a crisis in perception":[1] what philosopher Thomas Berry calls "not simply the physical loss of resources in an economic sense. It is even more devastating to us inwardly than it is to the planet outwardly."[2] We can legislate environmental strictures forever, but until each one of us learns to reperceive and then restructure our own personal relationship to the environment, nothing much is going to change. Given that very personal assessment of it, redefining a personal relationship to place suddenly takes on a new and urgent meaning.

This book takes the position that gardening probably offers us a clearer pathway for acquiring a sense of place than any other activity in our lives. The garden is already the place where many of our cultural attitudes and personal perceptions about nature are forged. But the connection between the garden and a sense of place is hardly unambiguous. Almost none of the nature writers who rave on so much about a sense of place also promote gardening as a primary path leading to it. For some reason, the two paths do not easily merge.

There's a good reason. Merging the paths involves far more than simply giving a few tweaks to contemporary horticultural principles. Before gardening is able to serve the environmental exigencies of our time, our perceptions about this most popular avocation must first undergo some serious remolding. Consider, as just one example, the contemporary jargon of horticulture that treats plants as *elements*, soil as a *medium*, and the underlying strategy of gardening as the essential *control* of nature for aesthetic reasons. If gardening ever hopes to merge with a sense of place, it cannot continue to suffer such domineering language. Although some writers, especially garden writers, tend to extol gardeners as if they are ecologically aware by default, it simply isn't so. Developing a sense of place is hardly the inevitable outcome of getting one's hands dirty in planting soil.

Language affects perception. The above example indicates that merging the two paths starts with an overhaul of the standard language of gardening. That is the primary reason this book excises terms that promote domination and replaces them with more participatory terms that treat plants as living things (even living beings), soil as an ally, and the garden as a guide and a mentor aiding us in our struggle to reconnect with the Earth at the place we live.

Adopting a language of participation would seem to enhance one of the most sublime of gardening experiences: a sense that the garden itself is acting directly upon the mind and soul of the person gardening. Although this experience of gardening is not rare, discussing it in detail actually inverts the common fare of gardening books that set out to demonstrate the myriad ways *a gardener can act upon a garden*. This book prefers to stand that relationship on its head by imbuing gardens with a life and a purpose all their own.

Let's start right here at the beginning, by redefining gardening, not as control, but as nurturing—a nurturing participation with the natural processes of place. However, gardening is not an ideological pursuit. This revised definition is not proposed as an across-the-board refutation of contemporary gardening practices. Most gardeners already nurture their gardens in one way or another. This revision simply grants to nurturing a defining emphasis.

Nurturing brings to bear a different set of relationships to place than does control. Plants become collaborators. They are near to becoming neighbors. Gardeners can no longer force-feed them to grow, can no longer rip them out of the ground without a second thought, just to achieve some preordained plan. The word *prosper* takes on a new meaning. Nature is no longer regarded as the enemy to be held at bay, and therefore the nurtured garden cannot prosper apart from its effect upon the greater environment. Nurturing a sense of participation with nature through the garden expands the context of our attention—our watering, our planting, our harvesting, our enriching—beyond the garden wall, now to include the ecosystem we inhabit, our sense of community, and even the Earth itself. All these relationships insist that the garden is no longer merely the physical space where we grow big carrots and healthy rhododendrons. It is rather a process of which gardeners are the initiating aspect. Nurturance is the foundation of this exercise.

Perhaps surprisingly, in my research for this book I have consulted many gardening, landscaping, and environmental texts, and yet I have not found even one that tackles, as its central theme, the ecological and spiritual link that exists between gardening and a sense of place. I have found, however, a few books that focus on something closely related to this: the clear pattern that connects the microcosm of the garden to the macrocosm of nature. Michael Pollan's book *Second Nature* may come closest to developing this theme in its beautifully articulated description of the garden as the middle ground between human culture and wilderness.

Pollan argues that true wilderness is a place apart from human beings, a place that can only exist independent of all human management. In fact, there is probably no area left within the contiguous United States that fits this definition. But if wilderness has disappeared, if it is instead what writer Jack Turner calls "a problem to be solved by further human intervention . . . a relic,"[3] what advantage can there possibly be in arguing to either protect or steward that which no longer exists?

So long as we refer to the relic as if it were a real place, instead of a myth of a place, we obfuscate the crucial issues regarding the proper human relationship to that place so designated. Environmental organizations and nature writers often stand most guilty of championing this romantic view of wilderness.

For their own part, the land managers and commercial interests who sit on the opposite side of the debate table from the environmentalists too often end up defining wilderness as nothing more than a plot of real estate to be governed, supervised, and exploited. They seek to neutralize the emotions that the other side dredges up to defend this geographical entity by championing quantification, as if statistics were the ultimate arbiter of conflict. They end up relying heavily on a legal language that is largely based on categorizing the terms of ownership while it snubs other, more perceptual, subjective (but very real) relationships to the land. For instance, they too easily refute the intangible concept of the sacred in nature.

With each side caught up in a perceptual web of its own making, the ongoing debate often ends in conflict. But how could it be different while both the defenders and the exploiters choose to live in denial? Both sides are arguing for a lost dream.

Michael Pollan's thesis is political, social, and horticultural. He argues that the relationship between gardener and garden offers an important new model both for the nature lovers seeking to protect wilderness as well as for the administrators who must come up with ways to manage those places. In his own words:

> Gardens . . . teach the necessary if un-American lesson that nature and culture can be compromised, that there might be some middle ground between the lawn and the forest—between those who would complete the conquest of the planet in the name of progress, and those who believe it's time we abdicated our rule and left the earth in the care of more innocent species. The garden suggests there might be a place where we can meet nature halfway.[4]

Gardeners' decisions fuse ecological and pragmatic considerations with cultural, aesthetic, economic, and ethical considerations. Gardeners must deal with balancing the inherent qualities of land with human use. And a gardener's relationship to land and biota is based on nurturing. It is artful. And fulfilling. We might well ask how the land managers' view of their own job would be transformed if they started to regard themselves as gardeners and treated the various wild areas as gardens. Or how the backpacking public might change their own view if they started to perceive wilderness as a wild garden—if they learned to treat their manicured backcountry trails as garden paths.

The pattern that connects our perceptions about nature to our perceptions about gardening is one of the major themes of this book.

An enhanced sense of the garden as the creative seat of place has other political ramifications as well. It offers a basis for the *restructuring* of the environmental debate. As the problems about the appropriate uses of a place get knottier to solve, they tend to get played out at the top, centralized levels of government. As any local problem rises up the hierarchal ladder, the decision-making process becomes increasingly less personal. Faraway decision makers routinely restructure local needs and local processes into a generic, objective mold of rules, regulations, and definitions. It sometimes seems the only way that governance is even possible.

At the local level, many of us start to believe that our largest problems are somebody else's job to solve. And at the federal level, political leaders too often have no personal experience of the places they govern. The undeniable fact that so many of these applied policies corrupt the ecosystem they set out to fix implies that the faraway governance of land is not working. How could it? It is a government devoid of a sense of place.

A growing political movement called *bioregionalism* is founded on the premise that central governance is an oxymoron. Bioregionalists would have us reverse all prevailing trends for centralization and point them back toward their local roots. Social visionary Peter Berg has written that a bioregion "refers both to geographical terrain and a terrain of consciousness—to a place and to the ideas that have developed about how to live in that place. Within a bioregion the conditions that influence life are similar and these in turn have influenced human occupancy."[5]

Bioregionalism promotes a general migration of our current political, environmental, cultural context away from the centralized, the monolithic, the faraway, the territorially arbitrary; and toward an ecosystems context for governance and culture.

Despite what some bioregionalists assert, not every local decision is inherently more enlightened (or just plain better) than every centralized policy. What we can be sure of is that no person can react responsibly to processes or places he or she doesn't understand. Even worse is a local person dealing with local issues he or she doesn't understand. Without a sense of place, local decision making can be a most dangerous proposition. There is an example of this in the chapter called "The Political Garden." In general, nurturance, knowledge, and experience are essential preconditions for any understanding of local conditions.

As much as any other activity in our lives, gardening nurtures the link between personal lifestyle and ecology. In fact, local gardeners are often our unacknowledged experts of place. They bring many practical ideas and much commonsense wisdom to the greater task of learning to live within a place. The most successful gardens, the healthiest gardens, are those that work best with the local constraints of topography, weather, and siting. When gardeners fail to participate mindfully with place, the garden simply doesn't work. Gardening also offers opportunities for a local economy based on barter, leading to what bioregionalist Kirkpatrick Sale calls "a moral sense that the bounty of the people is to be shared by all the people and its personal possession or accumulation unthinkable, that the health of the community is measured by the health and happiness of each one therein."[6]

Perhaps ironically, national environmental organizations rarely honor the local any more than national governments or national corporations do. They tend to adopt the same game plan, corporate format, and lobbying techniques as the exploiters—oftentimes just to get to sit at the same table with them. Although their objective is to diminish corporate and governmental exploitation, in the process of doing so, they also become skillful players in that same centralized contest of wills. Policies get set and lobbied from a distance. Issues affecting real people quickly turn abstract. Because neither side has any long-term stake in the neighborhood or the land involved, victories are gained through the depersonalized conflict of court battles rather than through collaboration or conciliation with the parties directly involved. One result is that the large environmental organizations have become far more savvy at *forcing* change from the outside rather than *nurturing* change from within. That is the reason wilderness advocates so often seem to represent victories *against* rather than *for* things. In this case, the medium may not be the entire message, but it is certainly an aspect of it.

What the environmental community may lack most is an ability to engage people in their daily lives in a positive, creative, and joyful manner. Developing some form of environmental aesthetics could conceivably help matters. Traditionally, art was never separate from life. It was created locally to connect individuals with a sense of the sacred within their own local environment and to help entire societies better comprehend their place within the universe. These ideas are still with us, although we don't always think of them as artistic or sacred. For example, the photograph of the whole Earth taken from the moon has done more to instill a personal sense of living on a fragile Earth than perhaps any environmental platform or law could ever accomplish.

Gardening is probably our culture's foremost expression of an aesthetics of place: an activity that already connects artfulness to a direct experience of nature. However, permit one caveat before I proceed. My intent here is not to endorse gardening as an alternative to environmental activism. The planet cannot afford any such luxury. In a larger sense, any single-factor solution proposed to meet the complex challenges we face is usually simplistic and always risky. This advocacy for the creative garden is forwarded, instead, as a parallel development, one that involves a personal commitment to an ecological lifestyle. Gardening is a unique tool that can turn environmental education artful, sacred, and fun. More on this in "The Creative Garden."

That so many gardening books overlook the link between place, art, and environmental literacy seems a consequence of a contemporary gardening philosophy held captive by its aristocratic English roots. The traditional European garden was the exuberant outcome of a credo founded upon the control of nature by humans for aesthetic reasons. Our own culture's flamboyant use of pesticides and chemical fertilizers bears testimony to the fact that many gardeners obviously agree with this credo. I, for one, am part of a growing minority who disagree. I rarely feel like a despot, but often like a nurturing parent and occasionally like a love slave. I believe that the greatest gift of gardening is the control of humans by nature. I have bumbled along in my garden for several years now, slowly developing a general aesthetic that *does* take the leap to a gardening lifestyle that suggests a place we can meet nature halfway. As both "The One-Tree Garden" and "The Nowhere Garden" will soon reveal, I often favor Utopian solutions to my gardening problems. Besides that single indomitable trait, my sense of gardening is not that different from anyone else's. Grounding is grounding, no matter how we clothe it. I learned long ago that plants thrive only when we employ certain obstinate principles in tending them.

Like any other gardener, I often find myself looking longingly over my shoulder at the immense legacy of traditional English (and occasionally Japanese) aristocratic gardening practice. I stand with bowed head and heap on praise for the wonderful aesthetic sensibilities exposed. I honor them as the primer of my own gardening techniques, even as I spurn their message of control. One result of this conflict between legacy and vision is that my sense of aesthetics is not always completely satisfied by the ethical or ecological choices my ideals prefer. I sometimes resolve this dilemma by seeking a mythical solution: devising responses that tell a good story while they teach a good artful lesson about life. The chapter entitled "The How-To Garden" analyzes this struggle and this solution in greater detail.

I doubt that the maven of Victorian gardens, Gertrude Jekyll, would find very much that is outlandish or unsettling about my garden. She would understand immediately that, philosophizing aside, all gardens that flourish do so because we appreciate them deeply and bend to them incessantly. She might pause a moment to wonder why anyone would delegate such a vast amount of garden real estate (and for that matter, book real estate) to concepts like "The Weed Garden" and "The Semi-Real Garden"—not to mention all this talk about environmental gamesmanship—in a book purporting to confront a new garden aesthetic. Then again, building her famous gardens as she did during the turn of the twentieth century, she might scratch her head in utter bewilderment over any book of nonfiction written a hundred years hence describing a world so egregiously altered by the forces of human desire.

As far as choosing control or nurturance, Gertrude Jekyll's more outspoken contemporary, William Robinson, often railed against the Victorian predilection for tender bedding plants grown to perfection in humid greenhouses and then laid out to present clever color designs best viewed from a distant balcony. He has been my teacher in this regard. If he and I differ, it is because he promoted the bizarre English landscaping principle of exerting intense control over land and plants to achieve a formal effect best described as wild abandon. In hindsight, it seems that he molded the aristocratic foibles of his day onto a relation with the land.

It was Gertrude Jekyll and William Robinson, along with their disciples and admirers, who invented the contemporary gardener's relationship to place. This view has evolved over time, and today much of it is very different from the original gardening aesthetic the two of them refined a hundred years ago. Yet in its generalities, it is still the overwhelming view of gardening excellence. What most gardeners don't quite realize is that it is a view at all and not some universal precondition for gardening success. It is, of course, a well-entrenched view. In fact, a few of the recently published books that I read to find out if anybody had ever come up with a modern definition of gardening defined the garden in essentially Victorian terms: the control of nature by human beings for aesthetic reasons.[7]

It is no surprise to learn that gardening conventions do their best in the climates in which they originated. For instance, Great Britain has a wet, mild, temperate climate, which presents ideal conditions for cultivating a green lawn and borders overflowing with voluptuous flowers. Although most of us live in a very different climate, we continue to lavish the lion's share of our gardening attention on the pursuit of the English border—and on a lawn that doesn't necessarily survive on its own where we live without undue amounts of specialized watering, artificial fertilizers, and pesticides. But because our predominant gardening definition still stresses control over nature, it makes little difference to us *how* we garden as long as the finished picture meets the original English expectation.

The English sense of place has been so completely adopted by American gardeners—although rarely with the same lavishness and attentiveness of the English original—that some American gardening writers bemoan the lack of a distinctive *American* style of gardening. But wishing to codify an American style that fits both Minneapolis and Tucson actually suggests a monumental ignorance of place conjoined to a misguided longing for centralization on the part of writers, rather than any lack of wisdom by American gardeners. Ironically, the very idea of "national style" seems to endorse the British aesthetic premise. Great Britain is predominantly all of one mild, wet climate, whereas Americans inhabit many distinctive ecosystems.

The local garden seeks nothing else but a style based on a sense of place. Sometimes it proposes that the best style is no style at all. For instance, my own small plot of land offers so many microclimates diverse in soil, incline, sun, and temperature that I shall never discover a uniform style.

If gardening books have come up short in describing the garden as a breeding ground for a sense of place, then the explosion of books, studies, and proposals about fixing the environment—governmental and otherwise—also neglects the potential role of gardening in helping to forge an ecological society. Although some of this lack may be due to the contemporary gardener's objective of controlling nature, much more of it is due to general attitudes about environmental healing. Environmental leaders and their organizations are enmeshed in the business of crisis management, which causes the work of the environment to be overwhelmingly defined in terms of solving urgent but short-term problems. That is how the general public views the work, how environmental groups focus their own projects, and where governmental money is mostly spent. To redefine gardening by giving it an ecological jump start, and then to present this innovative version of it as a crucial aspect of some all-encompassing perceptual solution to the environmental crisis, seems much too obscure.

That may be one reason we sometimes hear environmentalists and legislators declaring that the job of instilling ecological perceptions about place and about the home should be the domain of the educational system. But it doesn't quite work out that way. At best, the schools categorize the garden as one of the homely arts. In suburban school districts, girls (and never boys) may spend a few weeks each spring learning how to plant seeds in Home Ec. In rural areas both sexes have the opportunity to join 4-H after school to learn more about monoculture, animal husbandry, and other basic farming skills. Either way, gardening is rarely promoted as a means for helping people understand local ecology. The chapter entitled "The Soil Garden" has much more to say about this. For the moment, realize that the poll taken by the National Gardening Association is nowhere heeded as the grounds for a change in educational policy. If it were, art classes, science classes, environment classes—all would teach gardening for what it is: one of our culture's most highly developed processes for learning local ecology.

But we get none of that. Nor do our churches seem very interested in resurrecting the deep and ancient well of religious ceremony that connects gardening to the enrichment of the soul. Yet the ritual observance of planting and the harvest resides at the roots of all Western religions. Churches and synagogues no longer know how to articulate the deep connection between the gardener's pulse and the pulse of the Earth. Why don't we hear sermons about gardening as the attempt to re-create a lost Eden in our own backyard? The long answer is unraveled in the chapter called "The Sacred Garden." The short answer is as follows: Like a tree, Western spirituality germinated by sending out roots to hold the soil. It broke ground and flung its branches high into the sky. But unlike a tree, Western spirituality eventually cut its own roots and kept floating upward. For the past few thousand years our spiritual center has resided in a place called heaven, while Earth was largely regarded as the prison from which our spirituality needed to escape if it was ever to find eternal salvation. Our spiritual center has not yet returned to Earth, although there are many murmurs indicating that reentry may soon be under way.

The garden offers us a glimpse of a new definition of the sacred that embraces the individual, the community, and the Earth as aspects of the same unifying spirit. This is an ancient connection, and it is still honored in traditional cultures. In her book *Refuge*, Terry Tempest Williams quotes a conversation with a woman from Kenya:

> My people believe if you are close to the Earth, you are close to people. . . . What an African woman nurtures in the soil will eventually feed her family. Likewise what she nurtures in her relations will ultimately nurture her community. It is a matter of living the circle. . . . Because we have forgotten our kinship with the land, our kinship with each other has become pale.[8]

We live in a culture that does not acknowledge gardening as an educational and spiritual opportunity linking history, art, science, religion, and community to the

Earth. Given that reality, how can we expect educators and parents to teach a connection that artists, scientists, and religious and environmental leaders don't encourage?

We are a culture grown distrustful of building our future on the ideals that shape our dreams. That same belittled confidence in the ideal upholds the social climate that prompted so many Utopians in the past to proclaim a bit too shrilly that their own brand of transformation held the answer to all the problems of the age. I prefer to remain modest about it. A sense of place—both as a concept and as a book subtitle—holds one key to a door with many locks. It furnishes one easy-to-use tool to help us construct the greater framework of our environmental destiny. *Why We Garden* tries to provide a whole-brained approach to bolster up our declining relationship to nature. The imposing number of gardeners in the world causes this writer to remain optimistic about the outcome.

Each chapter of this book is introduced by a short vignette that follows the almanac style of commenting on gardeners' concerns for each month of the year. And though each of the long chapters focuses on one type of garden, these are not your ordinary backyard gardens. There's no vegetable garden, no flower garden, no apple orchard. Instead, there are metaphorical gardens: gardens defined in terms of attitudes, perceptions, hopes, desires, and even bald-faced biases born from the dreams that arise when we become preoccupied by this grand process. That would explain why some of the gardens described herein sound rather like the transcendentalism of Luther Burbank filtered through the surrealism of Salvador Dalí. There's the local garden, the nowhere garden, the sentient garden, the soil garden, the how-to garden, the remedy garden, the sacred garden, the semi-real garden, the creative garden, the political garden, the one-tree garden, the weed garden, and so forth. These metaphorical gardens are my attempt to integrate the many varied perceptions and processes of gardening as they crystallize a sense of place. A sense of place emerges as a kind of unifying mantra, rather in the "Hindu God" sense of one principle possessing as many visages as there are people to worship at its altar.

Readers seeking savvy tips to bring home to their own yard should be aware, however, that this book necessarily falls prey to a few problems common to any first-person gardener's report. First and foremost, all gardens are local. Because I tend to praise this sense of locality to the skies, I would be remiss not to add that just about every specific recommendation this book makes is going to prove misleading in somebody else's backyard. In other words, much of what passes for "how-to" advice is actualy local advice. Some of my own individual beds grapple with two or more microclimates and three different soil types. Perhaps worse, the climate seems to be changing even as I write. Trying to gauge the start of spring from the vantage point of a cold winter night—with seed catalogs spread out all over the dining room table—has turned into a crapshoot.

Another problem is one that everybody, and not just gardeners, must recognize. Being creative means learning to feel good about defying somebody else's sense of beauty. There is much more about this in the chapter entitled "The Creative Garden," although for now, suffice it to say that aesthetic concepts are not rules but opinions. For instance, who says that tall perennials should be planted behind shorter ones? Who says that a garden is only as good as its underpinnings—its rocks, its trees, and especially its evergreen shrubs—all of which a number of very self-confident British garden authorities refer to as "the bones"? This is not to imply that the concept of "bones" is bogus. It isn't, and in fact I can vouch that my own garden never looked like very much in the wintertime until I started planting more bones.

But I would argue that aesthetic ideas such as bones are mostly structural details—even though sweating the details of a garden is often where the most fun is. In fact, details like bones suggest only one particular way of seeing and relating to place. The chapter called "The Weed Garden," especially its ideas about habitat restoration, repudiates all such human druthers. Collaborating with place also contradicts tried-and-true perceptions of paradise. The chapter "The Nowhere Garden" asks us to plot a new architecture of paradise to fit the ecological wisdom of the times we live in.

On the other hand, gardening is not much like modern art where a premium is often placed on breaking the established rules. Working out our own details never means we gardeners can ignore certain fundamentals. To succeed at gardening, we must all learn the difference between pure aesthetics on the one hand and the good health of place on the other. When the distinction is learned, it becomes a sixth sense. This sense is not defined in any gardening encyclopedia or in any scientific treatise about the senses. We don't necessarily think about it, and there even seem to be limits to how much we can study up on it. It is eventually understood on its own behalf. When that occurs, this so-called sense of place has already become an extension of ourselves.

Devising a garden aesthetic based on the good health of place ultimately ensures our own good health. That is perhaps the most selfish reason I can offer for promoting a sense of place as the foundation for gardening in the twenty-first century.

Why We Garden is written with much love and much faith. It is written in the hope that the discoveries revealed to me within my own garden may provoke some small transformation in my culture's sense of place. As a well-known Mexican song points out, from my house to your house is but one small step.

January

The Lord made the heavens and Earth in six days. On the seventh day he rested. Jews, following God's example, also rest and pray on the last day of the week, although more precisely, the Hebrew Sabbath spans Friday dusk through Saturday dusk. Jews regard their Sabbath as both an end and a beginning.

Early Christians held their prayer meetings on Sunday morning. Today the church services of most Christian denominations are still held on the morning of the first day of the week. Some Christian scholars assert that their Sunday Sabbath conveys a new beginning. It celebrates the resurrection of Christ following the symbolic ending of the crucifixion.

The roots of Western religion, including a good deal of its rituals concerning death and rebirth, lie in ancient Middle Eastern ceremonies for sowing and the harvest. Passover and Easter both commemorate a time of pain leading to rebirth. And both coincide with the traditional sowing of seeds at the spring equinox. Yom Kippur and Sukkoth coincide with the harvest, each in its own way. Both Christmas and Chanukah invoke the winter solstice. Each offers the hope of light and the renewal of the Earth at the moment of greatest darkness.

Garden endings invoke garden beginnings. However, January is no more the first month of the gardening year than an American Saturday is precisely the last day of the Jewish week. The gardener's calendar is always a moving target, altering its face each year to satisfy the exigencies of weather. If a precise moment must be assigned, let it be a moment defined by darkness and light: the winter solstice.

The solstice marks the longest night. It is a time of rest, the Northern Hemisphere's Sabbath, the gardener's own Sabbath. There is nothing to plant, nothing to harvest. By the time of the solstice, a plant's living essence has completed its journey downward from leaf tip to stem to root, down and down into the nest of the soil toward the fulfillment of dormancy. The surface of the garden beds stares up at us empty, covered over with a blanket of hay or sawdust to better hold the topsoil through the incessant rains, blustery winds, and occasional blizzards of January. This void at ground level tends to guide the human senses upward. We find ourselves watching the skies. The heavens seem to acknowledge our attentions, providing us with some of the wildest storms of the year.

I especially cherish the bleak silence of cold, windless nights. Not a frog to be heard anywhere. The Irish junipers and the Ellwood cypresses rise tallest above the otherwise empty garden beds. Their presence illuminates neither beginnings nor endings, but rather the stark permanence of ongoing life amid the winter's void. A lone boulevard cypress seems to be at its most prepossessing at the moment its curlicue blue-gray needles lie bent down by a heavy hoarfrost. I appreciate anew the native Douglas firs and jack pines for their ability to redefine the architecture of the borderline where cultivated garden meets the wild forest. To this gardener, a Christmas tree seems the solstice's version of a vase full of summer roses. This year it is a living tree, a noble fir, possessed of a perfect radial symmetry. More often than not, I have bad luck transplanting a live tree back into the ground. Its presence in my living room offers a reminder about the gardening challenges of this new year.

Because the solstice marks a birth, the days that follow display the first subtle signs of a new gardening year. I have gazed longingly at witch hazels displaying their stringy, salmon flowers in mid-January at a local nursery. In my own garden, it is to the hellebore genus that I turn for the first glimmer of yearly renewal. Most of the species bloom consistently before the first of February. One species in particular, the Corsican hellebore, seems like a samurai warrior of a flowering perennial. The plants bear sharp saw blades all along the edges of their leathery evergreen leaves. And every part of the plant is deadly poisonous to human beings, which may also help explain why no insect holes ever mar the surface of its luminous leaves. Yet how could it be otherwise? In a winter garden stalked by desperately hungry plant eaters, it is only the hellebore's impenetrable armor of sharp barbs and deadly toxins that allows it to indulge its unorthodox devotion to the cold January sun. The greenish-creamish bloom of the hellebore is always the first flower of the year to open. It is almost always in flower on New Year's Day.

Attending any birth signifies a fresh recognition of all things tiny in the garden. My daily walk among the beds is primarily marked by a close observance of the buds. Camellias and star magnolias are already starting to swell, although neither bush will bloom before mid-March. The bloodred stalks of a favored herbaceous peony have already started to break ground. They will remain there, seemingly inert, paying no mind whatsoever to the hardest of freezes, peeking just above soil level right into March. I stare at them and smile, knowing that one day soon they will suddenly start to sprint upward toward the light. The plant eventually bears many bloodred flowers, although none before their time in late April.

During this coldest time of the year, the empty beds make me especially aware of a gardening constant: there is always more life below the soil surface than above it. Deep beneath my feet the soil remains a constant fifty-five degrees. 'Tis the season of root hairs, millipedes, grubs.

The One-Tree Garden

It caught my eye from fifty feet away. A two-foot-tall potted-up sequoia tree stuck away in the back of a display of ornamental conifers at a local nursery. The nursery's fall inventory sale was in full swing. Conifers in two-gallon pots were going for just about the same price as leftover perennials in four-inch pots. I'd already picked out three little ground-hugging trees to use as foundation plantings along the south face of my house. I hesitated in front of the sequoia, knew its identity without searching for the tag. I stared at it and conjured up a vision of the full-grown sequoias I'd once seen hiking through the southern Sierra in California. The largest of those wild giants grew as big around as my garage. Even the medium-sized trees had a base diameter of six to eight feet.

Now I stooped down to examine the tree a little more closely. I liked its color, a deep green with blue highlights. I admired the succulent droopiness of its scaly, bristly, barbed needles and wondered what botanists were looking at when they aligned this species with the very different-appearing coast redwood. Although sequoia and redwood certainly share a deeply gouged red bark as well as a potential for large size and great age, the giant sequoia's needles seem to have more in common with a cypress than with a redwood. They grow like scales, integral to the branch itself, whereas individual redwood needles are much more distinct, each one jutting from the wood of a branch like ribs off a fish's spine. Each coast red-wood needle is soft, stubby, vaguely like a hemlock's. Or a more pliable version of a grand fir.

I picked up the peat pot and brought it back to the counter with the rest of my choices. Standing back a moment to study my little collection, the sequoia looked out of place—as if I'd gone ahead and stuck a baby brontosaurus in among all the cute toy poodles that pass these days for foundation plantings.

Back home again, the sequoia stayed in its peat pot while I quickly planted all the rest of the conifers near to the house. I placed the sequoia in a semishady spot on the front porch where I got to look at it every time I entered or exited the house. It was out of the rain. Two weeks passed. The weather was turning wet, cold. I needed to act on the tree. One afternoon I ventured out into a drizzle to deposit the tree, still in its peat pot, into a deep bed where the tree would grow to accent a nearby rose bed. A month passed. One night I read that giant sequoias grow slowly for a year or two but then start spurting five or six feet a season. The roses weren't going to be very happy about that. The next morning I got out my garden fork and levered the peat pot out of its hole. I placed it back on the porch, out of the rain and close to the front door. Now I felt a tinge of guilt every time I either entered or left the house. A week later the temperature dropped below freezing. I had to do something. I picked up the tree in its pot and started walking the property line. I found a spot along the west boundary of the property. It was at the edge of a forest, a bit south of a small apricot and cherry orchard. I dug a hole, dropped it inside, and then backfilled it.

I watched the tree from a chair by a window in my living room through November. December came and went. I realized one afternoon in January that the sequoia would definitely start cutting off the sun to the orchard within fifteen years. That duration may seem an eternity to some, but it's not such a long time for someone passionately growing fruit trees. The next day I dug up the potted sequoia and heeled it into an empty vegetable bed for the duration of the winter. If the tree was out of sight, it was never out of mind.

Two months passed. Spring was imminent. Buds started appearing on the willows. The little blue ground irises flowered first, as they always do. The daffodils and then the tulips broke ground. One afternoon in March I lifted the sequoia out of the ground. Its pot was soggy, deteriorating. I carefully placed the tree in a wheelbarrow and pushed it down the hill, far away from the house, through a section of fir forest undergrown with a dense thicket of salal. I stopped when I reached a rise next to a small pond located in the middle of an alder bottom.

The pond had been dug by a bulldozer in three noisy hours the previous September. It was twelve feet wide and long, just under eight feet deep. It served my family as a secondary water catchment and had, in fact, filled to the brim by January. I had planted the dug-up clay sides of the dam in clover to keep it from eroding. The only time I ever visited the pond was to turn on a water pump.

I positioned the pot on a low mound of topsoil skillfully shaped to look natural by the very fastidious bulldozer operator. The sequoia seemed a good choice for the site. Here was a tree quite capable of fending off any incursion from the rampant alders. It might even flourish, insinuating its roots deeply through the mounded topsoil, eventually drawing its water needs from the boggy alder grove that lay just twelve feet away.

I placed the sagging pot on the mound, walked back ten feet, and turned around to admire the tree. Unfortunately, however I looked at it, the site seemed as much a gulag as a garden. Despite the early spring growth of clover, the ground around the tree still looked ripped up. Bulldozer tracks crisscrossed the clay dam. I distinctly remember feeling that I was *relegating* the tree to that spot more than I was *planting* it there. But it had to go somewhere. I dug a hole eighteen inches deep and eighteen inches wide in the blue clay and backfilled it halfway again with the black-as-coal topsoil taken directly from the floor of the alder bottom. The peat pot was pushed unceremoniously into the hole and immediately fell apart. It was starting to rain; I noticed the pond was near to overflowing. No need to water anything anywhere on such a wet day in March.

I admired my brand-new one-tree garden for a few seconds. But then, rather than dash back up the hill to a warm, dry house, the newly planted sequoia seemed to demand that I linger just a moment longer. I leaned on the long-handled spade and stared and stared at it, conjuring up images of that tree's momentous growth in twenty years, two hundred years, five hundred years, a thousand years, three thousand years. I guess that's what sequoia trees do to people. It comes with the size, the age, even the ostensible fact that one of the largest national parks in the entire United States was established to protect this one very special species of tree. Then and there I decided not to plant anything else around the pond. This would be a one-tree garden, a three-thousand-year-old garden whose birth I would midwife. It would be my private refuge. Certainly, no one else would visit it unless I led them there personally. Only then did I run back to the house. I was totally soaked.

I started visiting the pond about once every other week. During that first spring I was gratified to notice several new gray-green budding branches that quickly added two inches to the sequoia's height.

I commence a visit to the sequoia by examining the tree like a doctor giving a physical to a baby: taking a branch in my fingers and turning it this way and that just to reacquaint myself with some ephemeral temporal charisma I believe the tree possesses. Physical completed, I take a few steps back on the hard clay ground and find myself fantasizing about how this scene will transform as the baby sequoia matures. How big does it grow in a hundred and fifty years? Is it five feet wide? Is it a hundred and forty feet tall? I have found that my ability to imagine this future version of the tree depends, curiously, on how often I visit the tree, as if the image of the five-foot-wide tree progressively clarifies in my mind's eye through regular practice.

The sharpness of the futuristic image prompts another peculiar effect. The other nearby plants—the wild honeysuckles, the ferns, the wild roses, the red-osier dogwood, even the alders—always drop back into the shadows of my imagination. I am not certain why this occurs, although I sometimes attribute the difference in lucidity to the fact that individual ferns and vines and alders that surround me at this moment will be long gone in a hundred and fifty years. For much of the year it is also quite dark down here by the pond. The water is black from the alder tannin running in the creek that feeds it. The alder trunks themselves are charcoal gray. The alders grow tall and quite dense; their canopy sometimes seems as opaque as one found in a tropical rain forest. Even the ground is dark from a thick covering of blackened alder leaves. Only the sequoia and, to a lesser extent, the clay itself, seems to offer up much color.

My ability to project the tree—but not its surroundings—clearly into the future occasionally bothered me, implying that I had transformed the sequoia into a celebrity species much to the detriment of its noncelebrity extended environment.

This realization caused me to visit that wet setting even more often than before. Now I employed the sequoia more as a beacon, a guide to help me envision the ecosystem within which the tree flourished as its most long-lived aspect. The evocative powers of that exquisite little sequoia tree cannot be underestimated. It metamorphosed in my mind as a kind of TV channel tuned to a sweeping panorama of the entire future ecosystem I call home.

The original old-growth forest of huge Douglas firs and red cedars that once wrapped my own land in silence was clear-cut to feed the local lime kilns back in the 1930s and early 1940s. Although almost none of these giants remain standing anywhere around here, giant stumps can be seen just about everywhere one walks in the woods. Some of the stumps are awe-inspiring in their breadth, and it can be quite terrifying to realize that an entire forest of these ancient beings was cut down in just two or three years.

Actually, referring to these monuments as stumps seems a bit of a misnomer. The vast majority of them are waist-high cylinders of still-intact bark that contain nothing but a bright orange powder, which is all that remains of the wood. I see that powder and imagine the termite feast that must have occurred all through this country during the years preceding World War II. Some of the so-called stumps also contain thirty-foot-tall living trees growing right out of the orange powder. Although I have always felt an indistinct sadness over the current lack of very large trees in this place called home, I feel contented to have built my house surrounded by the substantial architecture of a fifty-year-old second-growth forest already attaining heights well over a hundred feet with base diameters of two feet.

Neither the firs nor the cedars will grow where it's overly wet, and that is where the alders, the willows, and the occasional cottonwood flourish. These are deciduous trees, some of them also quite tall, sixteen inches thick, with their branches heavily draped in green stringy moss. Alders produce a lot of leaves, drop them each fall. The soil that grows around their roots is usually very black, acidic, and fertile. That is the same soil within which I planted the sequoia.

Time passes. The tree starts to expand upward and outward in its own slow way. Sitting on the ground in front of it quite a lot these days, knees clutched by my arms watching the tree grow, I sometimes smile at the goofiness of the gesture. I am not unaware, however, that what is actually being kindled here at the site of this little stuck-in-the-ground sequoia tree is an impalpable vestige of what I believe to be a "totem" connection that has always existed between large trees and human beings. The power of certain trees to evoke either past or future or both certainly offers an important reason why the largest old oak trees were regarded as sacred totem beings by my own European forebears. But the tiny fire of this revelation is not an easy one to keep lit. I am a member of a species bent on perceiving nature primarily as commodity. Often forced to heel to the anthropocentric bottom line, I still believe that the temporal charisma of certain trees and forests holds far greater value to the human species standing and growing than cut up into pencils and paper. But imbuing our lives with this kind of value system takes constant attention and very few of us get a chance to visit large trees very often. Because the little sequoia grows right here in my own yard, it keeps the fire lit better than anything else in my life. I permit myself to become permeated by the temporal charisma offered up by a baby sequoia and understand tree totemism as something very real, very hopeful. The past, the present, and the future, they all seem jumbled together in one place in one moment, and through one entity. The sensation of it feels both erotic and peculiarly voyeuristic: the result is my newfound ability to peer at a little tree and watch Mother Earth mating with Father Time. The link with this tree in this place comes as close as I'll ever get to sensing a sacred grounding in nature.

I have made a few pointed references to the made-up term *temporal charisma*. It means not only that sequoias provide an expanded durational context between human beings and place, but that this particular species probably accomplishes the task better than any other living being, either plant or animal. What might we, as a species, make of such temporal talents? Actually, thinking about such gifts in an economic or political sense probably necessitates a wildly poetic (what some refer to as an all-species) view of the world. On a planet parceled out to a human political scene overflowing with diplomats representing every country, city, trade group, biome, and special interest, people would have to start viewing nature with much more care and respect if the diplomacy corps suddenly expanded to include other species representing the ideas, processes, and places they clarify best. We might commence this so-called all-species process by regarding the sequoia species for what it is: one of planet Earth's foremost living ambassadors to the distant future.

A few other tree species do almost as well. Coast redwoods of course. Certainly bristlecone pines—the planet's oldest living plants—growing in the White Mountains of California. Cedars of Lebanon. The huge cryptomerias that grow on the Japanese island of Yakushima. The sacred thule trees growing along the road south of Oaxaca in the highlands of Mexico. More local to me are the native species of my own extended neighborhood: the red cedars, Douglas firs, garry oaks. Nor can I leave out one particular bigleaf maple that grows just a few miles away from the baby sequoia. It seems not so much a single tree but rather a fused community of three or four very large specimens that over a period of centuries grew so close as to lose their own separate identities. The maple shades an area as large as half a football field. There are reports that the alerce trees of Chile grow nearly as large as any sequoia during a four-thousand-year lifetime. Tragically the alerce forests are so overlogged that the big trees are now about as rare as grizzly bears shuffling through the northern Rockies. More is the pity that I have never seen an alerce offered for sale in a nursery. Cryptomerias are common garden accents, although a tiny cultivar seems to possess none of the temporal charisma of a baby sequoia. I don't know why.

Temporal charisma is not only a trait of the most majestic species. Yews can live many hundreds of years. There are ancient rosebushes growing in France reputed to have been planted in the Middle Ages. Peonies can thrive for a hundred years or more and, in the process, accrue more temporal charisma than any other herbaceous perennial. The Japanese achieve that same temporal context in a very different way, by building small ponds in which they place koi, which can swim about contentedly for thirty years or more.

Planting any of the above tree species holds another temporal benefit as well. It can take us thirty years to establish a garden. When we formalize a tree planting by calling it a garden, we start to notice that most of the gardens we admire most have developed at just about the same pace it takes a living tree to grow to maturity. If our lives are filled up with such gardening, the pace of our lives must inevitably start to slow down even as our sense of duration expands outward. Or look at it another way. If tree planting has anything at all to do with that other widespread recreation, sports, the winners of the tree-planting race are never hares and always tortoises. If we run the race long and hard enough, we start to acquire a slow-as-molasses metabolism established by the trees themselves.

What other processes of nature besides the growth of trees can so insistently cause us to envision a hundred or even a thousand years hence? The ongoing erosion of the Grand Canyon might prompt some of us to future visioning. The glaciers of southeast Alaska—which have receded a remarkable fifty *miles* over the past one hundred years—seem another notable candidate. One doesn't actually need to live on the Alaska coast to start wondering how many glaciers will be left there several hundred years in the future. And what if the climate starts getting colder again? In such a manner, the glaciers remind us that another ice age could conceivably kick into gear sometime within the next ten thousand years.

Although our deductive mind can precisely measure the immense time scale that the Grand Canyon and the Alaska coastline represent, and although our imaginative mind may wonder long and hard about their eventual fate, neither of these "events" serve very well as temporal ambassadors. An ambassador is different from either an exemplar or a site of pilgrimage. These places, and the events they represent, are simply too grand, too remote, and too aloof from human sensibilities. When I visited the Grand Canyon, it left me feeling awestruck. But my senses proved inadequate to the task of detecting any of its monumental processes at work. That temporal context even had a name; I heard it referred to as *eons and eons*. The phrase conjured up a vision of Mesozoic swamps filled with giant salamanders snapping at giant dragonflies. It was an obscure vision at best, derived mostly from perusing too many science illustrations when I was a child. This is hardly a criticism of the experience I felt at the rim of the Grand Canyon. Rather, the Grand Canyon offers us a wonderful context in which humans are inconsequential. A sequoia may also offer us a substantial duration for visioning, although it is still less than the extent of previous human history.

Accessibility must also be taken into account. If one doesn't happen to live in Juneau, Alaska, glimpsing the Mendenhall Glacier through a photograph, or reading about its humbling features as they leap off the page in a passionate account by some talented nature writer, is incapable of affecting me in any way commensurable with the daily experience I glean so easily while sitting with that little sequoia tree. A long-lived tree or even a peony bought at a nursery and planted in our own yard accomplishes the key task of any ambassador. It interacts with us both directly and regularly.

Is there anything *man-made* capable of eliciting such a strong sense of the future? Two candidates spring to mind. Neither is optimistic, and perhaps ironically, neither seems a deliberate attempt at human monument building. The first is a collective artifact: all those barrels of plutonium no one knows what to do with, although they will still be with us and poisonous in tens of thousands of years. And second, much closer to home, a drive down any highway in the Pacific Northwest reveals the massive clear-cutting of the old-growth forest. It causes me to tremble as I envision the once green and wet Pacific Northwest mutated into a desert incapable of supporting large temperate conifers. Will this small sequoia be able to weather those changes?

Ecologists tell us that something similar occurred here about ten thousand years ago when the glacier trudged down from the north to cover the land all the way into California. It retreated only after hundreds of years of scraping the soil down to bedrock, leaving behind a treeless landscape not unlike today's Alaskan tundra. Trees finally started to grow. But the land stayed fairly dry for millennia— transformed into an oak savanna. Precipitation increased only within the past few thousand years to support the fir and pine forests we all know as the signature of the Pacific Northwest.[1] But the great expanses of forest I knew just fifteen years ago are all but devastated in the mad rush to get it all cut before the laws, the politics, and/or the economy changed.

One beautiful, carefree afternoon last February I visited the sequoia tree feeling especially effusive. The one-tree garden greeted me with something new this day. One set of tiny deer prints were impressed into the mud—probably made by a doe or a yearling browsing through the area. The prints suggest the animal stopped to drink from the pond, then stepped up to the tree, perhaps sniffed it a moment. But for some reason she decided it wasn't quite to her taste. She passed it by and walked back into the woods. It has been a cold and snowy winter this year, which has proven especially hard on the deer. Some of them have taken to browsing on conifers. Even the red cedars with their formaldehyde resin are not exempt. The little sequoia tree may not be so lucky the next time a deer passes through the alder bottom.

Staring at the scaly-needled little conifer, I try to project my visioning a thousand years into the future. The tree now stands fifteen feet in diameter. But only a few other things in this particular version of the future look as they do at this moment. The noisy juncos, kinglets, and nuthatches poke among the cones dropping from the fir trees. The dirt road that currently lies just beyond the first ring of alder trees has vanished. And the pond is an empty hole, half filled with dust and sand. The alders have also vanished, a sign that the water table must have dropped beyond the reach of their thirsty roots. Whereas the fir branches in my own time decompose quickly into forest duff, the fir branches in my fantasy are bleached white, signifying that they decompose much more slowly. The skeletons of dead junipers litter a forest floor that contains few shrubs and no herbaceous perennials. These are all sure signs of a much drier climate. I sit staring at the living tree and consider the clear-cuts that are occurring everywhere these days. I think about the eventual drought some long-term weather forecasters have predicted as the result of the destruction of the Northwest forests. But I can't decide if the aridity I envision is the sign of a naturally evolving climate, or if it's something far more deadly: a sign of global warming caused by clear-cutting and pollution and leading to an irreversible heating of the planet's surface. Either way, the future seems grim. My contentment vanishes.

The French impressionist Paul Gauguin, who lived in Tahiti for many years, painting the brown-skinned native people engaged in their everyday tasks, scrawled these three questions on one of his better-known canvases:

Where do we come from?
Where are we?
Where are we going?

Good questions all, and somehow worth posing to myself as I stare at a little tree. The first question: Where do we come from? The tree answers this one pointedly every time I visit it. Despite what we modern people may wish to believe about our own ancestors, we all come from a tribe of tree worshipers.

Where are we? In fact, where I sit the log feels uncomfortable. I stand a moment, bend to touch my toes, and then sit squarely on the damp ground. A hundred seasons pass. I do not move. But what season is it? If I fend off mosquitoes, it may be June. I watch out for yellow jackets zipping back and forth inches above the ground every August, wear a raincoat in November, and trade it for an insulated jacket on a cold sunny day in January.

I prefer the late fall for tree gazing. It is barely drizzling. A month later, in December, the pond is full. The seasonal creek is flowing strongly, trickling over the bank to ripple the black surface of the water. Four or five times each December I carry a noisy gasoline pump down to the pond's edge to draw the precious rainwater into a larger pond located fifty feet uphill and on the other side of the property. More months flicker past my vantage point. If it is early summer, my eyes glance at the pond surrounded by ferns, its shiny surface covered with a mayfly hatch. A foxglove is in flower. In September the clover is dying. If there's ice on the pond, it must be sometime in midwinter. Except the ice is never smooth here. The center sinks under its own weight, lifting the edges above the pond's slope like a tortilla covering a frying pan.

If it's February, the one-tree garden may look just as it does today. I sit on the frozen ground and notice the sequoia covered in a wonderful rime. Once again, a thousand years pass in an instant. I free-associate silly little glass-and-plastic machines driving on a cushion of air down the dirt road across the far side of the pond. There are no human beings on board to command the movements of the vehicles or even to offer a glimpse of the vehicles' ultimate purpose. I feel like Gauguin. I want to know where they come from. I pick up a stone and skim it on the ice of the pond. It slides and then falls into a crevice where the surface never quite meets the slope.

And where are we going? I recall a long-lost future vision from my own childhood. I was eleven years old, visiting New York City and traveling the Staten Island ferry. Staring across the harbor at the Statue of Liberty, but actually seeing her as she might appear several thousand years in the future. There she is now, lying in another desert, the New York City desert. She's buried up to her neck in the sand of a deep dry canyon where the Hudson River once flowed. Vultures sit on her spiky crown. I admit it, the statue appears precisely the way she appeared in her cameo role in *The Planet of the Apes*. Except this was years before the movie was made. I never read the book.

Are there any other buildings out there to remind me that this is now three thousand years into the future? My sequoia is silent about the subject of buildings. All deliberate human monuments to future generations seem primarily an opportunity to recite the famous poem by Shelley. A desert traveler chances upon ancient ruins. On one well-eroded statue are written these words:

> *My name is Ozymandias, king of kings:*
> *look on my works, ye Mighty, and despair! . . .*
> *. . . Nothing besides remains.*
> *Round the decay*
> *of that colossal wreck, boundless and bare*
> *The lone and level sands stretch far away.*[2]

Gauguin must have read "Ozymandias" as well, because his painting also asks where we are going. In fact, that better than anything else explains why I visit this glade on such a cold day. The sequoia answers the question in its own way, forecasting the vicissitudes of change by illuminating all possible futures within the environment of my mind. Given the contingency that no nuclear winters intercede to kill off my little sequoia, or that the potential desert scenario proposed by a few doomsayer meteorologists never actually manifests itself, or that a volcano doesn't suddenly erupt in the neighborhood, or—far more likely—that the progeny of the local developers don't clear-cut that alder bottom in twenty or two hundred or even two thousand years in anticipation of some future subdivision; given all that, in three thousand years that little tree should have grown at least twenty feet thick and over two hundred feet tall.

By that time the little rise upon which the sapling was planted should have increased many times in size, the tree creating a veritable hill from the bulk of its massive roots and needle fall. Such a tree may itself stand responsible for sucking that seasonal pond dry, thus offering an alternative explanation to my earlier fantasy. Given that the weather remains stable and that we aren't all living inside a Gary Larson cartoon where fifty billion humans stand elbow to elbow across the width and breadth of the planet, by then there should be several more half-grown sequoias standing like sentinels around that same pond.

I find this vision to be a cause for some rejoicing. There *is* something we can all count on. Sequoia trees outlive civilizations. They outlive most ruins.

I have recently made a discovery. My own fantastic musings are not an unusual response of the human species when confronted by a baby sequoia tree. I must acknowledge, however, that my control group—the few friends who have been guided through the salal thicket to the one-tree garden—already appreciates plants. They already recognize the sequoia as uncommon garden fare. Most stoop down to gaze at the tree in admiration. They feel its prickly fused needles just as I do. They may even comment that indeed, this tree will one day achieve great things. The more horticulturally minded among them may shake their heads at the unruly wildness of this so-called garden of mine. One visitor wryly asks if I had planned the emptiness of this garden in accord with the sequoia's eventual proportions. Ah yes, yet another two-thousand-year-old garden. Despite the kidding, everyone seems to recognize that the sequoia's bountiful relationship to time is its greatest virtue.

Then again, planting any tree in any corner of any size garden encourages a gardener to anticipate at least the *near* future of the place where the planting occurred. Yet whether our temporal context is near or far, peony or sequoia, the two visions seem more a difference of degree than of kind. Taken together, the two remind me of yet another aspect of any tree's temporal charisma. Trees are much more than a temporal *medium* for prophecy. These plant beings are McLuhanesque, their own best *message* as well. A tree is a veritable creator of its ecosystem's future.

The tree planter's vision is thus participatory because people who plant trees go a long way toward creating the future of place. In grand terms, if enough human beings start caring enough about the land to plant enough monumental trees as ambassadors to any place's own future, the future of many more places will quickly become more predictably auspicious. My sequoia planting, for instance, bespeaks a relationship I have created with a place I obviously care about.

While such an activity shares quite a few things with traditional ideas about gardening, it shares almost nothing with tree *farming*. The gardener's viewpoint disavows the exploitive mind-set that generates a *need* for mass tree planting as the only viable conclusion to mass logging. It has occurred to me that I often regard my own tree-planting activities to be a kind of eulogy in praise of old-growth forests. Opening up one's heart to the process offers a requiem for the 95 plus percent of that forest already cut from out of the heart of this country I call home.

While the gardener's view of tree planting is visionary, it shares very little with standard futurism. Compared to most forms of prophesying, this one is refreshingly mundane. Whatever it is I may imagine while sitting beside the tree, it always seems a plausible revelation, always grounded to the place I call home. It implies a future people living approachable lifestyles. Despite the occasional oddball vehicle I may imagine zipping down the dirt road, this is no futuristic image devoid of all present-day context. I remember one drizzly October morning when I had brewed a cup of tea and carried it down the trail, through the Douglas fir grove, and into the clearing I call the one-tree garden. I sat down on the alder log, sipped the tea, and stared at the sequoia. I soon found myself turning pleasantly sentimental, wondering if a great-great-great-great-grandson or -daughter of mine, seven generations down the line in one hundred and fifty years, would someday be standing in this same place visualizing his or her own future generations standing in this same place looking up at that same tree.

Admittedly, such generational reverie is not my own invention. It has been primed by a relatively obscure and yet notably profound Native American political notion that lately has been sticking to my thought processes like a leaf to a mushroom cap. It takes a moment to explain but will seem germane to those contemplating a visitation from their own tree oracle.

I am referring to the forum of the Haudenosaunee or Iroquois tribal government. Whenever the six nations of the Iroquois confederacy held a council meeting, they first took a moment to invoke the presence of the seventh future generation. Thereafter, any vote among the living council members also included an equal vote cast for the needs and dignity of those who would live a hundred and fifty to two hundred years in the future. To the Iroquois, the rights of future generations never became an *issue* of policy because they were, instead, the actual *context* of policy. This generational context was built right into the heart of government. As Onondaga elder Oren Lyons has observed, "When we walk upon Mother Earth we always plant our feet carefully because we know the faces of our future generations are looking up at us from beneath the ground."[3] Planting a sequoia tree achieves a gardener's version of that same perception. There is a difference, however. Lyons doesn't seem to need a garden. He has learned to revere future generations by planting nothing else but his own two feet. The garden remains my own lovely crutch. And it was a sequoia tree that taught me how to plant my own feet in this place I call home.

Thomas Jefferson, who was probably our tree-plantingest president, was said to have gathered much inspiration from the structure of Iroquois democracy in the process of drawing a blueprint for the American system of governance. It makes one wonder about things that might have been. For example, how would our own lives be different today if Jefferson had gone a step farther and included the rights of the seventh generation in the U.S. Bill of Rights? How would the health of our forests be different?

Although these ideas may seem academic—somehow difficult to grasp in terms of anyone's actual life—embracing the seventh generation should, in fact, be as natural and as mundane an endeavor as gazing at a tree. Even as I conjure up my great-great-great-great-grandchildren, I soon flesh out the scene with a quaint domestic vision of life around "our" pond in a hundred and fifty years. Two little girls, at five and eight, about the current ages of my own daughters, are swimming and giggling at the edges of the pond. A ten-year-old boy swings back and forth above them Tarzan-style from a great rope tied on one end to a foot-thick branch that had been carefully pruned forty years before (in the year 2103) for the specific purpose of one day securing just such a rope. An adult who looks suspiciously like me lies on his back with a piece of straw in his mouth. He is feeling lazy today, content to watch a raven feeding her young in a nest built high up in a crotch. The grass clinging to the edges of the pond is brown and wispy. The pond has no algae this year. I can see why—there are a few goldfish sucking in air off the surface of the water. Goldfish love algae. It looks like late summer. Quite hot today. The alders have receded quite a bit from around the base of the tree. I also notice that this time around, the road is no longer a road. This time it is a well-worn footpath.

All such visions about the seventh generation formulated while sitting on the ground at the base of a baby sequoia tree are going to offer a very striking contrast to our culture's prevailing science-fiction stereotype of the future. Our pop future always feels so gloomy. Individuals are more subjugated to fancy gadgetry than they are today. Homes are often devoid of trees, birds, gardens. We favor flying machines for getting from here to there. Entire cities have evolved into singular structures that look like art nouveau wedding cakes. Metal and/or ruins predominate the immediate sensory environment. We simulate nature with a holodeck viewer.

Is this what we have to look forward to? The sequoia tree's intimation of the future gives me enough hope to say maybe not—no matter how unrelenting the opposition may appear. Commercial interests are always goading us to buy what's new, exotic, and alluring. They assure us that this is the path to contentment, and we, being at the other end of the same process, tend to believe them. We envision progress as the newest grab bag of things to buy. One result is that we continually pit our deepest spiritual values against the possession of material and sensual riches. Another result is that we lose our ability to imbue family, place, community, nature, or home with any temporal context beyond the foreshortened horizon of next year's gadget, next year's payment, next year's benefit.

These are some of the reasons so few people are willing to plant their feet and sense the seventh generation as their own extended family. These are the reasons that the escapist fantasies of space and time travel seem so much more alluring to the majority than any mundane vision like watching ravens—despite what the former may portend for the Earth's own environment a hundred and fifty years from now. This same allure of a resource-dependent, escapist future may also explain why a future environment healthy enough to contain ravens can no longer be assured. Ironically, who can rightly say which is the less plausible of the two visions?

But criticism is necessarily limited. The comparison is moot. Science fiction is fiction. Despite Oren Lyons's recommended technique for experiencing future generations directly, we are not meant to plant our feet while reading it or watching it. Although its images and its ideas are often wonderfully thought-provoking, science fiction is still escapist entertainment. We are not part of its story. It possesses none of the sacred generational linkage that lies at the heart of both the one-tree garden and the seventh generation.

There is another issue to take into consideration. Although there may be no direct linkage between our own world and myriad science-fiction worlds, there is still a connection between them. Many of the events of the best science fiction— its images, stories, heroes, emotions, and archetypes—offer a powerful reflection of what is not so much a prescription for the future as a metaphor about a present-day crisis in the perceptions of our own species. Turn on the TV. Drive down any urban freeway at 5:00 P.M. The pace of urban events assaults our senses. The fact that most of us today inhabit milder versions of those same treeless landscapes explains why so many science-fiction dramas deal with some evolved aspect of contemporary technology gone bonkers. That is why so many of the heroes we get in science fiction are often portrayed as masters of the very emotions that numb our lives today. They stalk a violent society permeated with the most fantastic and least praiseworthy aspects of human desire and personified by the likes of Darth Vader, the Blade Runner, and the Terminator. Our pop mythos of the future is seen to be both violent and overwhelmingly masochistic—as if we have gone out of our way to encourage a distressing, anti-nature, and techno-tense dream of the seventh generation. This is a world where all the unresolved desires (and recurring nightmares) we collectively apprehend about our own contemporary society continue to grow and mutate. And a hundred and fifty years in the future a veritable monster confronts us. That monster is us.

We are what we make of ourselves. And the simple, earthbound, present-tense act of planting trees encourages a very different relationship to the future than any science fiction. Tree planting encourages a direct responsibility to the environment. It promotes a future founded upon a genuine commitment to the local, the precise spot where the trees are planted. This is the real future of somebody's actual neighborhood. Here is the birthplace of a sense of place.

Planting trees also suggests a paradox. Since this mundane act appears in the public imagination far less often than the techno-paradise, in many circles it offers up a far more *radical* vision about our common future than most of what passes for science fiction. It is radical—and yet so straightforward. Even as we plant, we are also creating the future environment in which the seventh generation will actually reside. People participating in the future of the place they live. And the trees themselves growing huge: first in our imagination and second in the explicit act of digging holes and planting them. Where I live, many are heeling in native cedars and firs and hemlocks. Nor do I feel shy to welcome a few emigrant species such as the giant sequoias that succeed so admirably well in my own Northwest climate.

Is it possible to expand this tree-planting foresight into other aspects of daily life? Or is it simply too idealistic to imagine a future where officials of the nuclear power industry start to exercise as much farsighted perseverance in the disposal of their poisonous wastes as the average gardener does when he or she plants a tree. Or conjure up a vision of members of Congress visiting the polluted areas within their own domain, carefully placing gravel and dirt around the roots of some native or nearly native tree capable of surviving the harshly altered landscape: planting trees as a formal element of their own swearing-in ceremony. A hundred years hence, that little sapling planted in a few minutes would have perhaps reproduced into a grove: a little tree that costs just about the same amount of money as a container of popcorn costs at the movies, potentially providing wildlife habitat and oxygen for a healing planet.

More time passes.

The clover seed I sprinkled on top of the pond's earthen dam has taken root and spread rampantly to stifle any chance of erosion. The wildflowers, brambles, and grasses are also establishing themselves admirably. I've done little more to cultivate the area than spread a few foxglove and feverfew seeds around the margin of the bog. I believe they will flourish with no more work on my part. My visits to the pond have become less frequent. Sometimes I jog down the slope from my house to turn on the noisy pump. I still break out in a smile when I catch sight of the sequoia tree. Given that update, naming my original task a tree planting seems a wholly accurate account of it. The pond hardly looks dug at all anymore. Someone with less developed sensibilities for local ecology than my own might think it was always there. The reclamation seems nearly complete, although the tree stands just four feet tall.

Although the job of reclamation originated in direct response to laying the ground bare with a bulldozer, the planting of any sequoia tree in the Pacific Northwest does not precisely fit the purist's definition of restoration. The sequoia is an "introduced" species, a tree that grows naturally in a few protected preserves strung out along the western slope of the Sierra Nevada. But that same newly coined gardener's term *temporal context* sheds a slightly different light on the sequoia's nativity. Although no sequoia has spread its boughs or dropped its seed in this place since the last ice age, fossils tell us that the species did flourish here before the onslaught of that fatal cold.

In other words, what we refer to as a "native" sometimes bears directly upon our own temporal context. The relationship I enjoy with the little sequoia has obviously set my mind to regard a protracted time span. If the advance and eventual retreat of the glacier cannot exactly be called a contemporary event, its handiwork is still noticeable just about everywhere I look. I built my house on a flat scoured rock that clearly displays the polish and scarring caused by that momentous ice sheet. That rock is my front yard, my children's playground. Within its deep crevices, full to the brim with ten thousand years of rotting moss transformed into a wonderful black soil, I have marked out and planted my various gardens.

If planting a "native" sequoia seems, at best, an oblique use of the term *restoration,* I side with Humpty-Dumpty, who offers this good advice: "When I make a word do a lot of work like that, I always pay it extra." That also explains why I sometimes employ the terms *tree planting* and *gardening* synonymously. Many gardeners would, no doubt, voice some concern over my lackadaisical use of synonyms. Some would no doubt express the sentiment that this so-called one-tree garden of mine is not a garden at all. It may have been a garden when I planted it. And it may become a garden again if I would only start tending to it. In other words, what it primarily lacks at this precise moment is the controlling hand of the gardener. Perhaps so. And yet, if not precisely a garden, and not a restoration, then what is it I have created here? The Talmudists were famous for answering questions by asking another one. Likewise, in my own skewed attempt to find an answer I consider this question: How many trees does it take to grow a proper sequoia garden twenty-five feet on a side?

Actually, there are three correct answers.

The first answer is four. If we follow the advice of most gardening books, we would *fill up* the space with various planting "elements" to achieve an aesthetic "balance." A small grove of four of the largest sequoias one might find at the local nursery—perhaps ten feet tall—should fit the bill. However, this four-tree garden is inevitably going to look a bit scraggly for at least a few years. So the four-tree gardener will interplant several shrubs, possibly ornamental grasses, and may I even suggest naturalizing bulbs and perennials like daffodils for spring, lilies for summer, and Japanese anemones for fall. The soil will need to be amended. The invasive alders and thistles will need to be rooted out with some regularity. The grass will need to be cut every two weeks during the summer months.

This garden should take about twenty-five years to fill out properly, which means that the gardener may not actually live to enjoy it although his children will (or even more likely the children of strangers). In twenty-five years' time the four trees will have grown about forty feet tall, each with a branch spread of twenty feet or more. If the heirs to this garden happen to follow the same traditional gardening aesthetic as the original tree planter, they will one day notice that the sequoias have outgrown their space. They will soon get out the saw to cut out some of the shrubs and possibly one or two of those tree "elements" just to let the light back into the understory. In terms of time-span awareness, this pruning job a generation in the future must be understood as a task implicit within the activity of planting four baby sequoia trees today.

The four-tree garden treats plants as if they were modeling clay utilized in the creation of a pleasing and ever-changing landscape. It also exemplifies the contemporary relationship between garden and controlling gardener.

The second answer is zero. If it's instant gratification one is after, a gardener does not want to bother with even one sequoia tree. Twenty-five years is an incredible commitment to a garden. Most people are too busy to care. They may not own their own house, and considering a twenty-five-year commitment to a stranger's property seems unrealistic. Their little twenty-five-foot-square yard demands a landscaping job that won't upset the neighbors, and so on and so forth.

They choose the zero-tree garden and plant a few carefree perennials instead. While doing so, they also notice that their busy ant of a next-door neighbor is laying out a vegetable garden. The neighbor on the other side, the one who does own her own house, has recently hired a landscaper to plant a few rhododendrons and roses. It makes sense for her to spend the extra money. It adds value to a property investment.

In terms of time-span awareness, even the instant gratification of a zero-tree garden refers to a period of time measured in years. It takes a minimum of four years to achieve a modest shrubbery, three years for a good perennial bed, and at least a season before a gardener is able to grow vegetables from seed to table. Even when it comes to instant gratification, the totem animal of gardeners remains the tortoise and never the hare. And this hypothetical zero-tree garden describes well the contemporary relationship between a garden and an inexperienced gardener.

The third answer is one. However, my avid promotion of the one-tree garden is not meant to chastise either the four-tree or the zero-tree gardener. In a world overflowing with serious problems, it would be fatuous to label gardening control, weeding, or a busy lifestyle as an avowed enemy of our common future. Nor is the point that the four-tree garden or the zero-tree garden is any less exalted than the one-tree garden. Rather, the one-tree garden offers a potentially new perspective on what a garden might be and could become.

Perhaps a personal confession about control will help set the record straight. I grow a very fruitful blueberry/apple orchard inside a chicken-wire fence just a hundred feet north of that same little pond. Keeping the alders, the thistles, and the quack grass in check has been my unrelenting challenge for nearly eight years. Weeding the orchard two or three times a summer helps matters. Last year I went so far as to place a mulch of heavy plastic sheeting on the ground around each blueberry plant. It was either the mulch or the assured loss of the berries to some very invasive weeds. Carefully pruning the fruit trees and bushes every winter ensures a bountiful harvest. Constructing that substantial fence has kept the deer out of an area that I visit only periodically. I anticipate no end in sight to these tasks. Meanwhile, the foxglove seeds I disseminated so casually last year have started to grow along the edge of the alder bottom. They look pretty, which, as far as I am concerned, is all there is to it.

The deep relationship that I describe between myself and the sequoia has little to do with the fact that there is precisely one tree in my own one-tree garden. That same tree could conceivably be found flourishing in a grove of trees. My sequoia is surrounded by alders. Ultimately, the "one-tree garden" mostly serves as a meaningful nod to the individuality of the relationship, rather than to the number of trees actually present. I have recently planted a tree peony, which elucidates its own version of temporal charisma upon a formal garden bed laid out along the front walk.

But all gardeners take note: too much human intervention in nature's tempo creates its own endless cycle of problems including excess pest control, constant weeding, soil and plant replacement. It takes far less maintenance (and money spent on chemical amendments) to keep a garden that melds with nature than one that constantly fights against it. Given the well-documented violence enacted upon the environment by some of the chemical amendments we employ in our fight for control—especially pesticides and herbicides—we must all become aware of just how little sense it makes to destroy nature in the cause of constructing an artificial landscape.

A new relationship to the garden engenders an ecologist's view of place. It is a nurturing view, a healing view, and certainly a long view. A long, long, long view. The four-tree gardener thinks in terms of a generation. The zero-tree gardener thinks in terms of a few years. And in twelve *hundred* years, that sequoia tree may be growing on a hill of its own making. If so, it should still be providing a splendid introduction to this concept I call a sense of place.

February

My journey to the gardener's paradise starts afresh each year on the third Saturday in February. That's the day I plant tomato seeds.

But that's not totally accurate. The task actually started life last September when I emptied out an overflowing compost pile and forked its contents into the vegetable garden. That same day I started producing compost all over again with the usual ingredients of rancid kitchen scraps, horse manure, and rotten hay. Now, five months gone by, the stuff exudes the sweet aroma of well-done compost. And never a penny spent on fertilizer.

I drop a heaping shovelful of the stuff into a pail. Then I add sand, not by measuring cup but until the compost no longer holds together on its own. Then I add a handful of either hardwood sawdust or planer shavings for fluffiness. I fill up eight four-inch plastic pots with the mix and place the pots in a sunny nook in the house and give the soil an entire day to warm up to room temperature.

By no stretch of the imagination could anybody praise the Pacific Northwest as a great climate for growing tomatoes. It's much too dry during the daytime in August and too cold at night. There are, however, certain varieties especially bred for this climate, and some of these are very good indeed. But they all need to be started inside as early as possible.

I planted the eight pots this morning. My index finger presses a small crater into the soil at the center of each pot, into which two seeds get deposited. I cover the craters with a pinch of soil and then water it. If both seeds germinate, I'll pinch out the weaker of the two plants. The tomatoes will grow in their pot for nearly two months. Occasionally, we'll have a cold April, and I'll be forced to transplant the growing plants into even bigger pots and keep them growing inside the house until late April or early May.

The first two pots get cherry tomatoes, and my cherry of choice has long been Camp Joy. It's a tasty nonhybrid variety and seems to withstand a bit more of the early spring chill than any other variety I've tried. In four or five weeks, I'll plant one of the two cherry tomato plants inside a tiny greenhouse built up against the south wall of the house. That way, with some luck, my family will be eating tomatoes by the second week in June. Camp Joy produces all summer long right up to the first killing frost of autumn. Supported by a trellis, it will grow ten feet tall.

I plant two more pots with an early fruiting, standard-sized variety bred for this area and called Oregon Spring. One of these will also end up in the greenhouse. If all goes well, it should fruit there by early July. We eat the tomatoes off that plant for about three weeks, or until the tomatoes out in the garden beds start to produce. At that point, I pull the Camp Joy along with the Oregon Spring to make room for melons that are starting to crowd them out.

I favor two other varieties possessed of large juicy, red-orange, slightly tart fruit that mature early enough to bear tomatoes by mid-August. Unfortunately, one of these is saddled with the rather moronic name of Ultra Girl. Luckily that name did not keep me from trying a package of it two years ago. If nothing else, that name gives some idea of the mentality of the people who specialize in poking eyedroppers into the sex glands of vegetables. You'd never find a peony or an iris named Ultra Girl. Peonies are Sarah Bernhardt or Feathers of a Heavenly Bird. Irises are Titan's Glory and Sultan's Palace. Who comes up with these names?

The last two pots are filled with the seeds of an heirloom variety, probably named after the town or the grower of origination. It's called Marmande, but the seed company that sells it, Thompson and Morgan, couldn't leave well enough alone, and so they insist on calling it Super Marmande, as if a gardener better beware of planting it in kryptonite-laced soil. You don't see it for sale very many places, which is almost certainly the result of its shape. Marmande is ugly—flat and ropy to a fault. But the taste is superb, the perfect blend of sweet and tart that always distinguishes the best vine-ripened tomatoes from the gray square fare found on supermarket shelves.

I've been selecting and saving my Marmande seeds for six years now, and each year the plants definitely fruit a few days earlier than the last. Seed selection is a fun process with a practical result. It eventually steers the evolving variety to meld better to the exigencies of one's own land and climate. Plants that are contented where they grow mean less work for the gardener. The tomatoes also seem to get more flavorful with each passing year, although I readily acknowledge that this latter attribute may exist nowhere else besides my own imagination.

The Nowhere Garden

Almost every weekday morning, no matter the season, rain or shine, I rise from the writing desk, give a good stretch, palm my eyes to reconstitute them to vistas beyond the vision-razing word-processing screen, slip on some waterproof clogs in winter or flip-flops in summer, and step outside to scrutinize the garden. Each day's tour usually starts with a specific agenda in mind. If it's June: Did those incarvilleas I raised so tentatively from seed last year finally unfold their buds? If it's April: Did the kohlrabi seeds I planted in flats last week germinate? If it's December: How are the corn salads doing under all the snow? If it's September: I'm curious about the color of those chrysanthemum volunteers.

Whatever the motive, it's just the start. On the way to the kohlrabi flats I notice a few slugs munching on the tulips and pause to pick them off one at a time. I linger a moment to peer inside the bowl of a bright red tulip bloom, delighted to notice the perfect twelve-pointed black star rimmed in yellow that adorns the center of the flower's cup. No one could ever dream up a black, yellow, and red tulip if this one wasn't already so common. Several years ago I bought twelve red Appeldoorn tulips and twelve Queen of the Night purple-black tulips. Every other year since then I have dutifully divided them and replanted them in clumps anywhere I thought they might flourish. Now, there are well over a hundred, and they surprise me each spring by popping up totally unexpected in the middle of the asparagus bed, along the edges of the strawberry patch, on a well-worn piece of hard ground next to the kids' swing set, and even at six or eight different places deep in the woods. The expectation of gazing upon all those iron-constitutioned tulips thriving so admirably in each of their varied environments now sends me down the hill to linger a moment among the tulip-blooming strawberries. It's colder here; the tulips still look a week away. I turn uphill and north and walk toward the swing set.

On the way to examining an isolated tulip bed along a deer path at the edge of the woods—one I planted four years ago as an outright gourmet gift to the local deer population—my eyes fall upon the Comice pear, which is also in full bloom. I never fail to stop and admire this tree whose white flower display outdoes any other fruit tree in the garden. The sight of it causes me to recall just how bizarre those pear flowers smelled last year. What was it? Apple blossom sweet, but with an undercurrent of fried chicken. I plunge my nose into the center of a pear flower and take note that the fragrance is not precisely chicken but rather hush puppy.

I break into a smile, take a step backward from the pear, scan the hillside, and notice that the Jacob's ladder growing beside a boulder has doubled in size from last year. Stooping down to admire the plant's ferny leaves, I see that the imposing but prickly sea holly I cut to the ground last summer has left behind twenty new plants growing in the gravel of the footpath. And what's that on the other side of the boulder? It looks like the Maltese Cross plant I forgot even existed. It must have broken the soil last night. The color of the new plant is an unusual yellow-green, not unlike the leaves growing at the tips of an apricot tree. My attention turns down the hill toward the newly planted Puget Gold apricots. They are showing no discernible flowers this spring. This puts me back on my feet to take a closer look. But on the way, a raven starts croaking my approach from a fir tree, which causes two mallard ducks to beat a swift retreat from the pond located farther below. The sudden bedlam of two quacking ducks and one croaking raven stops me in my tracks. Time passes. I don't know how much. I forget where I am. Who I am . . .

. . . I regain my senses staring at a mossy bedrock covered over again in the tiny sapphire wildflower known locally as blue-eyed Mary. I reckon that no more than ten minutes has passed since I left the computer screen. Time to end this midmorning break. Venture inside, get back to work. And yet there is still something incomplete. I was on my way to check the kohlrabis. Or was I?

In fact, it's the same every day. I end up nowhere in particular. Only the voyage matters, rarely the destination. I am an impulsive wanderer led passively around the garden by secret garden voices heard only by me, veritable devas guiding my steps, offering specific instructions about where I may turn, when I may stop and linger.

These daily sojourns remind me of a pilgrim's progress along the holy labyrinth inscribed onto the floor of Chartres cathedral. It is recorded that some pilgrims are able to maneuver the twisting path blindfolded, as if led by the Holy Ghost himself. But the path of the Chartres labyrinth eventually leads a pilgrim to a physical center point. By contrast, my own garden path never directs me to the same place twice. I prefer it that way because attaining the center point of any labyrinth seems a mixed blessing. The objective has become the only draw; it offers a greater thrill than anything found along the path. Although the center may indeed divulge an ultimate revelation, all roads from there on in lead back to the edge where a mundane world awaits. Undertake the same journey again, tread those same bricks a second time, make the same turns, and the revelation loses all elements of surprise. Although both my garden and my daily walk through it contain no nucleus, no endpoint, no unifying path, my devas have taught me well that the center can reside wherever I am located at any particular moment. Although this may sound like a statement in praise of conceit, in fact it is the exact opposite. To wander in this manner, one must first surrender one's ego to the equanimity of place.

The ancient Maya of Middle America possessed a compass distinctly different from our own navigational compass. The Mayan compass possessed not only the standard four directions but a fifth direction as well, located in the center. Whereas a standard navigator's compass leads one onward and outward—which in its own way offers up an apt symbology for our own restless civilization—the Mayan fifth direction informs an inner journey: the place where a person already is. Because the fifth direction *grounds* whoever consults it as much as the other four directions *lead*, it instills a sense of place anywhere a person may be at any particular moment. The fifth direction offers its navigator a kind of self-awareness Post-it Note reminder about the here and now. In truth, there is no place we might venture any better than where we already are.

This five-direction compass of the Maya was further distinguished by the peculiarity of each of the five points possessing its own distinct color. North was white and presumably implied snow, which the Maya encountered on their northern trade expeditions, or which may have even survived in mythic form from ancient tribal memories of migrations over the land bridge. South was yellow, perhaps alluding to the sun. East was red, where the sun rises. West was black for the night.

The fifth direction was green.

Although linguists have recently made some progress translating Mayan hieroglyphs, both the written and symbolic records defy most of our attempts to render them explicit. Commenting on this, the poet Charles Olson once expressed the wonderful idea that although Mayan culture may befuddle archaeologists, it offers a deep well of inspiration for poets because most of its rich symbology—and there is plenty of it—will never be translated. Because anything can mean anything, every interpretation is as credible as any other. And no interpretation is disallowed.

In just that spirit, I find it eminently plausible that the fifth direction of the Mayan compass, this green heart of the world, refers to a paradise garden. This device was a gardener's compass. All the ways a gardener might use such a tool I cannot imagine. However, this I do know: It seems the only compass worth consulting for anyone lost in the process of taking introspective and directionless walks through one's own garden. This is a compass for navigators trying to plot a course toward the here and now.

Charles Olson's assessment of Mayan culture also casts a shard of light on archetypal and historic notions about the place called paradise. Paradise has always been a concept as elusive as the Mayan fifth direction. Most of us have an idea what it looks like, what it feels like, although, at best, we have never experienced anything more than a fleeting glimpse of it on our way to and from life's more commonplace destinations. Perhaps that is the one reason we are not certain if the word refers to an actual physical place or instead a state of mind. In fact, its ability to encompass both place *and* perception without ever getting lassoed as precisely one or the other suggests that paradise is found at the intersection where enlightenment meets a sense of place. But the king has no clothes, or, in this case, paradise has no physical substance.

That may explain why so many accounts of paradise read like the Taoist text that insists words always mean their opposite. Those among us who insist they can picture paradise best are thus presumed to know it least. They display too little humility, and too much foolishness, while neither trait is encountered in paradise. And yet, even by declaring it to be so, I myself seem to be displaying too little humility. Too much foolishness.

To the Italian psyche of the thirteenth century, the compass of the spirit pointed in only three directions: up to God, sideways to limbo, and down to Satan. Dante's *Divine Comedy* expressed well the prevailing belief that heaven itself is the only paradise. Heaven was as real a place, as real a landmark, as the neighborhood church. But although it was definitely a place, it was also an emotional medium that encompassed all who were fortunate enough to reside within it. The angelic community and the paradisal mind-set could no more exist apart from the locale of heaven than a fish could live out of water. As a geography lesson, *The Divine Comedy* described heaven as a cloud-filled vista without ground and without corners. Heaven was an aerie, populated by angels floating in endless procession. It was a residence where night seemed never to fall. As our own residences are constructed out of nails and lumber, so Dante's paradise was constructed out of long shards of light cast by God himself. Heaven was also an acoustic environment where liturgical harp music would ostensibly be piped in forever. There was no water. No plants. No animals. No rocks. Besides God's mesmerizing physical presence, and his odd drillmaster's interest in making the angels march in precise columns forever, there was no other stimulus. These qualities alone make Dante's medieval vision of a heavenly paradise seem downright unparadisal to the modern mind. Pertinent to the subject matter of this book, Dante's paradise was not a garden.

If heaven is a place of the spirit although not of this Earth, then the concept of *Utopia* offers a far more earthbound vision of paradise. Unlike heaven, Utopia is not paradisal by definition. It is, instead, a problem to be solved, a conscious community *design* that attempts to encompass a perfection of spirit, economy, and politics—a place that idealistic city planners and community leaders have been envisioning and attempting throughout history. Although many Utopian communities have been blueprinted, and several have been constructed and inhabited, none has ever achieved the paradisal perfection that exists on paper and in the human imagination.

Thomas More, social visionary and archbishop of Canterbury under Henry VIII, invented the term *Utopia* as the name for one of his own perfect city-states. That name, Utopia, seems nearly offensive in its aptness. This term we now use to label any peaceful, happy human state is actually a mix of Greek and Latin words that translate into English as "nowhere." As that translation is meant to counsel, Utopia is a paradox. It will continue to exist *nowhere* as long as human beings remain human, as long we retain all our cumulative frailties.

Until the middle of the nineteenth century, most Utopian visions paid special attention both to the soil and to an enlightened sense of place. Whether this was the Renaissance ideal city controlling the necessary land for its survival, or the citizens of another of Thomas More's city-states, Amaurote, taking turns at farming, all stressed the importance of working closely with the rhythms of nature.

The industrial revolution introduced a mass migration from the countryside to the city, cleaving human experience from the soil, introducing a schism between human sensibilities and a sense of place. Utopia took on a new meaning, now promoted as a happy human beehive, the source of humanity's greatest hope on Earth, a guide to action, the embodiment of reason, the solution to all social problems, the happy outcome of progress.[1] But the development of heavy industry in the mid–nineteenth century soon warped this sunny vision, changing it again, this time from an intellectual exercise illuminating the characteristics of an ideal midsized town to something much less desirable, much more ominous—the bleak outcome of the dominant industrial society. The idea of "progress" itself had lost much of its sheen. Today, the very term *Utopia* sometimes accrues this same disheartening connotation: any unrealistic project doomed to failure.[2]

By the middle of the twentieth century, a bleak, totalitarian vision of Utopia crystallized, perhaps epitomized by Aldous Huxley's *Brave New World*, where even the process of giving birth was moved into a factory. No matter how bleak it seems, the historical realization of the sundering between the human psyche and a sense of place that *Brave New World* describes can be found in many aspects of modern culture. We find it in the modern suburb where malls replace towns, cars replace walking, franchises replace stores related to place, and aggregations of human population replace real community.

But our vision of Utopia keeps changing as it continues to mirror contemporary visions about human society both present and future. Historian Theodore Roszak has written that modern visions of Utopia can be divided into two philosophical camps. "The first—it may be called the *reversionary* scenario—was begun by wishing the industrial world away. The nineteenth century socialist leader and artist William Morris typifies this viewpoint. . . . Morris envisaged a post-industrial future that recreated the preindustrial past, a society of villages, family farms, and tribal settlements. In contrast, other Utopians—the *technophiles*—have enthusiastically embraced the urban-industrial system, hoping to see it mature into a wholly new order of life in which science and technology have permanently mastered the forces of nature."[3]

In his prepresidential role as spokesperson for GE, Ronald Reagan told us that "progress is our most important product." In other words, progress is good, and the newer product is better than the older product. EPCOT Center in Florida, a techno-Utopia offered to the general public in the form of a theme park, was founded on the inherent goodness of progress. Visitors are guided into a future where an array of incredible gadgets is meant to leave the impression that life there is better than it is today. "The dominions of the Future World literally knows no bounds," declares EPCOT's official park document.

But there is a fatal flaw to all of this. There can be no final product that achieves this longed-for perfection. Were it true, there would be nothing more to buy. The system would crash. In his book *In the Absence of the Sacred*, social critic Jerry Mander has written that commercialized visions of sterilized perfection, whether packaged as tourist destinations, shopping malls, or even space colonies,

> are symptomatic of the same modern malaise: a disconnection from a place on Earth that we can call Home. With the natural world—our true home—removed from our lives, we have built on top of the pavement a new world, a new Eden, perhaps a mental world of creative dreams. . . . Though we still live on the

Planet Earth, we are disconnected from it, afloat on pavement, in the same way the astronauts float in space.[4]

Whether we seek William Morris's past or EPCOT's future, Utopia seems as much a tense as it is a place. Morris would have us believe that we lost our chance for Utopia the first time around and should now get busy reconstructing an old and often difficult preindustrial lifestyle around a new enlightened mind-set that knows how to appreciate it better. EPCOT turns the clock in the other direction. It asks us to look to the future. Yet no matter which tense we choose, the Utopian vision of paradise still remains as Thomas More first defined it: nowhere as ever.

Most designed Utopias favor the trickle-down theory: the concept that an ideal social plan fosters a community of happy, well-rounded individuals. Jerry Mander's suggestion that happy homes lead to happy communities takes us in the opposite direction. The concept of *home* offers another example of a term we believe has always existed much the same as we comprehend it today. It isn't so. Whereas most every language has a word for *house*, a separate word for *home* is invariably unique to the languages of northern Europe. The only attribute common to both house and home is *shelter*. According to architect Witold Rybczynski, this new word, *home*, was invented by the seventeenth-century Dutch.[5] What so distinguished the Dutch home from all its predecessors was that the Dutch themselves regarded home not only as a physical "place" but also as a "state of being." The unique attributes of the Dutch home included convenience, comfort, domesticity, privacy, intimacy, and beauty.

But Rybczynski's idea of a successful home is one that does not even attempt to attain paradisal status unless the four walls are themselves surrounded by exemplary grounds—when, in short, there is a garden. Whereas the garden serves as an adjunct of a house, it is, in fact, an integrated component of a home. The purpose of the garden within the scheme of an ideal home lies in its ability to imbue a lifestyle with nature's own rhythms. The soil, the plants, the beds—the resident's own creative participation in the process—all of them are as much a part of the essential home as anything that occurs within the four walls. It becomes impossible to tell where the home ends and where the garden begins. They are a unit.

Whereas home and Utopia are meant to coax the human mind to tranquillity, both places remain physically external to one's own mind. Buddhism teaches something very different—that the only place to search for paradise is within oneself. More precisely, the Buddha preached that desire is the basis of all suffering. Whether that desire gets expressed as a striving for a techno-future, a longing for a simpler past, a nice home, or even the eventual attainment of heaven, paradise eludes us. The Buddhists did, however, believe that paradise exists. Its gates can be thrown open at any moment. By anyone.

Certain Buddhist sects promote a spiritual regimen known as the path of the Bodhisattva. The Bodhisattva may be best described as a *nearly* perfect human being. He or she knows how to throw open the gates but has consciously decided against taking the final plunge to enlightenment until all other sentient beings are also enlightened. In such a manner, the Bodhisattva dedicates his or her own life *to help bring about* the enlightenment of all beings. Here is a spiritual path founded on good deeds, good lifestyle, and deep compassion for others. Because Buddhism preaches reincarnation, this dedication may even span several lifetimes.

In its own way, the concept of the Bodhisattva offers a temporal paradox as striking as Thomas More's paradox of Utopia. Bodhisattvas succeed best at teaching their path when they themselves exude a life lived in the here and now. For all intents and purposes, they have attained paradise *within*. Yet they must keep one eye firmly focused on a distant future when all beings will be enlightened. In other words, they dedicate their lives and their own enlightenment to attaining paradise *without*. Although it would seem that the Bodhisattva thus bears two contrary visions of perfection at the same time, in fact there is only one. Paradise is integrative. Paradise exists in the present for whoever lives in the here and now, *and* it exists in the future when all sentient beings are enlightened.

The Bodhisattva's legendary peace of mind is not dissimilar from the mind-set of Dante's heavenly angels. The difference is that an angel resides in a perfect heaven, while a Bodhisattva lives on a suffering Earth. Yet perhaps the greatest attraction of the Bodhisattva path is that unlike angels, Buddhist aspirants do not need to die first to find a paradisal peace of mind. A Bodhisattva's feet are firmly planted in this world. Unlike angels, Bodhisattvas are not perfect beings. Nor are they precisely saints, either. They bumble along from incarnation to incarnation, living the compassionate life, and working humbly toward the ultimate goal of combining a paradise within and a paradise without. Since it is the Earth itself that is without, the true focus of a Bodhisattva is healing a suffering Earth and *all* the sentient beings thereof. The Bodhisattva's life is thus revealed as an unequivocally ecological act.

Unlike traditional Christianity and Judaism, which focus on the individual attainment of heaven by overcoming the pitfalls of society and Earth, Buddhism preaches that the attainment of personal paradise by any individual can never be separated from either social or ecological paradise. There lies its major pitfall. Aspirants to the Bodhisattva path are constantly being reminded by scripture not to confuse the expression of their zeal with its objective. Finding the balance between the personal and the social extremely difficult to sustain, aspirants often reach for the golden ring of paradise by working only on their mind, their home, their garden, their happiness, to the exclusion of community and planet. But the Bodhisattva path is very forgiving. It counsels this: when personal happiness does not willingly harm others, it helps heal the planet in its own humble way.

There is far more to mining the wealth of place than the seeing, the touching, the digging, and the planting of it. As my morning walk leads me from the mossy bedrock to the tulips to the pears to the blue-eyed Mary to the kohlrabis, my mind empties of chatter even as it fills up with the wealth of relations I have with rocks, moss, kohlrabis, weather, insects. Sometimes I sense that the garden is best defined as the walk itself—the commencement of a long, aimless sojourn from relation to relation. Setting off on that endless journey seems to offer a more substantial glimpse of paradise than any social recipe or even religious path.

But we are creatures of ideas and explanations, and they have a way of popping up no matter how successful we become at emptying our thoughts. Walking back in the house with paradise on my mind, I reach for the dictionary and discover that Webster is particularly prosaic about the emotion called happiness. He dredges up mere one- or two-word synonyms like *contentment, joy, luck, good fortune, pleasure,* and even *appropriateness,* with no attempt made to offer a more complex definition.

William Morris was much more astute about it when he wrote: "The secret of happiness lies in taking a genuine interest in all the details of daily life, and in elevating them to art."[6] According to Morris, true happiness would seem to be best found through the creative experience of the home life and not through external channels such as a striving for heaven or some perfect state called Utopia.

One of our contemporary champions of the organic farmer's life, Stanley Crawford, has described a so-called Pascalian room in his own home on a New Mexico garlic farm, to which he "retreats to write, daydream, and reconstruct the world on more acceptable lines." He too strives for a modicum of personal happiness working creatively with the place he lives and wryly compares his own pocket paradise with the greater "nowhere" paradise we call the American dream:

> Each time I buy a newspaper or reach to turn on the radio or open a magazine, I make the conscious decision to keep up with the mechanical rabbit of official cultural life; and each time I refrain, or refuse, and leave the paper at the store and the radio silent during dinnertime, and the television eye dormant through the night, I make another kind of decision, for another kind of center to a life.[7]

Paradise is elusive, which may explain why this writing about paradise tends to wander about its central premise as much as I wander about my garden. Zooming in on the word itself, we find that *paradise* is an English adaptation of the Persian *pairidaeza*, originally meaning "walled garden." The first paradise, Eden, offers a suitable description of the perfect self-contained, walled-in Middle Eastern garden. The symbology of Eden is steeped in metaphors of the paradise garden. *Adam*, for instance, is the Hebrew word for mankind, while also insinuating the word for soil (*adamah*). The root of both *Adam* and *adamah* is *dam*, meaning "lifeblood"—signifying that the same lifeblood flowing through mankind also flows through the soil and the rest of creation.[8] Dust to dust. Everything Adam or Eve ever needed was right there for the taking. The oldest profession was foraging.

Ultimately the paradise garden represented by Eden proved as "nowhere" as any gloomy Utopian vision to emerge from the industrial revolution. The presence of snake and apple added a worldly measure of stress and tragedy to this peaceable kingdom. Not incidentally, the biblical Fall from God's grace makes it abundantly clear that the same Judeo-Christians who proselytized a heaven apart from Earth also believed that neither curiosity nor women have any place in an earthly paradise.

The facts that we human beings are incessantly curious and that half our numbers are female demonstrate just how adamant Western religion feels about withholding any hope of locating paradise here on Earth. The legacy of Eden treated Earth as a kind of prison, a punishment we must endure for eating the forbidden fruit from the tree of knowledge. God, the gardener of Eden, chastises Adam like a tyrannical orchardist discovering a trespasser stealing apples from his prize trees: "cursed is the ground for thy sake." Then he turns to castigate Eve: "I will greatly multiply thy sorrow."[9]

Ever afterward, at least within the Judeo-Christian tradition, the very idea of an earthly paradise was regarded as an oxymoron. Many have since argued—most recently the Creation Spiritualists within the Catholic church—that the Western spiritual view of Earth as a prison rather than paradise laid the conceptual foundation for the current environmental crisis now raging here on Earth.

Despite the rancor left over from Eden—despite the pall that its preachment to dispel nature from our hearts has cast over the modern world—a strong link still connects gardens to paradise. Working our own garden on a warm June morning—listening to the birds, smelling the flowers, popping peas or strawberries into our mouth—may be as close to achieving the original Eden as most of us can ever hope to experience.

Bioregional writer Joe Hollis promotes a lifestyle he calls *paradise gardening*. He defines it as a way of life in service to a garden and which, in turn, is equally maintained by that same garden. But this is different from our current notions of farming. Whereas a farmer plants primarily to sell, the paradise gardener is sustained by "planting to forage."

The garden walk I described at the opening of this chapter suddenly takes on a new purpose. Not only does it empty the mind and unburden the soul, but, depending on the season, it fills the stomach as well. That's just the start. In Hollis's words, the objective of paradise gardening is nothing less than "a reintegration of human needs attained through one activity."[10] With a lot of tender loving care, good landscaping design, and savvy plant knowledge, most everything a human being needs in this world—including food, comfort, recreation, exercise, entertainment, medicine, church, museum, university, social clubhouse—will be there for the foraging.

In such a manner, paradise gardening skillfully coalesces notions of a Buddhist self-aware paradise with the Utopian social goals of an agrarian anarchist. The vision strongly reflects the nineteenth-century artisan philosophy espoused by the aforementioned William Morris. Like Morris, Hollis asks us to perceive paradise gardening as a juncture where artfulness directly serves life. In fact, we might go so far as to define this paradise as the place where art is indistinguishable from life, and where simplicity is codified as the best path for achieving happiness. The resultant work/art ethic reflects what any person is able to achieve with his or her own two hands and without resorting to the gasoline engine. This hand/hand tool "limitation" provocatively redefines the size of any person's individual plot and thus, in its own way, prods an outright revolution in the human relationship to place.

Modern agriculture does not survive unscathed in a world planted to paradise gardens. Hollis maintains that even the "good" farmer loves nature in the context of plowing it up every year. Meanwhile, an eye to basic ecology will demonstrate that the constantly disturbed environment favors invasive life-forms that are fast-growing and short-lived. Over time, agriculture has precipitated the global mass destruction of slower-growing forests. The result is that "our addiction to annual crops and disturbed habitats has put us at odds with the main thrust of the biosphere."[11]

Paradise gardening also provides a political and social agenda. Hollis distinguishes the paradise garden from modern commerce. He considers the division of labor (my back for your brains, etc.) to be an "insulting premise" because it makes "everyone less than a complete human being." Perhaps more to the point, the modern concept of work-as-money-drudgery is anathema to paradise gardening. Hollis takes his cue from Eden when he describes work as "whatever you are doing when you'd rather be doing something else. . . . Genesis refers to the same matter in saying that only outside the garden do we have to earn our living 'by the sweat of our brow.' "[12] Paradise gardening is the cure. Because the institution of gardening has always served as a splendid social lubricant, Hollis insists that a growing society of paradise gardeners will exert a grass-roots momentum to the future direction of society. It will deliver bioregional politics to society.

In such a manner we are subtly coerced away from an intriguing lifestyle choice and asked to take a long look at yet another contender in the rabbit's race for social Utopia. Were life so straightforward. As the thumbnail sketch of Utopian history cautioned earlier, ideals that work for strongly motivated individuals rarely succeed when repackaged as political blueprints. There is a danger here of turning the finely crafted vision of paradise gardening into just another nowhere garden. Paradise gardening fails not because it doesn't have many good things to offer, but because its objective is too explicit. It turns gardening into something it is not: a breeding ground for political revolutionaries. Paradise gardening's implied Calvinist rigidity also confronts us with another single-issue solution that overlooks the bewildering complexity of modern life.

We might wish, however, that certain aspects of this vision of Utopia were far more established than they are. Certainly there is an urgency to promoting a sense of place. Gardening does encourage self-awareness. It does crystallize community. Gardeners do connect with one another, and that connection likewise clarifies an important function of gardening. Is it even possible to garden successfully *without* tapping into the deep well of local community knowledge? Maybe so, but only if one possesses, instead, a bottomless pocketbook and a fool's willingness to plant and replant by trial and error. Obviously, the best way to gather together enough healthy plants to fill up one's own garden is to discover what plants and techniques already work locally. Gardeners exuberantly encourage the sharing of information, stories, guided tours, cuttings, and seeds with anyone interested enough to value these gifts. This does not, however, demand organization in the same way that, for instance, raising children does.

But although most of us perceive our gardens to be the same tool as Hollis's, we use it for a different purpose. My own is a love affair and not a social blueprint. It serves as a place for emptying out the cares of the world rather than plotting its overthrow. The directions it offers are nonstrident, spiritual, and creative. I thrive on its mystery; it's rather like consulting the green center of the Mayan compass to find out where its lessons could possibly be leading. Therein lies its power.

Inside my own garden, I walk awhile. Plant my feet awhile. Smell the roses. Search for meaning in the squawking of ravens, the pulse of duck wings beating on the air. I spend my time envisioning the distant future through the branches of a sequoia tree. And then I rise to my feet and walk some more. It may only be an oversight, but the paradise garden glaringly overlooks this exceedingly *sensual* relationship that exists between gardener and garden. I might go so far as to say that the sensual side of gardening is the creative glue that holds gardener to garden. It is neither overtly political nor overtly ethical, although it achieves both. In that manner, my own pocket paradise of a garden serves me (and my society) best when it remains built on solid ground. And an empty mind.

My pocket paradise makes me as prone to impassioned hyperbole as Dante's description of heaven. Because it is surrounded by a tall forest on all sides, shards of dappled light stream through the Douglas firs and onto the dazzling old rosebushes on any sunny morning in June. I too am dazzled. This is what it must mean to inhabit the land rather than simply own a piece of property. The robins, goldfinches, and house finches provide a music seemingly as sweet as an angel's harp recital. The Anna's hummingbirds zoom a hundred feet straight up into the air and then dive-bomb within inches of my nose just to float there and stare deep into my eyes. These indefatigable birds seem as close to angels incarnate as any person might hope to encounter in this life. The powerful destructive gales of January, the warm rains of April, the dry heat of August, and the harvest of October all hint that a neutral and powerful sky god indeed rules this garden from above. Amid such splendor, the place itself acquires a life and a purpose all its own. It bespeaks the practical value of emptying one's head. Only by doing so am I able to hear the quiet whispers telling the tale of that life. And that purpose. It leverages me to do the right thing.

But there are problems to glimpsing paradise. Like a person who suddenly finds the meaning of life in Jesus, gardeners who glimpse pocket paradise sometimes want to convert all their friends to the religion of gardening. Joe Hollis's enthusiasm is an example of what we might refer to as the paradise syndrome. It develops like this: Gardening is such a fine blending of art and nature that we gardeners are obviously very evolved people. We are the ones who get it. We don't just talk about air pollution; we also grow our own broccoli, which keeps a few more broccoli-toting, exhaust-spewing trucks off the highway. Other gardeners are comrades in the just cause of promoting a sense of place. But why doesn't everybody garden?

Were that the extent of our elitism, all might still bode well for the nongardeners of the world. However, these essentially positive feelings about weaning ourselves from the teat of petrochemical commerce occasionally show another negative side as well. What started out as enthusiasm, "I enjoy gardening and gardeners," sometimes develops into this autocratic statement: "Everyone should garden." We born-again Utopians stop praising other homegrown broccoli *growers* and now don the mask of a grand inquisitor bent on reviling supermarket broccoli *shoppers*. There is us, and there is them. *They* stand guilty for putting ever more broccoli-toting trucks on the road. How can *they* be so irresponsible? Don't *they* care about the greenhouse effect? Don't *they* know that every nonlocal purchase *they* make at the supermarket activates a commensurate amount of added air pollution?

Ironically, the shadow we cast over nongardeners darkens whatever aspirations for sunny paradise we engender by growing our own broccoli. And the lesson of the paradise syndrome is this: gardening works its magic only when its Utopian message gets dug into the ground along with the bonemeal. It is always there. Always doing its job, winning converts, aiding the planet. You just never see it. And if you do, it's not helping anything. Hoe it down deeper where the roots can get at it.

I cut away the chicken-wire, deer-proofing ring from around the trunk of a six-year-old prune-plum this past spring. I noticed this April how becoming the tree's wide architecture of bare limbs looks when covered in pure white blooms attended by honeybees. Certain plants at certain times definitely instill a sense of paradise more than others. Each to its season.

The humble bronze-leaved fennel, evergreen in a mild winter, may be capable of achieving this grandest of natural statements more often than any other plant in the garden. Whether winter or summer, the plant is capable at any time of stopping me dead in my tracks. This is mostly due its depth of color—an improbable turquoise-chocolate-copper-maroon foliage as softly luxuriant as a mink's coat. I stare at it, quite unable to discern any one color; staring and then staring again, trying to achieve some focus to its filigree finery. Yet all to no avail. So I keep staring and am transfixed like a tourist standing at the rim of the Grand Canyon working hard to make unpracticed eyes focus on an inconceivable depth of field.

In every respect besides color, the bronze fennel is identical to the common green garden fennel. Just like common fennel, this bronzy cousin possesses one of the most intoxicating fragrances in the garden. This attribute is a bonus, and it causes me to step quite a bit closer than I might otherwise wish in my visual bedazzlement. I boldly pinch a leaf and inhale the licorice fragrance deep into my lungs. Perhaps the combination of similarity to and difference from the common fennel is what enhances the plant to my eyes and nose. It makes me wonder why Dante has nothing whatsoever to say about the fragrance of heaven. Light and sound are everywhere. He certainly wasn't a gardener.

I am on my feet again. More paradise. A ten-foot-tall pyramid of green beans on the day of harvest. A peach tree so laden with heavy, golden fruit that its branches are starting to break. A gaggle of giggling little girls reaching into a row of raspberry bushes while covering their faces and clothes with a fruity red stain. Each in its own way invokes pocket paradise.

Or if it's September, my feet carry me eastward to the artichoke patch. Artichokes provide ripe buds for over a month. And yet I insist upon leaving the largest and roundest of the buds on the plant. Let them open up into bushy purple everlasting flowers. To my mind, leaving the best is an act that demonstrates a Buddhist respect for the plant as a living being. Working for the enlightenment of all sentient beings sometimes means relating to the artichokes as co-creators. This is a give-and-take relationship. It honors a good provider's natural urge to go to seed.

It also carries with it a certain quality of creative naughtiness: snubbing one's nose at the work ethnic—the prudent farmer's money-bound avowal that food plants are only an economic consideration. I stare at the purple flowers rimmed in their gold calyxes and huff at the scientist's cold insistence that neither plants nor gardens are sentient beings. Who says they aren't? Where's the proof? Much more on that in the pages that follow.

March

Depending on weather, the march of the flowers commences between the first and third week of March. Usually leading the procession are the Galanthus, the snowdrops. Best loved for the green dot that blushes each cheek of the nodding bloom.

Following in the procession, some of the names familiar, others among them less familiar, faster now, open the crocus, *Chionodoxa*, hyacinth, star magnolia, daffodil, wild currant, *Muscari*, laurustinus, *Euphorbia wulfenii*, saxifrage, shiro plum, anemone De Caen, frost peach, bleeding heart, calypso orchid, tulip, pheasant eye, wood hyacinth. Did I miss any? Certainly, I always miss some. Did I get them in the right order? Not a chance, although that is how it happened one particular March I happened to write them down in a notebook. Microclimates on my land affect bloom time as much as genes do. For instance, identical twins, divisions from the very same bulb, my south-facing daffodils growing alongside the house have long fled the scene while daffodils planted at the edge of the forest are still gathering enough heat to burst their sheaths. Microclimates ensure that a few plants from every species of bulb are in bloom at the same time. What a sight.

What a spring. Every year it's the same. Every year I am as astonished by the pro-cession as if I were a visitor from Mars experiencing spring for the first time.

What *is* the best-smelling March flower? Why not ask what's the best cloud? Yet I am certain it is not the daffodil, which smells like a stale balloon. Meanwhile, the daffodil's close relative, the pheasant eye narcissus, smells so undeniably sweet. The little purple-and-pink calypso orchid that blooms through the forest duff demands I sprawl flat out on the ground to glean its pale fragrance of cinna-mon and apples. So much work makes the scent that much sweeter. Is the subtle fragrance of the calypso orchid better than the more potent vanilla fragrance of the star magnolia? Does the star magnolia smell better than the still more potent *Viburnum burkwoodii*, which bowls me over with its heady gardenia fragrance? And what of the still more potent hyacinth? The fragrance would be pleasant enough if there just wasn't so much of it. If this flower were a woman, she would be stat-uesque. If it were a man, he would be a bodybuilder.

I do have a March favorite, but not because of its scent so much as for the sen-timents that accompany that scent. The fragrance of the blireana plum flower im-mediately transports me back to a long-lost event from my childhood. I am seven years old, sitting contentedly in the back seat of a two-tone blue Nash. We are driving home from a Sunday visit to the penny candy store located down the street from the Wayside Inn in Sudbury, Massachusetts. I am sleepy but con-tented, clutching a bag full of, among other treats, wax lips and tiny wax bottles filled with flavored sugar water. My teeth are picking at the best candy of all, a paper strip approximately four inches wide and twenty-four inches long upon which pink sugar-dot candies have been deposited. I had forgotten those candies ever existed. But here they are again in the fragrance of the blireana plum flower. In my reverie, I smell the frayed Nash upholstery upon which my boyish cheek is resting.

The Soil Garden

Our schools diminish the lesson of history by restricting it to the story of a few motivated Caucasian men doing battle and avoiding battle, conquering lands, administering government, creating works of art, and inventing and/or selling new technology. While this singular slant certainly has its place as one subplot of the greater story of civilization, the current global situation begs for other subplots— other versions—for instance, a revisionist history that emphasizes, instead, the changing human relationship to soil.

The relationship to soil is not the same thing as the history of agriculture. This is not precisely the story of what man invented what plow or what man crossed what seed to extend the harvest and grant a survival advantage to what empire-in-the-making. Nor does this history recount the oft-repeated tale of some ingenious man tapping certain natural resources to produce artificial plant stimulants, engineering new tools, or altering genetic materials. This is, instead, a bastard history: part agriculture, part gardening, part ecology, part nature worship, part feminism, part war, part perception, part marketing, part property rights, part resource development, part urban isolationism.

Some of these topics will be covered in this chapter. The rest will be examined later on. For the moment, if paraphrasing helps us comprehend the history of the

soil a little better, then regard it as the long-term relationship between human beings and place.

If teachers taught the history of soil in school, they might begin by unveiling
certain of its most revealing secrets through a series of recurring bell curves—up-
tilted spurts indicating various city-states in blossom, but which eventually peak
out and finally start to sink under the weight of what has been a recurring historical disrespect for the soil. Consider the case of the Middle Eastern city of Petra,
which was one of the most vibrant centers in the Roman and Byzantine empires.
But the citizens loved their cheese and meat more than their soil. After years of
overgrazing goats, the soil became depleted. Ground cover disappeared. Desertification reared its ugly head. Petra was finally abandoned sometime between A.D.
500 and 900. Now, more than a thousand years later, that area is still desert. The
bell curve would show us a similar situation at the ancient Mayan city of Copán.
The inhabitants suddenly abandoned their magnificent priestly city and evidently
disavowed their centrally organized religion in favor of withdrawing deep into the
jungle where they re-formed into much smaller villages. This exodus was at least
partially caused by slash-and-burn farming wrongly attempted on an urban scale.
The thin topsoil eventually degraded. People couldn't feed themselves. They left
Copán rather than starve.

The metropolitan areas that flourished longer often exhibited no better record
of local soil nurturance than Petra or Copán. These temporal winners in the violent thrust called civilization survived instead by expanding the land base upon
which their food-getting and natural resource system was based—a state of grace
achieved most often through warfare. For instance, a major reason the Mongol
hordes set out to conquer the known world in the thirteenth century was to
search for new grassland to graze their horses.

The clear pattern that connects armies to soil often displays an inverse ratio: as
the fertility of the soil depletes, armies grow. Given this unambiguous relationship
between the history of war and the history of soil, we might conclude that much
of the language of patriotism that promotes personal sacrifice and civic glory cam-
ouflages the real business of war, which is soil grabbing. In their rush for glory,
how very few young men were ever told that it was not honor, not country, but
rather the dirt itself that they were being shipped off to win.

Circumstances change. The industrial revolution has definitely altered the inverse proportion that formerly existed between armies and soil. Since the introduction of the steam engine, and later the gasoline engine, wars have been fought not only *with* machines but also *for* machines. In the process, aggression itself has lost much of its historical organic impetus. Desert Storm, for instance, was fought entirely on sand where almost nothing grows; fought entirely in the cause of the petrochemical products lying far beneath those sands which are used only to feed and maintain human machines.

The cold war was even less organic. This was a "conceptual" war founded on and waged for ideologies that existed nowhere else besides the minds of human beings. It posed an intellectual question: Whose abstract socioeconomic model, the USSR's or the USA's, would be adopted worldwide? Even the very similar-sounding names of the two combatants are inorganic acronyms that stand for political concepts (union/united, soviet socialist, states/republics) and not for any geophysical location. The only word in either country's acronym that is *not* conceptual is *America*. Perhaps ironically, this recognizes a man, Amerigo Vespucci, who never stepped foot on that country's soil.

Our history of the soil shows us one other version of modern inorganic warfare. This one is also conceptual: a contemporary manifestation of ancient tribal warfare waged in the cause of fundamentalist autonomy. The organic difference between modern tribal wars and ancient tribal wars is subtle. The modern version is not fought *for* soil so much as it seems a stand *against* foreign concepts. Islamic jihad, for instance, might be understood as a primal reaction to the modern age itself: a result of the well-grounded fear that the predominant global macroeconomy is geared to extinguish any tribal identity, any religious or cultural disposition, any localized sense of place, through formidable weapons like women's lib, Coca-Cola, and reruns of "Dallas."

Many futurists warn that we live perched at the brink of a gloomy age increasingly affected by human overpopulation and resource depletion on a global scale. National boundaries no longer have primacy in defining the resources accessible by any nation. Given that reality, the only way that the old soil/army model of war could ever reestablish itself would be if there were another nearby inhabited planet with vast amounts of virgin till. In other words, the perennial civic habit of sending armies out in search of new virgin till is no longer an option. The land has run out. The original organic premise of war has lost its center. Although the shift from organic to inorganic war was a gradual one, 1914—which marks the start of both World War I and the fait accompli of the global macroeconomy—seems an appropriate benchmark for punctuating the end of organic war as it had always been fought.

The history of the soil also demonstrates that the old organic alternatives to war don't always fit the peace in the current era of agribusiness. Wise nations are no longer the ones that necessarily turn their swords into plowshares. Our history of the soil depicts the giant plows of monocrop agribusiness as violent weapons of destruction utilized in a chronic global war fought between human beings and the Earth itself. They are the agricultural equivalent of Russian roulette.

An education that includes a history of the soil gives us a new spin on our own society. The same bell curve that clarifies the fragile vitality of cities also depicts our fickle moment in time as the age of environmentally unsound agribusiness. It tells a tale about the unfortunate in Africa falling prey to mass starvation on a recurring basis. The upheaval is caused, at least in part, by the fact that the best soil in Africa has been given over to monocrops grown for export to rich first-world countries.

As the relationship between out-of-control birthrates and ecology heats up on a global scale, we start to notice that any nation's stable future may have less to do with material wealth and technology and more to do with an inherent respect for the soil. The people of poor nations already exist much closer to the soil than those of us living in the first world who currently consume so much more of the global resource pie. People living in the poorest nations have far less to give up. In that respect, they are better positioned than we are to achieve stasis within their own local environment. As the current lesson of the Brazilian rain forest already foretells, one of the third world's greatest challenges is finding ways to appease a populace who wants to be just like us.

We Americans will have a much harder time changing over to a less consumptive lifestyle, which is precisely the reason a history of the soil is such a crucial subject. Very few of us bother to reflect on the bell curve of Petra as a sign of what lies in store for us. Very few of us make the connection between those people who caretake our food-growing soil today—especially farmers—and the well-being of future generations.

It is not currently fashionable to blame the problem of the American farm on the farmer, and therefore the assessment that follows may at first seem a callous view of what just about everyone agrees to be a tragic situation. But whatever emotions this interpretation may dredge up, everyone can agree that it is a view rarely heard in the mainstream, although it has been voiced by a veritable tidal wave of organic gardeners over the past fifty years.

In contrast to commercial farmers, organic gardeners practice a so-called golden rule of organic gardening that declares we put back into the soil everything we take out. Any gardener who practices this rule soon learns that he or she is not so much growing produce as growing soil. The result is that the organic garden is perhaps best understood as a soil garden. This idea is important enough to deserve repeating: although the organic garden is often described as a place where chemical pesticides and fertilizers are verboten (which is true), in fact it is the place human beings grow soil. Farsighted organic gardeners grow soil so that plants, home, nation, and even planet may prosper. Our revisionist history of the soil lauds organic gardening as one of life's best tutors for teaching a sense of place.

Most organic gardeners would probably agree that the modern farmer *had* to destroy the soil. This conclusion seems all but obvious from even a cursory examination of farm practices over the past two hundred years. A disrespect for the soil was built into the American farm system from the very start. It was perhaps exemplified by the mythical nineteenth-century farmer *bragging* that he'd used up three or four farms in a lifetime. This legendary strong-willed man is the farmer's analogue to the logger's Paul Bunyan clear-cutting entire bioregions, the analogue to the rancher's Pecos Bill leading millions of cattle to tromp over virgin watersheds all across the American West.

These are a few of the more famous historical archetypes of the American dream. Each mythological character is larger than life: the very personification of the manifest destiny that has always been the locus where American idealism meets resource utilization. But manifest destiny is also the credo that justified the annihilation of the Indians and the destruction of the wilderness. It was, and still is, an arrogant thrust onward and outward. A man declaring that he had used up three or four farms was meant to leave the impression that he was an especially hard worker. But *using up a farm* is a euphemism for wasting soil, a result that can only be caused by a woeful ignorance of natural processes. That a man who destroyed soil was ever considered an exemplar offers an ugly reflection of what happens when an individualist credo like the American dream forgets to include a strict proviso to honor future generations.

The American farmer was well along the path of destroying the soil even as our boundaries expanded to encompass all the soil between two oceans. If American farms produced huge crops for well over two hundred years, it was largely due to the fact that America was a vast untapped land and thus already possessed of some of the richest previously untilled farming soils in the world. But what has occurred in that short geological time span couldn't have turned out any worse if the homesteaders had set out to destroy this bountiful bequest on purpose.

The evidence is just about everywhere we look. American farmers in the state of Iowa, the state with the greatest concentration of prime farmland in the United States, have already destroyed half the topsoil. In parts of Ohio, farmers lose two bushels of topsoil for every bushel of corn harvested. Back in 1950, J. Russell Smith wrote that "the soil washed out and blown out of the fields of the United States each year would load a modern freight train long enough to reach around the world eighteen times."[1] All the farmers and ranchers—as if working together—lose an inch of topsoil from these United States every sixteen years. It takes nature one hundred to five hundred years to replace it. The American history of the soil clearly demonstrates that we stand on the edge of an abyss. Our soil bank is nearly bankrupt.

The golden rule of organic gardening provides the best explanation for this loss. Nothing was ever put back in. We simply need to create a mental picture of an operating American farm before 1950 to understand how this actually occurred. In my own musing, I see huge fields of a single crop planted on the same soil year in and year out. But no attempt is ever made to let the soil regenerate by turning largely *nonmarketable* cover crops back into the soil and thus replenishing structural nutrients. The American farmer seemed set to a task of creating an infertile and highly erodable soil. With nothing covering the soil during the winter, the unbound, plowed-up soil simply blew away. The dust bowl that devastated Kansas and Oklahoma in the early 1930s was largely the result of bad soil practice.

It is November as I write this chapter. Where I live, November is the start of winter—a windy, cold, five-month-long rainy season punctuated by plunges in temperature causing frost heaves. Winter storms are capable of dropping two inches of hard, driving rain overnight. Any soil not properly bound up by plant roots soon gets washed into drainage ditches and eventually outfalls into Puget Sound. Although very little can be planted here until mid-March, yesterday as I drove into town I noticed two farmers sitting atop their tractors two miles apart plowing up fifty acres of native grass between them. I hailed one of the men and asked why he would want to be plowing at this time of the year. He answered that springtime was just too busy so he thought he'd get a head start during a season when there wasn't so much to do.

For well over a hundred years hillsides all across this country have been plowed up at inappropriate times by machinery in neat parallel lines as if to fit some abstract geometrist's grid optimized for little else besides the mechanical exigency of maneuvering the wheels of a tractor. This method seemed to optimize the erosion of hillsides, banks, knolls, eskers. It was standard practice, and to hell with any labor-intensive but conservationist terracing of hillsides to make them follow the actual contours of the land—a farming strategy well established in Asia for thousands of years.

Likewise, new machines were constantly being invented to further refine the process of turning soil. Heavier machinery meant that land could be "handled" in greater increments, ensuring that much larger areas could be cultivated by fewer people. But as the next generation of farmers sat ever higher upon ever-larger tractors, they also moved both literally and figuratively farther away from the dirt they now compacted beneath ever-larger wheels. As each farmer endured the roar of ever-louder diesel engines, he also seemed to grow more incapable of hearing the much softer sounds of the ecosystem he worked so implacably to control. And the soil farm was rarely being cultivated.

By 1950, observers of American agriculture had noted that the U.S. population had finally caught up with the available land base. There was simply no more land left to allow farmers to move on once their last farm was exhausted. Perhaps coincidentally, it was at that same historical moment that the long-promised fix of chemical fertilizers and pesticides finally made their dramatic entrance. This meant that any soil's *inherent* fertility was no longer the fundamental element in the farming equation. The richness stored in soil over thousands of years and washed out in fifty was now promised to be replenished by the laying on of highly concentrated amendments tapped from ancient soils long ago transformed into petroleum and coal.

Starting in the 1950s, chemical companies touted petrochemicals as the "modern" farmers' means to take full control over their own destinies by enrichening soil at will and by dosage. But chemical pesticides, herbicides, and fertilizers soon caused the family farm to transmute into a poisoned environment. Members of a farming family were counted wise to take the necessary precautions to protect their health during certain weeks of the season. This also caused a dramatic change in the relationship between farmer and soil. The fields were no longer as friendly as they once were, the land itself now transformed from a place to make a lifestyle into a place to make a living. In some fundamental way, the changeover to large-scale factory farming simply formalizes what was already a diminished relationship between soil and farming lifestyle.

Although fertilizers were now laid on at will, the soil—composed as it is of so much more than applied chemicals—continued to erode away. The reason is simple. Cover crops, which farmers used for thousands of years to add organic matter back into the soil, were now being cast aside in favor of a short-term fix of chemical nitrogen. The laying on of poisons and concentrated fertilizers destroyed many of the microbial organisms and earthworms that give soil its nutritive structure. Anyone who has ever repotted a houseplant knows that the exhausted soil at the very bottom of the old pot looks and feels like black sand. By contrast, healthy soil is sticky and crumbly. It holds together in little balls that can endure the strongest rain and winds. Once we forgo the process of adding organic matter, the once stable crumbs of soil are prone to dissolve into a black sand easily carried away by rain. The thick tires of heavy machines add insult to injury, ruining the essential tilth, or airiness, of the soil. Without tilth, wet soil eventually becomes compacted into hardpan.

The American farmer's two-hundred-year nonrelationship to the soil now cries out to be put on an ethical footing. Half the soil is gone. Over the past twenty years the farmers' independent way of life was sold out through a dependence on technology and chemicals they were never able to afford in the first place. What was once a way of life is now a food production factory.

The methods of organic gardening offer one solution. But farmers are naturally slow to come around. Farmers *farm*; a garden is something else entirely. Then again, perhaps not. Several farm writers searching for a cure to heal the ailing American food production system have commented that the Chinese, for instance, do not *farm* their soil as Americans do—planting vast rows of chemical- and machine-dependent monocrops—but rather they *garden* their farmland in much smaller plots. Plantings are diversified. The Chinese are the world's most avid soil gardeners, returning their organic waste back to the soil through the most comprehensive composting and mulching system in the world. There is even a national industry founded upon the conversion of human excrement into viable compost, perhaps the ultimate symbol of good-sense recycling in an overpopulated world.

The Chinese approach to agriculture is founded upon the golden rule of organic gardening. In certain areas of the country the land has produced crops continuously for five thousand years. And another particularly telling point: the Chinese soil garden still produces far more food per acre than the modern American farm. Former U.S. Secretary of Agriculture Bob Bergland has written that the Chinese feed their huge population by producing nine times more food per acre than what the American farm is able to produce using chemicals and heavy machinery.[2]

But when the approach of the Chinese farm gardener is suggested for America, it is usually rejected out of hand as too labor-intensive. The revised American dream of this late twentieth century no longer encourages children to want to be farm gardeners when they grow up. Somehow, we all envision this lifestyle in terms of a clichéd image of human "worker ants" eking out a hand-to-mouth existence in some third-world totalitarian regime. It is an image very far removed from the modern American mythos of the entrepreneurial agribusinessperson sitting astride any of several pieces of heavy machinery.

In China, a staggering 80 percent of the populace is actively involved in the process of food production. Food is local, bound to place, and thus no centralized disaster could result in mass starvation. In America, even as fewer and fewer farmers produce more and more of our food, the distribution channels that carry the food to our table become ever more complex and ever more distant from the daily business of our lives. On that note, let me repeat once again what is fast turning into a coda for this book. Gardening is the most popular avocation in the United States. It engages seventy million households on a regular basis.[3] Although that figure still runs far short of the 80 percent of the population that farm their gardens in China, a change in American food-growing policy seems just waiting to be activated. Given the number of gardeners, it seems nearly inconceivable that the American people will not revitalize local production as the heart and soul of this nation's food production. In fact, our unwillingness to decentralize may be partly a result of the same issue of image that also defines the American dream. What a food gardener *is* and what a farmer *is* does not translate easily between Chinese and American culture. But the point seems moot because the end of the farming lifestyle in this country offers a strong signal that the moment is upon us to start remaking that image.

If Americans have an image problem with gardening as a provider of local sustenance, they have a greater problem with the image of soil. We refer to it as *dirt*. We say a thing is as cheap as dirt. Essayist William Bryant Logan notes that "we have a dirty mind or a dirty job. We are dragged down into it. After unseemly revelations, her name is mud. The TVs of our TV culture spout out an endless stream of ads for Tide, All, Joy, and a whole legion of ionic surfactants that promise a world purged of dirt. True, it is not a bad thing to be an earthy person, the salt of the Earth, or to have grit. But when we have grit, we usually mean 'gritty reality,' and when we use 'earthy' as a positive adjective we are usually referring to the whole ball of wax, the capital E Earth. As often as not, dirt is beneath us to contemplate."[4]

Compare this to the fact that even in this century, the bride price of a French country girl was determined by the weight of the manure produced on her father's farm. Compare it to the fact that pilgrims still visit Chimayo in New Mexico and Esquipulas in Guatemala to worship a Christ whose souvenir is a little bag of dirt, which supplicants drink dissolved in a tea.[5]

In this country, the vast majority of people who raise vegetables do so in their "spare" time. Everyone but the most compulsive home vegetable gardener holds down a job to provide the money to purchase food. This job—this so-called living of ours—offers no direct relationship to our physical nourishment. That is the job of other people. It is what farmers are for, what agribusiness is for. It is what we have a complex food distribution system for, what we have supermarkets for.

For most of us who have been raised on the economic premise known as the division of labor, our own secondhand relationship to sustenance simply means that other people provide something for us just as we provide something for them. In toto, we celebrate the division of labor as the mechanism that supplies us with all the myriad products and services by which our consumer society runs and grows. For some economists, it is the very barometer by which we measure our success as a society.

But not without a high cost. Any move away from self-sufficiency and toward a complex division of labor can only be predicated on a parallel move away from the local—and toward centralization. In such a manner this view of progress actively negates our sense of place. We exist inside a faceless system of food growing, distribution, and advertising that voids any direct connection between ourselves and the health of the Earth. For instance, there is a well-documented link between cattle raising and the rapid, irreversible depletion of soil in the U.S. western range. But most of us know beef only as a red slab wrapped in clear plastic. We do not see the erosion, do not notice the soil disappearing. The direct responsibility we feel toward such issues as water pollution at feed lots or even cruelty to animals are, at best, unclear. Any connection between us and Montana's dirt ceases to exist because nothing is ever perceived directly. Nothing is local. Thus does beef advertising backhandedly implore us to separate our sustenance from any real concern for the soil. It also wishes us to ignore the studies that link the consumption of red meat to increased rates of heart disease and cancer. In such a manner does beef advertising succeed at something quite bizarre: it causes us to separate our sustenance from our health.

But we do not need to focus only on the beef industry to make the point. The issue manifests itself in many other ways. For instance, we find nothing strange in consuming fruits and meats and sweets and vegetables out of season; they are shipped to us from halfway around the world through a transportation system run on nonrenewable energy sources. Advertisers coax us into favoring prepared food products packaged in elaborate nonrecyclable containers. All of this is done in the cause of satisfying an important symbol of our societal success: our unique ability to enjoy everything possible and with no restrictions imposed by season, locale, health, or any other natural *ab origine*. This deeply complex nonrelationship between our "things" and place has turned us into the most overconsumptive society in the history of the world.

We cheer on this megalithic system *because* it permits us to buy broccoli grown on the far shore of the continent. One recent study concluded that there are thirty thousand items on the shelves of an average supermarket, up from nine thousand in 1976. Each food item travels an average of thirteen hundred miles before reaching its final destination at the human mouth.[6] Yet all of us appreciate the favor of ubiquitous availability—that all this plenitude can be bought on any day of the year no matter whether we live in Anchorage or Tallahassee.

How does an alternative food-getting system based on local networks of organic gardens measure up? The health advantages of fresh produce are obvious. Earth-unfriendly packaging is kept to an absolute minimum. The relationship between food and place also helps us rediscover the connection between the Earth and the earth. And maybe more people would support local networks if they were indeed operational. But why should we want to revert to a localized agrarian system that would turn back the hand of progress? In fact, promoting and subsidizing an American nation of self-sustaining gardens based (even loosely) on the Chinese farm-garden model would necessitate a veritable revolution in American society. For instance, we would have to alter the look of our cities to include extensive green zones where organic gardeners could produce the food for the rest of us. Urban pollution levels would need to decline drastically to nurture these green zones.

We might need to alter our perception of what an economy is. Since many more people would be encouraged to grow at least a portion of their own food, we would eventually need to transform our most fundamental ideas about *work*. Growing food is a job. As it now stands, we regard food as cheap, subsidized as it is by government and by chemical fertilizer. Who has the time to grow food? Not incidentally, this same lack of time is precisely what nurtures the contemporary processed food industry, which spends a significant share of the gross national product winning our hearts and stomachs through advertising. As the discussion on the local garden has already pointed out, such a change would also cause much of our politics to drift away from its centralized power base and toward the local.

Jobs would migrate out of the office and back onto the land. Even our tastes in clothing would need to alter.

And if the history of the soil were taught to us in grade school, more of us would know at a young age what can happen when the people of any society stop paying close attention to the relationship between the health of their soil and their own sustenance. We would know that even as the division of labor gives us more products and services from which to choose, so it harbors a hidden danger that destroys the linkage between ourselves and the soil. It would underscore the essential point that until very recently in history, tilling the earth and growing food employed more people than any other single category of labor. And when more people rely on growing soil for their own sustenance, soil itself accrues greater esteem than it ever could in a society reliant on monocrops, heavy machinery, and chemicals.

Yet it all starts to sound so out of reach, so Utopian. If so, then also realize that an increasing disenchantment with current modes of employment is an unmistakable sign of the times. In fact, investing our future in local networks of farm gardens makes much sense in a society where the cities are ever more unlivable, disintegrating into violence because so many people are out of work. It makes sense in a society that desperately needs new and innovative ways to revitalize a decaying economic structure while healing a degraded environment. It makes sense in a society where half the topsoil has already been lost while the farmer's traditional way of life has been destroyed. It makes sense in a society where pesticide residues in food are causing ever-accelerating health problems. As social visionary Rudolf Steiner put it, "So long as one feeds on food from unhealthy soil, the spirit will lack the stamina to free itself from the prison of the body."[7]

The greatest impetus to change, however, is one that differentiates this particular solution from so many other idealistic proposals on the table of our future. This one is molded to an American temperament that already embraces gardening, is in fact wild about gardening. The interest is already there. Given all the advantages of growing food locally, the barriers that stand in the way of instituting a national organic gardening movement seem mainly the same barriers that always crop up in the United States whenever any grass-roots solution is offered to status quo problems currently managed and administered by vested interests. It is the same type of barrier that so successfully impeded the emergence of a national renewable energy policy (especially solar) during the 1980s. In that case, the recipients were entrenched oil interests. This time the culprits are some of the very same people—for instance, those in chemical companies who benefit most from centralized monoculture farming. Add to them the members of an increasingly centralized food distribution system, who must inevitably suffer if people are getting taught how to grow a substantial amount of their own food. And trading much of the rest.

Although this thumbnail description of what it would take for our society to start reinvesting in locally grown food is certainly incomplete, it is not inaccurate. At the present moment, local food production networks based on soil gardening do spring up on their own and in all parts of the country. It is an inevitable process. Organic farmers *do* make a good living by growing and selling food as part of a burgeoning underground subculture. They *do* offer fresh local, good-tasting produce with less overhead than agribusiness. Given the real potential of a resource-limited future, the grass-roots movement for soil gardening must emerge later (as a matter for survival) if not sooner (as a matter of public choice).

I do not mean to leave the impression that the future of soil gardening is vocational, or even that the *avocation* of soil gardening is a first step on a path pointing toward vocational gardening. Nor is it especially Utopian, like paradise gardening. My own example may explain best what I do mean.

When I started gardening, I was a homesteading, back-to-the-land, grow-your-own-organic-veggies, thirty-something former hippie. Not unlike Joe Hollis's own depiction of the paradise gardener, my gardener's self-image was overwhelmingly oral: I imagined myself *eating well* inside the cell of a private Eden. Garden trees meant fruit trees. Ornamental trees chosen primarily for their aesthetic attributes were not yet part of my gardener's vocabulary. Shrubs were utilitarian devices, living screens planted to block the view of cars in the driveway. Flowers were an afterthought, considered to be little more than little bursts of gay annual color sited in segregated flower beds located close to the foundation of the house.

I wanted to live a life of voluntary simplicity, one far less product oriented than the one I saw promoted in magazines and on TV. My own version of the

American dream included that same stubborn sense of independence, although, quite unlike the standard model, it also embraced devolution and loving the Earth as its basic tenets. In the best of all possible worlds, I envisioned a trip to the supermarket eventually supplanted by foraging my own acreage during the spring, summer, and fall, and daily excursions to a well-stocked root cellar during the winter. All my neighbors would be doing the same. Barter would one day emerge as the primary synonym for economics.

That my own original sense of place obviously implied a paradise garden, but not necessarily a soil garden, may have been the result of my own American dread of laboring like a Chinese worker ant. In retrospect, it seems an issue of ideology and symbolism. A full-time soil garden meant dealing on a survival level with the vicissitudes of pests and weeds, droughts, floods, and late frosts. It meant hauling manure and seaweed in vast, backbreaking amounts. Yet plain old hard work seemed the antithesis of any Utopian lifestyle. As if that wasn't bad enough, the idea of establishing a network of farm gardens implied proselytizing a kind of communist political platform bent on organizing the larger extended community into land and food cooperatives.

This disavowal of hard work also demonstrates how firmly I refused to consider myself a farmer, even an avocational farmer. To me, farming meant an utter lack of Utopian dreaming. It was the business of dirt, the drudgery of a landed peasantry with dirty fingernails working the soil in dirty overalls. Farming was a job undertaken by someone without a clue about the future, a person devoid of ideals, who mined the soil as a land developer mines real estate. Whatever farming actually connotes to those who practice it, whatever goodness that occupation strives to accomplish in this world, whatever farming *is*, to my own tarnished dream of paradise gardening, it signified full-time mindless work, sweaty callused hands, fundamentalist perceptions about God and nature, going to bed at nine o'clock and rising at four, an eminently boring lifestyle surrounded by clucking chickens and made oppressively dangerous by large diesel machines that occasionally toppled over onto young future farmers about my age, severing arms and snuffing out lives in the process. There was farming, and then there was paradise. The two were diametrically opposed to each other.

Looking back upon my bigoted outlook from the vantage point of years, I realize I was a child of my culture's viewpoint. My contempt for farming was mostly a function of an East Coast suburban upbringing. It seems a paradox in hindsight. Long before I ever felt outraged about the farmer's long-term abuse of the soil, I actually scorned farming because I believed it was bound up in a *love* of the soil. Farmers lived from the dirt, while the rest of us would just as soon have the whole mess of it paved over.

Yet farmers destroyed the American soil because they had no more love for dirt than any of the rest of us did. That might even hint at why so many children of farmers abandoned their homes for the city at just about the same time the children of the middle class started the back-to-the-land movement. As we tried to escape the ennui of the strip malls, young farmers longed for a life free of dirt.

This young, middle-class, liberal-arts-college-educated-in-the-sixties, Vietnam-protesting strip-mall denizen of the late twentieth century soon started a working farm garden but wished to regard it, rather, as something else: as the "supermarket garden." This name speaks volumes about my own emphasis. A supermarket garden functions as an alternative to the *destination* of its baroque distribution system rather than its *source*. Yet soil is where it begins, where it has always begun. Unwilling to acknowledge that source, I pursued a perceptual legacy that led all the way back to Petra, to Copán, to the farmer who bragged of how many farms he'd used up.

But the source remains the source. That is why I choose to call this chapter "The Soil Garden" and not "The Supermarket Garden."

I soon laughed off my original objective of growing *all* my own food and declared to the world that I wanted to grow *as much as possible*. As much as possible. It meant I had to recognize my own limitations and attempt to live in contented harmony with my culture. It also implied a realistic garden built around the Mayan compass, that device always pointing firmly to where we are while it likewise points anywhere else we may choose to journey. The Mayan compass may be the best tool available to help us keep paradise within our sights.

Now, many years later, I find myself living in a place where I am surrounded by real honest-to-goodness farmers whose mothers and fathers farmed the same plot and whose great-grandfathers and great-grandmothers first pioneered this place a hundred years before I ever called it home. As if they ever needed my approval, I can only relate how much I have come to admire their lifestyle, their incredible knowledge of place, and especially their radiated inner strength garnered from a life dedicated to working the soil and paying attention to place. I would apologize to every one of them for the outrageous antifarmer bigotry of my youth, although not for the soil revelations of my middle age. Though I have now come to admire them as neighbors, I continue to find ample grounds to abhor the way so many of them abuse the Earth. Just as important, and as trivial as it may seem, I no longer envisage a trip to the supermarket as a failure of either my gardening prowess or my Utopian politics.

Every other afternoon of late I have been driving my Ford pickup down to a local stable where I shovel it full of horse manure. It is a good time of year to do so. The weather is cool, the flies are gone, and yet there hasn't been enough rain yet to saturate the manure, doubling its weight. Arriving home again, I dispense it around the various beds by wheelbarrow, using it mainly as a three-inch-thick winter mulch on top of all the established beds. If lime is needed to neutralize its acidity, I apply it last and let the rain take care of mixing it into the manure.

I also fill up my newly constructed stone terraces with four or five feet of nothing but composted manure. I pile it on a foot higher than the rim to permit for compaction and decay. By spring the terraces will be ready to plant. Employing simple labor-intensive techniques at the start of the terrace construction process produces crops for years afterward that are every bit as large as and far healthier than anything modern chemistry is able to throw at the plants.

I also adopt a technique known as double digging, which truly involves twice as much digging. All the dirt is taken out of a garden bed to a depth of *at least* a foot. Then the hard bottom of the bed is further broken up to a depth of another four to six inches. Partially decomposed compost is deposited to a depth of six inches and spread evenly across the bottom. Finally, the original dirt is mounded back into place. Since rotting compost produces heat, the rise in temperature quickly draws the roots downward into the heart of an organic furnace. With larger root systems reaching and exploring and finally tapping directly into a nutrient-rich stratum, crop yields start to exceed what many of us imperfect humans deserve in this world.

If that is all it takes to achieve paradise, then I suppose paradise has been attained. Except paradise is still nowhere because, quite honestly, *not* dying of starvation, no matter how elegantly accomplished, is not much of a measure of perfection. Nor will very many soil gardeners ever seek happiness as foot-soldier gardeners in the Chinese sense. Few of us long to become salt-of-the-earth farmers as long as we are products of aristocratic gardening traditions—whether English or Japanese. Ours is a relationship to the earth that is inherently avocational. We are as captivated by the aesthetics and environmental potential of gardening as by any mere utilitarian motive. Most of us have uprooted far too many vegetable beds in the cause of nonutilitarian flowers bursting with color. We delegate too much prime orchard ground to too many columnar junipers, Japanese maples, and croquet courts.

My personal evolution eventually led me back to American culture in the hopes of making it better. It was, almost assuredly, the same draw that sealed the fate of most of the other idealistic back-to-the-land communers who typified the counterculture of my youth. One by one, each of us discovered we wanted to do something in and for our culture. One by one, each of us learned something important about ourselves: that we never possessed the psyche to devote so big a chunk of our lives to sustaining life as a dropout. Even so, I sometimes wonder if any of us children of the cold war will ever be able to relinquish a basic wariness that warned us to keep the potential of self-sustainability tucked away in reserve—just in case the civilization does one day alter as dramatically as we all believed it would way back then. If bombs are not quite the harbinger of apocalypse they once were, then maybe the greenhouse effect (or something completely unexpected) will soon take its place.

But at what point does the pleasure we feel at growing *anything* transmute into a self-righteous political lifestyle statement that dogs so many of the people who strive to grow *everything*? How many times have we heard successful gardeners rant on to excess about the benefits of knowing exactly what's "in" those salad tomatoes? I would answer that although it's certainly commendable to grow pesticide-free tomatoes, humility spawns more converts than preaching. There is a great danger in acting self-actualized while munching on peas placed on the dinner table just ten minutes after being picked. Any prideful platform of excess inevitably leads to self-delusion.

I now grow 50 percent of my own food. But I don't drive to the grocery store 50 percent less often than before. I spew just as many gasoline fumes into the air as my neighbor who grows nothing. In any case, 50 percent seems quite enough for me, although I still scheme about ascending onto what I call "the next food-growing level" by growing one or another staple crop. The dictionary defines *staple* as "most important." The word refers specifically to wheat, rye, oats, barley, corn, millet, rice, lentils, sorghum—any grain or bean crop we could survive on to the exclusion of just about anything else.

For reasons not immediately clear, growing a staple crop often involves a decisive psychological shift in commitment to the less-is-more lifestyle. It seems an act commensurate with consciously giving up the internal combustion engine to travel to work—not unlike rewiring one's house for solar power. In fact, experimenting with grains sometimes seems too radical a pipe dream for most gardeners whose roots grow deeply in the European aesthetic tradition. It conjures up a decidedly unparadisal image of a row of ragged peasants with scythes in hand harvesting the steppes. It seems a kind of gardening that exists on the edge of apocalyptic disaster. I consider planting a small field of rye and soon imagine the proverbial hordes descending on horseback to wreak havoc, carry off the women, and raze the fields. I rationalize these feelings. I would plant more grains if I only had a bit more land, a bit more time, better soil, a less exotic fantasy existence. If only the local bakers weren't so darned skilled.

Although tending to the soil is important everywhere we grow plants, it is in the vegetable garden that soil is cultivated most intensively and piled up most luxuriously. Every gardener knows that the quality (and sheer abundance) of such crops as lettuce, peas, strawberries, and corn fluctuates quite markedly in response to our ability to meet their specific nutrient needs. Unrelenting attention to soil may, in fact, offer the best reason why so many of us segregate the vegetables into their own special area. The soil garden is the place we grow food that surpasses in quality that offered up by any supermarket.

The history of the soil informs us that most classical gardening traditions—from the British to the Italian and the Japanese—also segregated the edible plants into the so-called kitchen garden and away from the ornamental plants in the various ornamental gardens. But this was not always accomplished out of consideration for the soil. The practice originated because food crops are also the chosen prey of such creatures as deer and gophers and locusts and therefore need to be contained behind some manner of fence. Likewise, no one can deny that it is much easier to tend and harvest food crops when they are strung out in rows, grown all together in one place.

In the British and French traditions, separating flowers from cabbages had as much to do with a segregation among the social classes as with any horticultural logic. The kitchen was the province of the cook and the servants, and thus the kitchen garden was pragmatically placed near the kitchen. It was a working-class garden. The orchard was the province of the orchardist, and he, of course, worked in concert with the cook and his staff. Over time, turnips and tulips found their precise place in society, just as the servants and the lord of the manor did. Although most of this is no longer pertinent to our own gardening experience, the segregation lingers on.

For no good reason, I have never segregated all the vegetables into one ghetto, ornamental flowers and shrubs into another ghetto, herbs into a third ghetto. This stubbornness may be a result of perceiving all the beds as mere variations on the one unified soil garden. Whatever the reason, this blurring of the distinctions long ago guided me to solve the problem of where (and where not) to place the so-called vegetable garden by cautiously integrating certain edible plants among all the rest of the cultivars.

I later discovered that *edible landscaping* is the term invented to describe the process of interspersing vegetables and fruit into the ornamental beds. It seems such a downright natural solution to what seems a silly outmoded convention that I am sometimes surprised that the idea has never caught on more generally. Were edible landscaping a political credo, it would inspire an eminently classless and holistic state of gardening. There is also a genuine psychological and physical advantage to this integrative perception of the garden. Our lavish attention to dispersing manure and building soil tends to be much more equitable when the vegetables are no longer segregated. The process also involves more work.

One gardening friend asserts that most landscape designs are flawed by our culture's proclivity to define *ornamental* as "something that primarily pleases the senses of sight and smell." He believes that plants meant to dazzle the taste buds possess an equal beauty to plants that dazzle the eye or the nose. He once swore to me that a fully ripened head of broccoli glistening with beads of dew in the early morning light was the most beautiful flower bud in the entire plant *kindom*. And then this semantic clarifier: "Did you notice how I left the *g* out of *kingdom*? It's my way of saying we all need to think of plant categories as kinships and not hierarchies!"

His enthusiasm is contagious. Visitors can be seen peering upon all his ripening broccoli heads with the same awestruck enthusiasm they usually reserve for the semi-real flowers, which are described in greater detail in an upcoming chapter. Like any good teacher, he patiently explains that a broccoli head is a collection of a hundred or more unopened flower *buds*. If allowed to come to term, each one of those individual green bumps would soon elongate on its own little stem to burst open to a display of pale yellow flowers. The flowers are quite distinctive by their sheer number if not by their color, shape, or size. Perhaps unfortunately, by the time the flowering occurs, the plant has also turned a sickly yellow color and is quite inedible.

This friend has designed his entire "ornamental" garden around the motivations of an ample belly. The pathway leading from his driveway to the front door is jammed with spiraling lime-green heads of romanesco broccoli, which look like normal broccoli wrung through a tornado. These he intersperses with deep-purple Burgundy Queen cauliflower, colossal gray-green cruiser broccoli, and Christmasy-looking Day-Glo red-green rhubarb chard. The total effect is not un-like the avenue of the kings in Cecil B. DeMille's silent screen version of *The Ten Commandments.* By mid-August, his front door is usually framed in a jungle of scarlet runner beans, making it nearly impossible to ring the doorbell without also munching on one of the ripe beans. He doesn't mind and tells any visitor who asks that it is the whole point of planting beans by the front door. My friend's garden is, just like him, surrealistic, colossal, and pleasantly eccentric.

I'm a moderate, a bit less botanically democratic than my friend, but far more of an integrationist than the norm. I prefer to segregate a large vegetable garden into its own luxurious ghetto located behind an eight-foot-tall fence of chicken wire and cedar posts. I started doing this mostly as a hedge against unavoidable deer and rabbit predation. I likewise started planting nothing but pretty flowers and shrubs closer to the house. I remain the traditionalist. To me, *ornamental* will always mean "colorful, shapely, or fragrant."

There are, however, two vegetables I choose to plant much closer to the house simply because I believe them to be among the most ornamental plants in the entire extended landscape. Although both are conventional food items, neither is, by any measure, a conventional garden item. The first is the artichoke. This plant seems everything that edible landscaping was meant to be. It can go from seed to a large fountain-shaped bush possessed of huge, three-foot gray-green, deeply serrated leaves in just three months. Any gardener seeking an instant ornamental shrub should take a close look at this perennial kin to the common thistle.

Somehow, it never occurred to me that the part of the artichoke we eat is actually—as with broccoli—the unopened bud of a very substantial flower. And the flower is absolutely gorgeous: a blue-purple shaving brush of a bloom possessed of all the best traits of a fuzzy thistle-flower but with none of the thorns. Pin it upside down from ceiling rafters, and within a few days you have one of the very best everlasting flowers in the entire garden. It dries to a beautiful deep pastel blue surrounded by a striking corona of satiny bronze leaves.

The commercial artichoke industry is located in a frost-free belt spread along the cool and foggy coast near Santa Cruz in central California. The artichoke thistle doesn't really get into maximum production until the second year. A prolonged hard freeze can kill the roots, yet despite the problematic nature of growing the plant in a garden where temperatures can drop below freezing for an extended period, using it as an annual still seems well worth the effort. The plant demands two feet of space on each side. It devours nitrogen-rich compost like nothing this side of a kiwi vine. Where the artichokes grow is where the soil garden is most ardently cultivated, and where I can be found digging in my much-hoarded chicken manure and bonemeal more often than any other place in the garden.

Like tomatoes, corn, peas, et cetera, a homegrown artichoke left to ripen on the plant and then picked just minutes before serving tastes entirely different from anything one might find in a supermarket produce department. It is thick, buttery, and in a word, heavenly. On that premise, I planted six artichoke sprouts into a raised bed near the house. The plants grew fast and by early August were starting to put out their first fruit. Unfortunately, as an annual, each plant produced no more than two buds. And as a crop for a family of four, all that attention and all that precious garden real estate seemed hardly worth the trouble because we never had more than two ready to eat at any one time. The twelve artichokes we harvested that first year tasted very good, although not extraordinary.

After the first frost of November, I cut the plants back to a stubble and covered them over with six inches of hay in what proved to be a fairly mild winter. Unfortunately, by next spring, only two of the original six resurrected, and so I found myself buying four more starts and essentially beginning all over again. I added four more inches of well-rotted compost made from kitchen scraps. If the artichokes weren't developing quite as I had hoped, the soil was.

The two overwintering plants started growing so fast that I was able to discern a subtle difference in size each morning. The two buds on each of those two plants were ready for harvest by mid-June. These tasted sublime. I remember sitting at the table one evening, scraping my teeth along the inside edge of a scale, watching my little daughters also scrape their teeth while grunting contentedly, and concluding that here was an eating experience worthy of a Fellini movie. My four-year-old commented with a deep sigh that she'd eat one every night if we only had that many. We never would.

By mid-July, the two overwintered plants suddenly stopped producing altogether and, inexplicably, soon died. Meanwhile, the four starts were just coming into their own. These artichokes were also superb, although definitely not worthy of quite so many mythic adjectives as the overwintered two. It was apparent to all that we needed to learn more about growing artichokes. A neighbor dropped by one afternoon and taught us that the best way to get a tender artichoke to survive a harsh winter is to cut the plants right to the ground after the first heavy frost. Then cover each one over with a bushel basket, and cover each basket with several inches of dry straw. The air space inside the basket keeps the crowns from rotting, while the mulch keeps them from freezing. I perceived the baskets as extensions of the soil.

I expanded the raised bed to hold ten plants and waited in anticipation as the plants slept through the chilliest, wettest, windiest winter in Northwest history. To put my obsession into perspective, I remember one momentous night in December when the temperature plummeted to near zero degrees Fahrenheit, accompanied by a ninety-mile-an-hour wind that toppled trees all over the roads and cut our power for three days. The temperature never got close to thirty degrees for three weeks. But while everybody else in the neighborhood fretted over frozen pipes and dangerous driving conditions, I fretted over those artichoke roots. Would they make it? I kept my fingers crossed.

They didn't make it. Actually, one plant made it. That February I added four *more* inches of rotted compost to the bed, three inches of horse manure, waited eight weeks, and finally planted nine more artichoke starts. By early July, we started the harvest. It must have been all that new compost. Dinners started approximating *Juliet of the Spirits*, or was it the oyster-eating scene from *Tom Jones*, or maybe the climactic noodle scene from *Tampopo*? And after the plants finished producing in late July, the stalks turned spindly, and the leaves shriveled. It caused me to cut the plants right down to the ground again. I added more compost, and, lo and behold, every bush started growing again. By late October they had produced a smaller, second crop of buds. I cut them down again and covered them over a second time. The winter wasn't so harsh, and the plants were much better protected. This time, they all made it.

The second plant worth all the trouble of growing ornamentally is the asparagus. It is a wonderfully diaphanous vegetable that can eventually attain eight feet in height. Like artichokes, asparagus is a perennial crop. But asparagus asks us to take an entirely different approach to the soil garden. Unlike artichokes, asparagus send out invasive root runners, and thus they demand their own bed. Dig an eighteen-inch-deep trough. Shovel two or three inches of a mix of bonemeal, hardwood ashes, and compost into the trough, and then hand-pat the roots on top of the mix at twenty-four-inch intervals. Just cover the roots with more of the mix. Then shovel back all the original soil. If such care is taken at the time of planting, an asparagus bed rarely needs any amendments or even any watering from that point on. The plants will thrive for fifteen years or more without any more attention besides an occasional weeding. But it takes three years for the plants to mature to harvest size. In sheer domestic terms, the sight of asparagus growing in anybody's backyard is as sure a sign as any that there lives a gardener who has committed to living in one place over the long haul.

Like kiwis, ginkgoes, hollies, skimmias, and marijuana, asparagus plants are *dioecious*, meaning there are distinct male and female plants. By early autumn, the female of the species is starting to display translucent red berries that are set aglow by the intense yellow light of a winter's afternoon. These berries will often stay affixed to the standing husks all winter long. The sight of these drooping and ferny beige husks dotted as they are with glowing red berries and partially covered with snow is positively arresting. It is easily one of the most beautiful sights of the winter garden.

I constructed two raised beds to which I added plenty of homegrown compost made from local seaweed, sawdust, and kitchen scraps—turning and mixing the ingredients for three months until they slowly transformed from a rancid mess into a rich, black, sweet-smelling growing medium. I then planted twenty asparagus roots. During the first year, asparagus puts out skinny chopstick-thick spears, which soon grow tall and transform into green fernlike plumes of great beauty. During the second year, the plants push out a few eating-size spears and many more skinny ones. Although I was sorely tempted to pick a few, I abstained, knowing that the roots might deplete without enough greenery to replenish them. At this juncture I also realized that each and every one of those gorgeous red berries hanging in what looked like a green mist contained a very fertile seed. They soon produced an exorbitant number of baby volunteers growing like weeds in and around the bed.

Late in the third week of the third April of their existence, I started picking the spears. I felt like an alchemist growing his own gold. In fact, there were so many spears available that I gave them away to friends. The opulent expressions of gratitude that I received in return made me comprehend for the first time in my life what it must feel like to run a major charitable foundation.

A lunatic problem arose. Eating a lot of fresh-picked asparagus is not quite the same repast as occasionally eating the not-so-fresh asparagus we find in the supermarkets every April. This is a potent herb, and when we consume it every other day, our urine starts to stink all the time. By the second week of the harvest, I was convinced that my pores must have stank as well, although, granted, a bit less repulsively than my urine. Neither did my gastrointestinal tract feel quite right, although it wasn't actually indigestion, and I wondered if I was queasy from all the adulation my grateful neighbors had been heaping on me lately. Then my kids started appending the adjective *yucky* to every dinner that included asparagus, while proclaiming loudly that they didn't like it and didn't want to eat even a single bite—"But Daddy, when are the artichokes going to be ripe?" By mid-May I actually felt relieved when the spears started to fern out, signifying that the beauty stage was beginning and the harvest was finally over.

It took two years of this before I admitted to myself that fresh green asparagus possesses a very mild level of whatever toxin it contains, but that it is toxic nonetheless. It was then I learned that the plant was originally cultivated not as food but as a medicine high in iron. Asparagus has diaphoretic properties, meaning that it causes excess sweating. It is also a diuretic, increasing cellular activity in the kidneys and therefore increasing the rate of urine production. Ironically, the seeds of the asparagus were once prescribed by doctors *as a relief* for nausea.[8] Perhaps we would all do well to munch on the seeds to counteract the effects of eating the fresh spears.

Asparagus spears are eaten blanched in just about every country in the world exept the United States. In Italy the farmers pile more and more dirt around the growing spears, which, when eventually uncovered, tend to look as pallid as mushrooms. I began to suspect that the toxic effect I experienced had been produced by the same chemical process that turns the spears green. Perhaps we never notice the negative side effects in store-bought asparagus because so much of the vitality has also fled. In other words, this perceived toxicity is mostly an issue with exquisitely fresh, homegrown asparagus.

I adopted the European solution, mounding dirt around the spears as soon as they break ground. By the time I pick them they are blanched, although never quite as pale as one might find them in Italy or France. Unfortunately, this process of employing the soil to impede the greening process also destroys much of the nutritional value. A compromise: picking the spears no longer than one day after they first break soil seems to neutralize the potential nausea without destroying all the potential nutrition. These young spears are exceedingly tender and very tasty. I turned one of the beds to raspberries. With only half as many plants now available for the table, asparagus does not get served quite so often, causing it to win back most of its gourmet status. My kids still refuse to eat it. Who didn't before the age of twelve?

April

The winter of 1991–92 was the warmest on record in the Pacific Northwest. Something was awry. Everyone I talked to seemed aware of winter's disappearance in their gut if not always in their mind. I remember feeling disoriented listening to the Seattle TV weatherman assure me that "we're all in for more good weather" when what he was really reporting was that the rains had failed us and the January temperature never once dropped below freezing. Who hires these people?

The columbines, mallows, and sweet williams never froze to the ground. The slugs never hibernated. They went into hiding only during the one hard freeze of the entire winter, which lasted for three days in mid-December. My family burned a cord less firewood than usual. Can you imagine, the calendulas kept blooming past the new year. I never bothered to dig up and store the dahlia tubers. Now it's mid-April. Dahlia leaves are already showing their green a solid five weeks before they usually do. I am amazed to declare that some of the roses will bloom before the fourth week of April.

April blesses us with large groves of blooming wild bulbs including trout lilies (*Erythronium*), chocolate lilies (*Fritillaria*), calypso orchids (*Calypso bulbosa*), and shooting stars (*Dodecatheon*). While both the cultivated and wild bulbs advanced their normal bloom time by several weeks this spring, the trout lilies followed a different drummer. They alone seemed quite unaffected by the eccentric weather.

The trout lily is an all-around gorgeous flower. The stem grows from a base of two shiny leaves of the same general shape, size, and texture as those of a tulip. But the leaves' dominant green is deeply stained with a mahogany mottling, ostensibly resembling the coloration of a trout, perhaps a brown trout; although by my reckoning the pattern suggests a pickerel or a lingcod. The trout lily's stem rises above these lingcod mottled leaves and opens to a demure, downward-pointing white lily about three inches wide. During its two-week tenure, the flowers cover a nearby forested area with hundreds of blooms.

In a normal spring, trout lilies bloom at the same time as daffodils, during the last week of March or the first week of April. But the daffodils bloomed in early March this year. The trout lilies were still nowhere to be seen. In the warmer springs of the past, trout lilies bloomed with the tulips and the wild calypso orchids during that same period in April. But this year the little forest orchids bloomed during the third week of March. The tulips bloomed during the last week of March.

I started to worry that some rare disease known only to trout lilies had surreptitiously visited the forest floor and annihilated them all. I chalked it up, prematurely, as one more case of the greenhouse effect subtly altering the ecology of the planet.

My mistake lay in consulting the daffodils and the tulips rather than the height of the sun in the sky. The trout lilies finally broke soil. They huddled together in their little grove and then bloomed precisely on the seventeenth of April. I conclude that they must be the fundamentalists of the bulb world, refusing to recognize climatic trends and never forgetting that warmth is hardly the only measure of spring.

I have never seen this admirable bulb blooming in a cultivated garden, although I have seen it listed for sale in bulb catalogs. Despite its beauty, I have never desired to dig up a wild bulb. The community of trout lilies emerges into my life from out of nowhere. They flower gloriously, nodding, and then just as quickly vanish back down into the leaf mold of the earth by the first of May. To lift it during this brief period would be to deny its need to replenish its bulb storehouse. It seems a violation of some unwritten natural contract. I shall never do so. Pity that this contract is not universally recognized.

The Sentient Garden

The more I learn about the garden, the less objective I feel about it. Now that I can rattle off the Latin names and vital needs of so many landscape plants, you might think I would regard them as botanical specimens, each possessed of a unique genetic recipe and species-specific traits. Call me sentimental: I think of them as friends.

I'm no expert; not a professional gardener, and certainly not a botanist. I learned in the ninth grade that science mandates an emotional separation be maintained between observer and observed. If so, then what I do has little basis in science. I can be a keen observer but not always an objective one. I treat gardening as a cooperative affair. I rather feel like a part of a neighborhood in which plants, animals, dirt, rocks, and a human family all participate collectively in a love affair with place.

Neither the language nor the forthright pragmatism of horticulture is able to plumb the depths of what I consider to be a mostly unspoken, intuitive relationship with the garden. My mind treats its own growing stockpile of horticultural information not as the basis of gardening but rather as a background hum to the more immediate aims of digging, wandering, smelling, enjoying, and critiquing.

This confession also explains a hunch of mine: that the sentient garden is best written about in the first person. I believe the instincts that apprehend it turn tentative when clothed in the garb of dispassionate observation. There isn't much that is objective about it, so why obfuscate its many insubstantial traits by falling upon a scientific jargon that does no better than transmute pure delight into an objective posture? We are all the heirs of this jargon, the innocent children of the reductionist idiom it represents. I pity the gardener who peers into the sentient garden and perceives nothing but solid resources exhibited to the senses through biological processes bound up in laws of causation and ticking away with the precision of a machine possessed of molecular tolerances. Look again. See that ornamental plum tree over there? That one's a warrior. A survivor. An interspecies communicator. Or look at these cabbages. They are the gift givers. Sentient beings possessed of a shy and humble integrity.

Most of us read such descriptive prose and our education immediately puts up a stop sign to keep our senses from proceeding any farther down this garden path. We might conclude that such descriptions smack of too vivid an imagination. No, I protest, look again. Look differently. Refocus your eyes on the spaces between the imagination and the resource. There! See the cabbages? The plum tree? The sentient garden is beckoning to us.

This is hardly a game. I sometimes believe that acknowledging a consciousness and a conscience within nature actually holds the last best hope for a humanity seemingly bent on destroying this fair Earth. But that is a very large idea. We do better to start this walk down the path of the sentient garden by avoiding grand conclusions. Let us commence this walk by conversing about humble experiences. And let's not be too timid to indulge ourselves in personal hunches. As we wander this sentient garden chatting about the personality of plum trees and the shy integrity of cabbages, realize that scientific terms like *species-specific characteristics* and *genetic makeup* tell us nothing about how we might connect with the plants. As a layman, I consider all such terms to be official language, "distancers"—words best reserved for people primarily bent on distancing themselves from their subjects as well as from their own emotional point of view. In my case, plant *personalities* is what I say. Personalities is what I get. Personalities is what makes sense.

*   *   *

Several years ago I planted two ornamental hawthorns, two pears, a peach, a blireana ornamental plum, and a prune-plum; all strung out in a skewed line along a deer path leading from the edge of a fir forest. Despite the well-known ability of deer to leap six feet over a barrier to get at fruit saplings—and which ordinarily leads all the gardeners hereabouts to string a six- or eight-foot-tall fence around the young trees—I remained a stubborn aesthete. Not a chicken-wire fence in sight.

Over the years, the deer arrive to browse my property during the latter half of the winter when the wild browse is at a minimum. I notice that they avoid the hawthorns and the blireana plum, which are right on their path. They usually grab no more than a nibble at the leaves of the pear trees before moving on. They show no interest whatsoever in the peaches. Yet they would have destroyed the prune-plum years ago if I hadn't immediately initiated a campaign to prune off all the lower branches and then circled the trunk with a fence. I strung up a thirty-inch-tall barrier of chicken wire just inches from the tree trunk and held up by a single bamboo stick.

I call it my *ideogram fence,* because it reminds me of one of those characters in the Chinese alphabet that represents an object or an idea rather than a phonetic sound. More than a fence itself, this chicken-wire-and-bamboo-stick sculpture *represents* a fence. Any deer could break through it in a second if so motivated. My ideogram fence seems to work far better than no fence at all, which is good enough for me. I am not sure why it works.

The ideogram fence means that I have never had to get nasty with the local deer population. I have never considered buying a gun. Nor did I acquire a dog to keep the deer away. I have never needed to construct a high fence around any of the fruit trees as I would later do around the vegetable garden. Explaining why the ideogram works on the fruit trees and not on the vegetables seems mostly a matter of thinking like a deer. If I were a deer, I could easily forgo a few plum leaves each spring if that idea were communicated to me. Of course no communication would sway me if, as a deer, I chanced upon a winter garden filled to the brim with Russian kale, mizuna, and beet greens.

In the process of recognizing this ideogram as a solution, I have discovered something important about doling out garden advice. Although the local deer obviously display very distinct preferences in their choice of browse, I am convinced that no general rule of thumb can be ascertained from this very local lesson. The ideogram fence *may* work for someone else. And then again it may not. Deer are not instinctoids, blank-eyed no-brainers possessed of nonpersonalities and generic taste buds. Nor do they exhibit any *predictable* inclination to linger near or far from the houses of human beings. The best "how-to" advice I am willing to offer anyone else is to recommend trying an ideogram fence around the base of any favored deer tree. It appears to work for me. However, no one can convince me that if I went so far as to rip out that well-scarred but productive prune-plum, replanted the exact same hole with another prune-plum, that the exact same fence strung around the new tree would repel the local deer as it did before. In other words, the map is not the territory.

Every tree and every deer has a distinct personality. The people who build fences have distinct personalities. Even the fences—whether real, symbolic, or wholly imagined—have distinct personalities. The relationship between all these beings and structures, each one of them bursting with personality, seems to exist beyond the reckonings of any logic. Scientists will never plumb the depths of this relationship through any wile of statistical analysis. Does it exist? Let's withhold judgment a bit longer.

This same relationship motivates me to recommend successful strategies to other gardeners, but not tactics. In this case, the strategy is simple: do not treat natural predators as a manifestation of evil. I personally regard the relationship between gardener, predator (such as deer), and prey (such as Russian kale) to be an important enough matter in the development of a sense of place that I have devoted an entire chapter ("The Predator's Garden") to it.

Or another strategy: plant all the trees you like and rest assured that the deer will be just as finicky in choosing the ones he or she likes. Yet always treat that deer as a discerning neighbor. Talk to it! Communicate: build a sign, an ideogram fence. But don't build a great wall of China unless you like running a prison camp for fruit trees. And one more strategy: follow the tortoise's example. Plant two each of every fruit tree you like and then sit back and watch the deer. Watch the trees. In five years you'll know which ones the deer prefer. In eight years the trees will have grown too large for any deer to harm. Only *five years* to run a fruit-growing experiment? Feel blessed when a hundred golden peaches start ripening on a tree that is a mere four-year-old stripling and takes up about the same amount of garden space as a picnic table. Feel blessed that it's not sequoia cones we're waiting for. That would take decades. Then again, when we're in a hurry, we need to consider a hobby like sprinting instead.

There is another plum tree growing inside my sentient garden. This is the ornamental blireana plum possessed of a penny-candy fragrance and striking bronzy leaves of a color seemingly appropriated from a coral reef. It grows off by itself at the very edge of the forest where it serves as a one-tree garden. I have observed over several years that of all the trees in the larger extended landscape, my cat sharpens her claws only on this ten-foot-tall sapling. It seems that the cat actually goes quite a bit out of her way to visit that tree. I was recently nonplussed while visiting a friend. I was admiring the distinct coppery coloring of her own blireana plum when I noticed scratches along the length of the trunk. Was it possible? She soon informed me that *her* cat also prefers to scratch *his* claws on the blireana plum tree. Perhaps paradoxically, I have since talked to yet another neighbor whose own blireana plum was recently destroyed by a deer. Mine seems completely deerproof.

What can we learn about that blireana plum during its tenancy along the deer path? Although my own particular plum has nothing to fear from the local deer, I would certainly think twice before recommending that someone else plant an unprotected blireana plum on a deer path.

But enough earnest advice about cats and deer, enough proffering of folksy wisdom about plant personalities. Let's up the ante to a different level of perception.

I feel certain that my own blireana plum tree has formed an alliance with the three or four deer who frequent this neighborhood. Is this conclusion mystical? Is it sentimental? Is it merely anecdotal? Does it square with recent botanical evidence demonstrating that certain species of trees possess rudimentary communication skills? Apparently, a species of rain forest tree is capable of signaling the presence of predators to other nearby members of the same species. The other trees alter their chemistry accordingly. But what is the effect of this alteration? Do beetles and sloths suddenly find the leaves inedible? Or is this rather an announcement, a kind of arboreal stop sign, an ideogram of unpalatability? No one seems to know for sure. The predators aren't telling.

What we do have to admit, however, is that this much-publicized "objective" example lends a bit of credence to my own cockeyed hunch. I notice the plum tree while out on my garden tour and wonder if it is even more sentient than those chemistry-altering trees, which, after all, can only discuss their sense of well-being among themselves. Does the blireana plum with the scratched trunk communicate to the black-tailed doe with the crooked hind leg? Does it talk differently to the big buck? And what does the cat sense? I notice that most of the scratch marks have healed during the past year, signifying that my cat has quit her own blireana claw-sharpening predation. Did the tree have anything to do with it? Or is the cat responding to my own emoted annoyance over the scratch marks? Is the plum communicating a tree's own version of a fence ideogram directly to a predator? Maybe it communicates lots of other things as well to anyone able to hear it. Maybe I could hear it. I want to learn how to do that. I don't know how to begin.

So many maybes also reveal why the sentient garden is found so seldom in books about gardening. We live in a culture that devalues the intuitive. As this diminishment refers specifically to garden literature—a subject composed of unequal parts science, craft, aesthetics, and mysticism—the result is a steady stream of books written about the science, the craft, and the aesthetics of gardening, and only a few books that set out to elucidate its mystical side.

The most famous of these is *The Secret Life of Plants*, which is probably the most controversial, best-selling book about the vegetable kingdom published in the last fifty years.[1] Paradoxically, *The Secret Life of Plants* is better understood as a history of various experiments in plant sentience viewed through the rationalist lens of scientific analysis. The book is overwhelmingly the product of two savvy science writers who spent much more time in libraries than in gardens. The result is a text that masterfully expands the envelope of scientific plausibility, a kind of new-age botany text that carefully sidesteps any personal message of transcendence except through inferences to specific experiments. Yet there are almost no references to the experiential aspects so crucial to any gardener's ongoing relationship to the garden. Then again, *The Secret Life of Plants* was never intended to be a gardening book.

Why do garden writers avoid the subject of garden sentience? In fact, writers are as privy to our culture's devaluation of the intuitive as anybody else. Most work hard to present themselves as experts of one stripe or another. As every potential expert soon discovers, dabbling in the intuitive for its own sake emphatically diminishes one's projected sense of authority. But authority is essential for anyone bent on doling out practical advice. This may explain why magazines such as *Sunset, Fine Landscaping, Horticulture,* and *Country Living* have all been remarkably silent about the sentient garden.

Not to say that garden writers haven't explored the intuitive side of their relationships to the garden. One of the best of them, Gertrude Jekyll, was an artist who treated the garden as a loving and living canvas of color and texture; in the process she forever changed the tone of gardening away from a pretty view and toward a process of high participatory art with plants and space. Another English author, Vita Sackville-West, composed chatty prose that added a touch of the mystical to the greater discussion of gardens and gardeners. She was a gardening sensualist, obviously enamored of fragrance, who gushed about the relative aromatic merits of her roses as if they were special friends possessed of sensual genius. Luther Burbank, the great turn-of-the-century plant breeder, often wrote about his plants as if they were his peers collaborating together to attain new forms and useful traits. The Japanese Masanobu Fukuoka wrote *The One-Straw Revolution*, promoting a sacred view of plants and soil as allies. Of the contemporary garden writers in English, Allen Lacy, among a few others, occasionally hits a stride that is pure inspiration from the heart of a gardening visionary.

Were more gardeners to consider the ways that plants relate to human beings, they might fall on these words on the subject of sentience offered by fabulist Leo Lionni:

> In our everyday garden grow the rosemary, juniper, ferns and plane trees, perfectly tangible and visible. For these plants that have an illusory relationship with us, which in no way alters their existentiality, we are merely an event, an accident, and our presence, which seems so solid, laden with gravity, is to them no more than a momentary void in motion through the air. Reality is a quality that belongs to them, and we can exercise no rights over it.[2]

Were plants sentient, it would imply that they smell their own fragrance, see their own petal colors, hear the thunder of a neighboring tree as it falls to the whine of a chain saw. Were plants conscious, it might imply that they *choose* their own fragrances or admire their own long silhouettes reflected by the low winter sun. Consciousness also implies that plants possess a sense of place. Luther Burbank, who drew as close to the plant world as any human ever has, insisted that his own plants existed primarily to accommodate place. They altered their traits to fit certain places and climates more quickly than genetics warranted.

Speeded-up film animates flowers doing things our own sentience is incapable of perceiving. A trick of technology lends the plants a metabolism more like our own. I, for one, could watch flowers bloom this way for hours on end, quite willing to withhold my own unkinetic, unevolved perception of plants if even for the brief time. But it is a trick of the human mind that causes these now fast-paced plants to seem more alive and more conscious than they appear in my own garden. I submit the obvious: Faster equals more conscious because plants start to look just like animals acting out behaviors and reacting quickly to their environment. They seem nimble. Talented. Bold. Aggressive. Even vain. Whereas before they seemed only beautiful in their stasis. Fast motion strongly hints that plants do possess a temperament a bit like our own, merely acted out at a different tempo. Then again, their temperament may all be a hoax, not unlike humans observing the dolphins' frozen smile and believing these creatures must be happy-go-lucky.

Watching these racing, hugging, attacking, unfolding plants causes me to wonder about yet another maybe. Maybe it is our own scientific and patently extractive wiring that no longer lets us accept the idea of consciousness in other beings unless those beings *are already* like us. Some of us obviously won't accept the idea of seeing our own intellectual reflection in creatures like deer, octopuses, or millipedes, not to mention plum trees. It does not serve the present regime. As environmental philosopher Michael J. Cohen has written, "How convenient for us to conceive mud, water, and stones, to be dead; to decide that other life has no consciousness, pain or equality. What an incredible alibi we have created to soothe our guilt of killing for profit."[3] The sentient garden not only speaks to us about the limits of the rationalist worldview but also reveals its arrogance.

There is inherent ecological value to acknowledging the sentient garden. People who believe that plants are conscious invariably treat them with greater respect than those who don't. If we all believed that plants are conscious—that the very garden itself is conscious—we might, as one example, be less willing to continue killing the soil with chemicals.

I'm out on a limb here. Many sober people refuse to grant consciousness to monkeys and dolphins, who are like us in so many ways, and here I am ascribing similar characteristics to plum trees. I even wonder if the vegetarians may have gotten their salient argument about consciousness all wrong because, in fact, plants are every bit as conscious as animals are, albeit quieter and far less restless. Isn't that the reason a sizable minority of gardeners talk to their plants? They do talk to them, you know. Even though many won't admit it.

To know the sentient garden, we must first learn how to look for it. Let us begin our search by sifting through some of the intellectual baggage we all bring to the task of gardening. Two perceptual ideas soon emerge from the heap: The first one is our culture's devaluation of the intuitive. The second one is called anthropocentrism.

The devaluation of the intuitive occurs as an unfortunate result of science influencing our perceptions about reality. Science is based on measurement. Careful measurement establishes objectivity. As stated above, the quest for accurate measurement also mandates that a separation be strictly enforced between observer and observed. In field biology, when an observer interjects his or her own personal intuitions about the behavior of an observed animal or plant, the results are called anecdotal. Anecdote makes for weak science. Too much of it makes for no science at all.

Our perceptions of the way the world works are deeply affected by scientific principles of analyzing measured data leading to objectivity. Our schools teach us to believe that nonmeasurable and intuitive experience does not offer as credible a model of reality as another experience gleaned from objective observation. One result is that scientists as often as not turn a blind eye to phenomena that cannot be reduced to measurement. Science class teaches the rest of us to subordinate the subjective—for example, any qualitative expression of animate intelligence in nature—because it doesn't "measure up." But there are deep-seated problems implicit within this worldview. The case has been made many times that the predominant scientific worldview itself is one cause of our steamrollering the world. We do so as a result of forgetting how to honor nature as an animate being. The devaluation of the intuitive causes us to suppress nonrationalist masculine feelings while it utterly disempowers the feminine. It also may cause some members of the rationalist establishment to throw up their hands in exasperation to read this proclaimed non-expert promoting a plum tree as a warrior, a friend, and a sentient being.

To understand anthropocentrism, we must dig deeper into our heap of perceptual baggage. We discover that the contemporary relationship between gardener and garden (and most of the rest of nature as well) originated during the latter half of the seventeenth century. This was a period of breathtaking perceptual transition. Europeans were starting to perceive of nature not as the penitential leftovers from a divinely inspired Eden but as something new—a perfect, maintenance-free machine designed by God as the home for these bipedal creatures made in his own image: the human race. Whereas the old view had taught that everything on Earth was a temptation, either a weapon or a trap in the epic struggle being waged between Heaven and Hell, the new view treated Earth as an ergonomic vehicle. Everything in nature was made for human use and accommodation.

Today we remain the heirs of this human-centered notion about the relationship between humanity and nature. We call the view anthropocentrism. We call the ergonomic vehicle spaceship Earth.

This book makes much of the fact that certain ideas common to our lives—like love, home, and a sense of place—are only dimly present in our consciousness and are sometimes difficult to articulate plainly. Like aesthetics, anthropocentrism has to be understood as an opinion of culture rather than as reality itself. This opinion gained much momentum during the seventeenth century when Europeans wrestled to square the defunct heavenbound perceptions of nature with the brand-new earthbound ones. Just like us today, they too found themselves caught between two mutually exclusive perceptions of reality. In our case it is the old anthropocentric worldview versus the new biocentric worldview; in their case it was the old God-centered worldview versus the new anthropocentric worldview.

It fell upon the ministry of the time to justify the ways of the new God to the masses raised to the beat of a different God, whose every act had been adjudged beyond human comprehension. To keep the new conceptual bubble intact, the learned men of the day churned out anthropocentric arguments to explain what must have seemed like ungodly flaws in the divine handiwork. Justifying the ways of God to man became such a common activity that it soon got a name attached to it. Called *theodicy*, it was all the rage in the sermons of the European Enlightenment.

For instance, if this new rationalist God had constructed the world to accommodate humanity, what possible reason could He have had to design the likes of smallpox, aphids, poison ivy, and sharks? Answering this fundamental question, the seventeenth-century physician George Cheyne wrote that the Creator made the horse's excrement smell sweet because he knew men would often be in its vicinity. Horseflies, vouched the Virginian William Byrd, had been created "that men should exercise their wits in order to guard against them." Even the lowly louse was indispensable, explained the Reverend William Kirby, because it provided a powerful incentive to habits of cleanliness.[4]

Over the centuries we have grown much more sophisticated in our ability to certify a human center to the machinery of nature. Still, the signs of this center can be witnessed just about everywhere we look. From the Amazon rain forest to the Arctic National Wildlife Refuge, our actions demonstrate over and over again that our civilization still endorses the basic belief that nature exists for human accommodation.

But what our actions tell, our thoughts often dispel. Like the men and women of the late seventeenth century, more and more of us are today starting to realize we are caught between two vastly different views of reality: the first one human-centered or anthropocentric; the second, life-centered or biocentric. We are starting to sense that human beings are no longer at the center of the Earth's purpose. Our species is, rather, one integral aspect of the greater interdependent network of nature.

Commentator David Suzuki makes the case that many scientists are now becoming painfully aware of their own role in bolstering the anthropocentric worldview. They seek to discover scientific methods that embrace biocentrism. Suzuki quotes biologist and author E. O. Wilson declaring, "Well what we have to do is discover our kin, to discover our relatives, who are the other animals and plants who are related to us through our evolution and DNA, because to know our kin is to come to love and cherish them."[5]

Our culture sits squarely between the two views. Most of us are unsure of its implications, misread the message of conflicting realities as an issue of jobs or resources. Some of us strike out in a different direction, looking to the trunks of plum trees or the taste buds of deer to find some visible sign of a biocentric network. Still others among us throw up our hands in anguish and repudiate the very idea that anthropocentrism is just another worn-out opinion about reality, and not reality itself. We all want to know: whose nature is this anyway?

The struggle to answer this question affects every human institution. Our old anthropocentric fences are being breached and replaced by new fencing even as every nation continues to assert that its own fence, its border, delineates and reserves its own resources for the citizens who reside within the fence. Meanwhile, the new fence defines something different from national access. The ongoing fight to develop or preserve North America's last great wilderness area, the Arctic National Wildlife Refuge, offers one striking example. The designers of the new fence don't want to keep out the Russians, the Japanese, or the Canadians. They want to keep out the humans.

How does all this relate to gardening? In fact, one of the twentieth century's leading gardening writers, Hugh Johnson, draws from the same deep well of anthropocentrism when he couches his fundamental definition of gardening this way:

> What, if anything, do the infinity of different traditional and individual ideas of a garden have in common? They vary so much in purpose, in size, in style and content that not even flowers, or even plants at all, can be said to be essential. In the last analysis there is only one common factor between all gardens, and that is the control of nature by man. Control, that is, for aesthetic reasons.[6]

The craft of gardening offers us, in our own little way and on our own little plot, an opportunity to come to terms with the monumental struggle to redefine reality that is now gripping all our lives. As the four-tree garden declared earlier, control treats the plants and the beds as elements, like paint applied to a canvas. Control sets up a hierarchy, with gardeners poised at the top as lord and master. This petit kingdom is created as an aesthetic triumph of human accommodation.

Control reenacts a horticultural rendition of the prevailing cultural paradigm that separates human beings from nature—what writer Loren Eiseley once referred to as "man's long loneliness."

Hugh Johnson's definition implies something else as well—that unruly nature is a dragon, the snake in our nouveau Eden intent on thwarting our every attempt to build a pocket paradise here on Earth by heaving a never-ending artillery of weeds, insects, deer, and unaccommodating weather our way. Reining nature in is every gardener's central task. With the dragon so ready to pounce, we must never let up our guard.

Granted, dredging up such a fire-and-brimstone tone to describe the likes of dandelions and tent caterpillars exaggerates the way most gardeners actually deal their own controlling hand. But if the allusion seems overblown—and admittedly it is—then it is not without reason. It is far *less* overblown than the herbicides and pesticides we now wield in our daily combat with the dragon.

The second half of Johnson's definition—gardening as the control of nature for *aesthetic* reasons—has a hidden agenda. As explained in "The Local Garden," art critics are often clever at disguising their own personal biases as if they represent a universal truth about art. And Johnson's aesthetic in the cause of control mostly displays his anthropocentric bias. His definition also implies that aesthetics are neutral; that a rose picked from a bush sprayed with pesticides is equally as beautiful as its twin picked from an unsprayed bush. A definition based on control also assumes that we get more roses, and thus more beauty, by instituting a spray program, and consequently fewer roses, *less beauty*, when we forgo spraying.

Although aesthetics may be nothing more than opinions about beauty, these opinions are hardly neutral. Aesthetics are inherently ethical. Misbegotten assumptions about beauty end up killing nature. The insects we seek to annihilate eventually become resistant to chemicals. As they adapt, our gardens lose a measure of their artificially sustained beauty. More powerful chemicals are applied. The insects adapt again. A spiral is set to spin. All across America individual gardeners set out to achieve the greenest lawn, the earliest tomato harvest, the largest roses, none of which could ever prosper without a control born of anthropocentrism. Too many dandelions growing in too many green lawns cause too many controlling gardeners to lay on too much herbicide, which ends up poisoning our aquifers. By attempting to keep nature out, even on a small scale, each gardener adds his or her own small contribution to the poisoning of rivers, coastal waters, and soil. Given that conclusion, which do we continue to eradicate: dandelions or green lawns? In fact, our point of view needs to change and not the dandelions.

The biocentric view asks us to take a fresh look at our choices. It shows us that a beauty dependent on excessive control is an arrogant beauty, even a vicious beauty. This perception of beauty keeps us from developing a more compliant, participatory relationship with place. For all these reasons, some biocentrists would argue that Johnson's aesthetic offers no beauty at all. At best, it is an outmoded beauty: a sense of beauty that is woefully naive about the challenges we face. In the end, God made horseflies, tea roses, green lawns, and yes, even Johnson's definition to rationalize human use and accommodation. And now the world is on fire.

Without meaning to sound contradictory, every garden *also* exhibits the controlling hand of the gardener. No gardener can deny that an untended garden soon reverts to a less tidy state. Despite the unorthodox example of the one-tree garden, a tidy garden is usually the desired objective. The tidy garden demands that weeds get pulled, edges be defined, slugs get evicted. I state the obvious to make the crucial point that gardening is always going to be *somewhat* about taking control of nature in the pursuit of aesthetic perfection. If this were politics, we might call the gardener an enlightened despot.

As the biocentric view suggests, the garden prospers when control is balanced by equal measures of humility and benevolence. A balance is struck. Control, servitude, respect, imagination, pragmatism, an ecological conscience, compliance, and a certain measure of mysticism and altruism all meld together to provide *nurturance*. Try to separate the various aspects into their constituent parts—grant any one of them the status of fundamental gardening definition, as Hugh Johnson does—and one soon skews the entire process. Put them back together again in the service of the two-way street called nurturance, and we express the state of grace called gardening.

So we seem to have backed into a different definition of gardening. If the anthropocentric definition hinged on control, the biocentric one hinges on nurturance. With our revised definition now in hand, we are finally ready to wander down the garden path leading into the sentient garden. We may feel unsure of ourselves; after all, it is no minor matter to cast off one view of reality for a brand-new one. We stand at the gate, take a peek through the slats of the ideogram fence, and give a sigh. Even as we sense the garden with fresh eyes, so we now notice that this garden also senses us.

I have been spotted, on one or two occasions, sitting in the sawdust of my own sentient garden, whispering sweet nothings to the cabbages. I'm not sure why I do this, although I recognize it as a manifestation of the co-creative point of view. It seems the natural thing to do.

This activity commenced after I discovered for myself what has been a truism for plant breeders for millennia: that every cabbage plant sprouted from the same seed packet is not identical. They may all display a common rosette pattern of nine leaves spiraling up from the center, but each one is also as unique as each human baby is unique, as unpredictable in its growth pattern as the weather that nurtures it. Two cabbage seeds planted just eighteen inches apart will grow in two different ways. One sprints to a broad four inches and then remains that way for two weeks or more. Meanwhile, the other one grows spindly. It falls prey to ear-wigs and slugs while its cousin has nary a mark upon it.

I pay a visit to the garden one June morning and am very surprised to notice that the two cabbage heads are about the same size. I suddenly start humming into the nonexistent ears of the two cabbages as my way of expressing an aes-thetic encouragement to their growth. I sing a Tibetan mantra over and over again in the same opportunistic manner that the walrus was found to recite sweet po-etry to the oysters in *Alice in Wonderland*. The act is spontaneous. There isn't meant to be much logic to it.

I stop singing and notice that the cabbage that was chewed up as a sprout has grown strong just to protect itself from further predation. This one grows quickly over the next several weeks. We harvest it at six pounds on the last day of July. Most of the tough outer leaves are noticeably beaten up, but the heart is as perfect as one might expect from a vigorous, healthy, organically grown cabbage.

Meanwhile, the other one is taking its sweet time to mature. The second cab-bage is harvested ten days later than the first, also at six pounds. My wife shreds it into cole slaw. We sit down to dinner; my two daughters recite "blessings on the meal," and the four of us set to the task of devouring it. It tastes superb. Life is perfect. A few weeks later, at a well-attended neighborhood barbecue, I tell the story of the two cabbages to the general throng. Someone mentions the auspicious timing of the two cabbages.

"The auspicious timing? What's that supposed to mean?"

"Well, my family doesn't like to eat cabbage more than once every ten days. Does yours?"

"Well, yes, I suppose you're right."

"And ten days is what you got, isn't it? Sounds like there may be something to it."

It is at this juncture that this admitted nonexpert recently seen discussing cabbages at a friendly barbecue is now seen hurling himself boldly off the twentieth-century rationalist cliff. I land not in cool water where I am brought to my senses, but rather on the warm August soil of a 1930s cartoon world where anthropomorphic plum trees dance the cakewalk while a bouncing purple cabbage points out the words of a Tibetan chant. Om Mani padme huuuuummmmmm! Some people spend their entire lives unsuccessfully trying to communicate to their spouse or their kids. Other people firmly believe that the government should invest more of the so-called defense dividend into communicating with dolphins because that species holds the key to planetary bliss. This crazy gardener wants you to believe that cabbages do it just as often. And just as well.

I am standing in the center of the sentient garden. This time it's February. I have wandered down the deer path to my sentient plum tree and wish I knew a way to ask it if its actions really do affect the deer's actions. And vice versa. Or it's September. I wear a foolish grin as I start singing an old Beatles tune—"Will you still need me, will you still feed me, when I'm sixty-four?"—to a row of broccoli. Or it's June. I stand before a flower bed and offer congratulations to the gallica rose Belle de Crecy, for honoring me with such an incredible display of color, shape, and fragrance. The arrangement of petals seems perfect, and yet the flowers are so much smaller than I ever imagined a perfect rose could be. Or it's October, and I find myself verbally apologizing to one of those same broccolis before harvesting the head.

But it's too easy to turn metaphysically effusive. Let us turn skeptical instead. What other stretches of elasticized logic might just as easily explain the case of the synchronized cabbages? There are many other explanations. For instance, let no one underestimate the power of circumstance. It could just as easily have been a coincidence. For that matter, if I orchestrated the ripening moment of the two cabbages, I must have also modified the eating habits of several insect predators. Do I believe my little mantras have altered the culinary druthers of local slugs and cabbage moth larvae? And how do I explain the fact that a nearby willow casts a slight shadow over the more northerly cabbage? Did I test the chemical variations in the soil? And why am I so unwilling to acknowledge that genetics played some part in this drama?

In other words, a simple scientific query easily evinces any number of other factors affecting the ripening times of cabbages. Evidence also suggests that I may be suffering from a common malady known as after-the-fact wishful thinking. I stand guilty of applying cause-and-effect sentience to my own desires. All may be true. Yet I still insist upon talking and listening to the plants. I sometimes wonder if I can affect four cabbages over thirty days next summer as I did two over ten days this summer.

There is something more at stake here than simply trying to justify why a gardener might wish to talk to plants. Traditional peoples around the world have always asserted that the process of food gathering is an act of gift giving from prey to person. It is said that the spirit of the gift increases even as the body of the gift is consumed.[7] The predator who expresses gratitude for the gift receives more gifts. The predator who forgets to acknowledge the gift suffers dire consequences. Lest this relationship be misunderstood out of context, let it be known that in the above story, I am a predator of cabbages. Cabbage is my prey.

Why is this important? Many aboriginal critics of contemporary culture believe that the environmental crisis is exacerbated by our own culture's neglect to honor the profound gift given *from* prey *to* predator. But how can we be expected to honor something we do not recognize? In fact, there can be no honoring until we first learn to acknowledge the consciousness of other creatures. This is the reason that Inuit people in the High Arctic express real fear over the consequences of a dominant civilization bent on denying the value of common aboriginal beliefs about animal and plant consciousness. They believe that unless modern people are able to revitalize and redefine these same aboriginal perceptions about ecosystems existing as neighborhoods—and on a global scale—none of us has much hope of surviving.[8] To the traditional person, the very idea of animal and plant consciousness promotes an atmosphere of mutual esteem across species. It instills humility wherever the relationship is honored. No matter if this relationship is sung, danced, touched, carved, planted, worn, hugged, dug, or eaten, it is always honored.

Paradoxically, the positive effect this ancient spiritual repertoire *could* exert on our society (such as treating food as a conscious gift from plants and animals) may be more important to the welfare of the planet in this late twentieth century than our society's unswerving desire to debunk it wherever it rears its nonlinear head. One might rightly wonder about our own skewed sense of "progress" that replaces traditional values with cold hard data—no matter how much wisdom the original belief granted to its believers, their families, and their communities. But let it also be understood that honoring the gift between predator and prey, recognizing the sentience of all life, is not the same thing as glorifying the primitive. To regard them as a paraphrase of each other only trivializes what is a genuine modern longing to reconnect with the natural world. Reconnecting is what biocentrism is all about. And biocentrism is rising fast as the reality for our children's generation.

In that sense, I like to believe my cabbage anecdote offers a kind of ecological *myth* (like the well-known case of the one-hundredth monkey) whose value—as with most myths—sometimes offers more to a person than its debunking ever could. I *wish* to believe in this idea of negotiated relations between human and nature because it enhances my life. Thus I continually find myself promoting its expression, even if my logical education constantly reminds me I may have my head screwed on backward. No matter; this belief makes more sense to me than the predominant depiction of nature as a vat full of names, categories, and resources.

Nor am I unaware of the fact that those of us who exalt cabbages may be guilty of grabbing at the same proverbial straws as William Kirby, who exalted the lowly louse in a parallel attempt to explain his own new worldview to denizens of the old. Yet the more we face up to these very personal biases, the more we discover that the relationship between ourselves and such as cabbages and plum trees and deer is just as much about truth as it is about ethics, simple faith, or even about the postmodern philosophy that depicts every view of reality as a personal preference. In such a manner, it becomes our working reality.

There is an old saying: If you look too hard, paradise disappears. If this is true, there is a risk to scrutinizing the sentient garden too intensively. Yet there are still important questions waiting to be answered. For instance, if not circumstance, if not weather, if not soil chemistry, if not genetics, then how *do* I explain the cabbages ripening at such a perfect ten-day interval?

Unfortunately, it is here that my reasoning turns most recondite. I have no clear answer, although, inscrutably, that is not quite the same thing as admitting I do not know. What I did was visualize an unspoken (and mostly subconscious) wish to have the harvest turn out well. Sounds innocuous enough. Regard it as a simple gardener's prayer mumbled directly to the sentient garden. But this is no hocus-pocus; I offer no burnt offerings to the god of this garden, don no feathers, bend no elbows to the four directions. Nor do I possess any hidden agenda of promoting myself as the next generation of consciousness athlete. Or perhaps I make too much of an event that occurred only once. The scientific method would beg me to repeat the experiment next year, and then again the year after that. Not a bad idea.

Which halfheartedly leads to a final series of questions. Cooperating cabbages is one thing, but claiming a unified conscience for the entire garden seems quite another. If what I contend is true, at what point in the process of constructing a garden from scratch does this bold leap to consciousness presumably occur? Is it sudden? Gradual? And to what extent is the mind of the gardener tangled up in the process? Is it just gardens that are loved intensely, sweated over profusely, or admired roundly that gain consciousness?

In fact, all such questions remind me of Victor Frankenstein sewing body parts together, giving them a jolt of electricity, and then forever agonizing how to regain control over a creation who had started making real demands on his peace of mind. This entire line of thought leads nowhere because it presupposes that we sentient gardeners promote a robotic (herbotic?) garden—some kind of naive pop mysticism for the horticultural set. This is not a case of listening to birds sing and hearing cabbages. Permit me to swap the word *garden* for *art*, below, and thus paraphrase author Ken Wilber as he paraphrases Schopenhauer to express the same idea this way:

> Bad gardens copy, good gardens create, great gardens transcend. What all great gardens have in common are their ability to pull the sensitive viewer out of him or herself and into the garden, so completely that the separate self-sense disappears entirely, and at least for a brief moment one is ushered into a nondual and time-less awareness. A great garden, in other words, is mystical no matter what its actual content.[9]

Or regard another image taken from Keith Thomas's *Man and the Natural World*, which earlier gave us sweet-smelling horse manure and instructive lice:

> One of the most treasured memories of an old lady friend of mine, recently deceased, was of her visits, some sixty years or more ago, to a great countryhouse . . . and of her host, who was then old, the head of an ancient and distinguished family, and of his reverential feeling for his old trees. His greatest pleasure was to sit out of doors of an evening in sight of the grand old trees in his park, and before going in he walked round to visit them, one by one, and resting his hand on the bark he would whisper good night. He was convinced, he confided to his young guest, who often accompanied him in these evening walks, that they had in-telligent souls and knew and encouraged his devotion.[10]

An old man wanders around his garden a hundred years ago, chats up the trees, and charms his young friend, who herself has recently died of old age. The image demonstrates that a sentient garden transcends purely ethical inclinations to do good work or good foraging or even attain a reintegration of activities. Here is an image of the sentient garden as a *charmed* garden where all the myriad parts—in-cluding the human part—interpenetrate to create a sense of place. The gardener who acquires such a sense connects more closely to the divine mystery of life.

May

Soaker hose seems an all-around winner. It is constructed from recycled car tires, the water forced out drop by drop. The hose soaks an area a foot on each side— and nowhere else. The paths between the beds stay dry. With a soaker hose, everything stays moist on half the water consumption of a normal hose.

I've laid each hose an inch beneath the surface of my various raised vegetable beds. Where it peeks out of the corner of the bed, it is clamped to an underground pipe that eventually leads back toward a hose bib located along the side of the house. I've interjected a piece of hi-tech poetry between the hose bib and the pipe in the form of an inexpensive watering computer. The gadget is cluttered with buttons, and although it may look a bit intimidating to the nonmechanical, in fact it is nothing more than a valve controlled by a digital watch that sets the hour and duration of flow over seven days. Once set, and if left as is, the computer repeats the cycle again next week. And so on until the battery gives out. The computer seems to run for one and a half summers on a single nine-volt battery.

The spring rains vanished earlier than usual this year. The second half of May has been as hot as early August. Whereas I usually turn on the water computer during late June, this year I screwed it onto the hose bib on May twentieth. I started punching buttons, programming the valve to open for precisely thirty-five minutes a day, four days a week, at 4:30 A.M. Early in the morning is the coldest part of the day; the plants won't be so shocked by the sudden influx of cold well water. Also, setting it for that time of day copies the atmosphere's own tendency to manifest dew. The water stays put in the soil until early afternoon. By the end of July I may need to increase the duration to forty minutes each morning.

On very hot afternoons in late summer I sometimes augment my hi-tech solution with an occasional hosing down of the leaf crops. Doing so, I must admit that I enjoy immensely the half hour spent among the green vegetables with hose in hand. But I no longer let myself get carried away. Water has turned precious in these days of receding water tables. I conservatively figure that the combination of soaker hose and computer saves five hundred gallons of water a month. The whole system cost less than one hundred dollars to put together.

The How-To Garden

Although there are many books and courses on the subject of how to garden, ultimately we learn about gardening by doing it. The how-to garden is thus defined as the place we go to encounter our own gardening education. Like the sentient garden, this one is an experiential garden. That is the reason the story of a how-to garden's planning, digging, and planting is also told most accurately in the first person. Also like the sentient garden, this garden clearly speaks to us, offering counsel in its own good time. Unlike the sentient garden, the how-to garden is rarely a self-conscious garden that persistently focuses our sensibilities upon itself. The how-to garden is more passive, more like a playing field that focuses our sensibilities upon the activity manifested within its borders.

So far, this book has referred to *my* personal garden only obliquely—as if it were a diving board from which I continually spring off into large notions about a sense of place, paradise, sentience, history, the future, and so on. It now seems an appropriate moment to step off that conceptual diving board to sketch in an experiential biography of one particular how-to garden as told through the eyes of its own pet gardener, namely me.

Because any account of the how-to garden is inevitably strung together from a framework of the first-person voice, its telling occasionally stumbles on the same problems of distancing that confront proud parents discussing their children. Before segueing into this discussion of my own how-to garden, we might all benefit from first considering the strange case of the fictitious botanist Kamikochi Kiyomasa, who ran into his own problem of distancing while studying the equally fictitious flower *Anaclea taludensis*.

> Kamikochi decided to take a closer look at the flowers and so started walking towards the hilltop. On the way he realized that something very bizarre was taking place. Unlike what usually happens when we approach an object we have seen from a distance—it gradually appears larger until, when we are near enough to touch it, it assumes its proper dimensions—these plants did not seem to get any bigger as the biologist approached them. When Kamikochi reached the hilltop they turned out to be just as small as they had appeared from a hundred meters away.[1]

I started my garden ten years ago by focusing entirely on masses of colorful annuals. The bigger and brasher the hybrid, the better it would look in my brand-new garden. I was the guy standing in front of you in line at the local gardening store juggling ten six-packs of those red-and-white-striped petunias with the blue-and-white-mottled rim that spelled out the message "Support our troops."

But seriously, although they provide an instant blaze of bright color, hybrid bedding annuals like petunias and begonias often trumpet a grand statement of impermanence born of gardening inexperience. By the end of that first season gardening on six very wild acres, I watched the petunias and the potted geraniums wither into oblivion and realized that I had planted nothing whatsoever to nurture a deeper connection between myself and this unique place that surrounds me—even though the connection to this place would probably endure through the rest of my life.

I sought an enduring garden.

There are annuals, and then there are annuals. The term *annual* simply defines any herbaceous plant that germinates, flowers, sets seed, and dies all in one season. This succinct life cycle also signifies that an annual follows a survival strategy that devotes all its energy toward effusive flower production capable of attracting whatever pollinator it needs in order to achieve the goal of generous seed production. As all this oversimplified botany refers to gardening, the primary virtue of any annual is providing an instant splash of color to patch up the tattered spaces in a garden bed.

Likewise, there are splashes, and there are splashes. Six-packs of so-called improved mixed colors actually means that some marketing person sitting within the bowels of some seed company office has decided to employ the great American advertising gambit of playing on the customer's vanity by naming something the slightest bit new and unusual as, well, *improved*. It is a word germinated in the very same bed as seed catalogs that describe each of twenty different broccoli varieties as being the best of the best; this fact is ostensibly demonstrated by the glossy inclusion of twenty one-inch-square photographs that look suspiciously like the very same broccoli plant shot from twenty different angles using twenty different lens filters.

Improved rarely means "better," only occasionally means "different," sometimes means "more" or "larger," and always means "buy." It almost always means "hybrid," going a long way to explain why the seed catalogs lavish so many extra columnar inches promoting them. A *hybrid*, for the uninitiated gardening penny-pincher, might be defined this way: If we happen to like that pack of "improved mixed colors," we are going to have to buy another pack of twenty seeds at $1.98 next year from that same company, because probably none of the thousand seeds we might have saved from this year's model will reseed true to form. The parents are different; the underlying genetics don't equate. Those thousand seeds will germinate, instead, into smaller plants bearing smaller flowers. If we are very lucky, we won't start cursing the progeny of the hybrids, referring to them as weeds when they start popping up uninvited everywhere we never planted them. We gardeners refer to these uninvited as *volunteers*. I suppose it is an attempt to put a positive spin on what often amounts to many hours of extra weeding.

Mixed is another dubious adjective. Unfortunately, mixed colors of just about anything planted in a garden rarely achieve more than a grand confusion to the eye while trumpeting a lack of clarity by the gardener. Mixed colors sit in the bed as a sampler of the hybridist's art, a summation of all the possibilities on the same order as those six-packs of cold cereal we buy to decide which flavor we actually like. Planted together, mixed colors treat the garden as a container of tints, and variations on some company's marketing scheme. At best, they may elicit the collector's curious emotion of having one of each. If there are annuals and annuals, splashes and splashes, then "improved mixed colors" might best be regarded as the horticultural equivalent to splashing into a kid's plastic wading pool. The one that was never meant to last beyond one season.

Despite the very striking petunias planted at key locations around the perimeter of the house, the flowers that actually held my attention the longest that first summer were the so-called old-fashioned annuals. If improved mixed annuals are the *Billboard* Top Ten of flowers, then the old-fashioneds are the old standards—the ones that have stood the test of time—like purple bachelor's buttons (*Centaurea*), yellow calendulas, and the extraordinary, spidery, gray-blue love-in-a-mist (*Nigella*).

Each of these species grew, flowered, and set seed without much watering on my part. And today, nearly ten years later, the progeny of those same three standards still grace the edges of several borders. All it takes to ensure their return each year is to grab a handful of seed heads and cast them a bit beyond what the plants are able to muster on their own. Sometimes I forget to do this. And yet, like reruns of "Star Trek," the "old-fashioneds" always return. Like rereading *Moby Dick* for the tenth time, they still pique my senses all over again. Significantly, the so-called improved species never last, which seems another way of saying that the ability to bond to place is bred right out of them.

At the end of my first gardening season, I had also learned the names, favored habitat, and flowering period of several of the tiny wildflower species that flourish at the edge of the woods. I paid close attention to the fact that early dandelions are soon followed in quick succession by pink filarees, followed by calypso orchids, buttercups, chocolate lilies, coral root, camas, and centaury. Roughly in that order.

By the following spring I added my first long-term investments in what was still a highly unformed gardening vision: in this instance, the relatively foolproof choices of a red-leafed Japanese maple and a star magnolia. In my ignorance I had thought I was buying trees that would eventually shade a substantial area. What I got was trees the size of shrubs. After nearly ten years, the maple has grown to seven feet tall, and the magnolia barely to six. In another twenty years, I am told, neither should attain more than twice its current height. I have long grown to love both trees, although for reasons a nongardener can hardly hope to appreciate second-hand.

The star magnolia's primary trait is its awesome ability to unfold a lavish spread of the softest white, fragrant, and exceedingly thick-petaled flowers. Quite honestly, if I did not personally experience my own front walk glowing with the show of those four-inch-wide flowers in early spring and someone chose to slip me a photo of this same tree in full bloom, I might believe the photo to be a prac-tical joke: the canny result of a trickster pinning huge tissue-paper blooms on the branches just to test the limits of my credulity.

This floor show of a bloom lasts less than three weeks. It leaves behind a fond memory of the flower's sweet vanilla fragrance, an occasional out-of-sync bloom in mid-August, and a thickly leaved, two-trunked shrub with otherwise unremark-able characteristics.

If the star magnolia had nothing to offer besides a three-week bloom—no matter how spectacular—I would have planted it at the end of some garden cul-de-sac, thus precipitating an annual spring pilgrimage just to pay homage to a very special tree in full bloom. But I planted it, instead, right beside the front porch. That's because I also observe it to be the most *hopeful* plant in the entire garden (although someone else might continue calling it a trickster). It wins that appellation by virtue of the forty or fifty flower buds that bloom to such excess in April. Those buds start showing themselves way back in September. Its display of swelling buds continues throughout the winter.

The general effect on my own state of mind is joyous anticipation. By late January—when almost nothing else in the garden is happening, and the ground is soggy and sometimes frozen, and a normal human being can't seem to put his finger on what the word *spring* actually refers to—chancing upon those magnolia buds growing slightly larger every day offers a generous ray of hope as well as a grand illusion of all that is to come. By late January, the buds have developed a furry silver casing that makes them look not unlike a hyperthyroid pussy willow. Every bud shouts out that spring is not far away. But it is still only January. Spring seems very far away indeed. And the hopeful magnolia has tricked me again.

The Japanese maple achieves an entirely different effect. Whereas the magnolia looks remarkable for a very short time and then transforms into a hopeful trickster for most of the rest of the year, the maple puts on a worthy display just about all the time. The leaves are a brilliant red, especially during the spring when they first unfurl. The high sun of early June reflects through those bloodred leaves, causing them to light up from right inside themselves. The tree glows as if it were a cultivar introduced from a collection Moses himself brought down from Mount Sinai. The maple puts me in a paradise garden anytime I choose to visit it.

If the effect of the magnolia is hopeful, the effect of the maple is unexpectedly nostalgic. I'm lying on the ground just to north of that tree on a breezy June afternoon, head propped up on my elbows. The tree appears to pulse in time with each gust of the soft breeze. The sun tosses shards of bloodred light through the shimmery fingerlike leaves; the audacious flicker soon causes me to reminisce about a time, many years ago now, when we were all younger and mind-altering drugs enjoyed a brief meteoric renaissance before being relegated, once again, to the death row of societal icons. Sixties songs like "Lucy in the Sky with Diamonds," sixties images like Jimi Hendrix in full psychedelic regalia, start flashing in front of my eyes. I see the rockets' red glare of Southeast Asia, and it rekindles in me the experience of that crazy, inspiring, youthful, dangerous counterculture.

But then the breeze stops gusting; the tree lies inert. Just as suddenly, I intuit what it was that caused the psychedelic generation to vanish until who knows when. No pun intended. Still, the answer, my friend, is blowing in the wind . . .

Nostalgic is the only word for that tree. Yet I also imagine the Japanese maple being favored by architects. The leaves possess a wonderful structure of their own. The Japanese Bloodgood maple is one cultivar whose twiny branches and bowl-like shape invoke a splendid garden architecture even when devoid of leaves. The tree is a sight to behold even during the dead of winter when the leaves and all their reminiscences are fast asleep waiting for spring.

Knowledge and experience. Some garden writers assert that a mastery of their art occurs primarily through an accumulation of knowledge wed to the direct experience of plant identification, soil chemistry, landscape design, and perhaps the finer points of the color spectrum. Once we learn enough of these basics, we should be ready to set off on our own to exert that blessed sense of control over nature that is the contemporary definition of gardening.

However, any thorough examination of the science of horticulture—when to plant, what to plant, why to plant, et cetera—will also be seen to offer nothing at all in the way of explaining the process by which a casual gardener suddenly explodes full-blown upon the scene as a *compulsive* gardener.

The analytical approach to gardening mainly offers up choice tips and pointers to aid in the education of a gardener. But mere knowledge rarely leads to mastery because it overlooks both the sweaty passion and the poetry. As the nowhere garden has already foretold, gardening is creativity on a grand Utopian scale. We consult a nonexistent compass and so set off on a journey to Eden, which actually ends when we encounter a sense of place. The how-to garden teaches us grounding: how to keep our eyes firmly locked on the path and not lose our way.

Our lives are constantly bombarded with information. One result is that most of us "know" more than we experience. Some of us go so far as to believe, erroneously, that knowing is in fact the same thing as experiencing. But what that conviction primarily lacks is grounding. To quote an old saw, experience is the best teacher—not our thoughts and stories about our experiences; and certainly not the data we may collect while experiencing. The *practice* of gardening offers one of the premier pathways leading to a direct experience of the Earth. It does so far more directly than any discussion about gardening. It does so even better than the product of that practice: the garden itself.

A first-rate education grows in our own backyards. This education displays all the characteristics of matriculation, final exams, degree credits, failing and passing grades. A gardening education combines the unexpected and the revelational with the methodical. I plant a Japanese maple in my own how-to garden not only because the color and shape are right for any particular spot but because the tree possesses an unexplainable charisma capable of lifting my spirits to crazy day-dreaming on a sunny June afternoon. The unpredictable process of choosing that tree thus borrows as much from spiritual development as it does from craft or science. I would submit that it is to the bones-throwing, entrails-divining, and especially sweat-producing aspects of the gardening experience that we must surrender if we are to transform our controlling hand into a nurturing one.

A key aspect of my own epiphany occurred shortly after I discovered the gift of the glacier. A glacier retreated across the land I garden about fifteen thousand years ago. I am told that the ice was three thousand feet thick, which explains why the surface of my front yard is mostly a slab of polished granite bedrock. The scarring and gouging of the rock runs decidedly southeast to northwest. The knoll drops off precipitously to the northwest. When my wife and I first moved here and built our house, the flat plain beyond the edge of this northwest-facing cliff was composed entirely of scrubby Oregon grape, alder, and willow. The very noticeable lack of forest trees indicated that the ground there probably had no topsoil. The presence of the moisture-loving alders and willows strongly hinted at a local water-retentive blue clay. When we dug a pond on that spot five years later, we were very happy, although not surprised, that the clay plunged below ground to a depth greater than our fifteen-foot hole. When the winter rains do their job and fill the pond to overflow, Tarzan himself could dive off that cliff and hit deep water.

The opposite edge of the knoll, the southeast quadrant, possesses a very different sort of geology. This is a gradual slope that descends into a second-growth fir, madrona, and pine forest possessed of an understory of serviceberry trees that fill the forest with white flowers each April. Between the bedrock knoll and the beginning of the forest there is a uniquely bumpy ground of widely spaced, stunted trees. While digging there seven years ago in preparation for an eventual artichoke bed, I discovered a jumble of pumpkin-sized boulders covered over by just a few inches of topsoil. Since no human being had ever lived here before, I deduced that the stone must have been deposited in the same glacial withdrawal that left so much clay on the opposite side of the knoll. These heavy boulders were the detritus given up by the ice in its northwest retreat across the boulder catcher that was my knoll.

The discovery of a seemingly bottomless pile of boulders has since proven to be the most influential factor in determining both the shape and the form of the resultant garden. I started excavating the fifty-to-a-hundred-pound boulders, one at a time, by pick and shovel and wheelbarrow and soon began mortaring them together to construct terraced garden beds all along the varying slopes of the bedrock. Over the years, these terraces have grown ever more sophisticated and ambitious as my skills increased. While most of the boulders are of the exact same mineral composition as the bedrock itself, I have also discovered bubbly pieces of lava, large quartz crystals, and even a heavy piece of lumpy iron that looks suspiciously like a meteorite. They are all gifts of the glacier—rocks, each one of them with its own shape, each one with a story of its own to tell. Each one adding to the composition of the growing garden.

I do most of the rock work in the late fall, during the two-month period when the garden is going to sleep but the cold weather has not yet arrived to mar the setup time of mortar. When the rocks are in place, I immediately start filling the boulder-framed beds with whatever organic material I have on hand. My main source of the gardener's gold and diamonds known as compost is kitchen scraps mixed with barrels of seaweed and bales of hay, augmented with the very abundant horse manure that I gather by the truckload from a neighboring stable. When the bed is full, I let the mass simmer for a winter or even longer, until nothing remains but rich, sweet-smelling compost. Since the finished product is much denser than the original, I start adding in more wheelbarrowsful of decomposed horse manure until the top of the terrace is overflowing with it. I let it sit for another few weeks and then plant.

I follow no recipe for building compost and therefore provide no fount of knowledge about how anyone else should proceed with the matter. With a plethora of how-to books on the market, I have preferred to consult my how-to garden directly. In fact there are many excellent books teaching a gardener how to build a proper composter. What every book will recommend is that we turn the mess regularly with a fork, add in as much air as possible for the benefit of the aer-· obic bacteria. Turning also kills the stench. I have not yet discovered, however, any how-to book that will tell me how to deal with garbage when it's thirty degrees outside, and the composter itself is already overflowing, and the breakdown of all that organic matter is progressing so much more painfully slowly than the how-to book says it's supposed to do. And every time I put a fish carcass in the composter, some dog or raccoon manages to get into it and makes a mess all over the yard. But I can't figure out *how* the animal gets in. Then again, maybe that dog is doing me a favor. She is turning the compost and I'm not, which accounts for both the overflow and the stench.

Actually, my own bottom-line advice about composters is less than clinical. It demands instead that we take a short side trip into the land of cosmic consciousness. Get whatever composter suits your fancy. Build it, buy it, dig it, do it. Place it as far from your house as is geographically possible without also getting yourself into a lawsuit whenever the wind shifts toward your neighbors. Turn it every so often. Buy a few bales of hay. Whenever you empty the garbage can into the bins, heap a few wads of hay on top. Besides that simple advice, *que sera*—let what happens happen. Flies, smells, messes; one or another of them is going to creep up once in a while, no matter how sanitary a person tries to be—and no matter how many times that how-to book says it doesn't need to happen.

My own rock terraces cum composters have been developing for several years now. Constructing the boulders into terraces, filling them with garbage, planting them several seasons later, and building stone stairways to connect them all have since turned into the most labor-intensive tasks of my life. Reiterating the goals of Joe Hollis's paradise garden, terrace building offers me the reintegration of my leisure activities. It is the ongoing source of my physical well-being—my jogging and aerobics. It is the largest art project of my life, a labor of love and spirit that now writhes across the knoll like a series of great frozen waves. I could never have imagined the extent of these terraces in advance. They are completed one at a time. Only when the current terrace is finished do I start imagining the placement and depth of the next one. They are all constructed to the shape of the land, out of the land, and filled to the brim with yet more of the same land.

Notice that this description of building the rock-terraced garden has made no mention whatsoever of the plants that ended up in the various terraces. This is meant to point out the major distinction between gardening and landscaping. If gardening is the experience of growing plants, landscaping is the experience of growing gardens. Gardeners keep their eyes to the ground and the greenery. Landscapers develop a peripheral vision, always scanning the larger environment called home. In many ways, the terms *gardening* and *landscaping* are not much more than two different viewpoints of the very same relationship to place. In this book, I sometimes use the two terms synonymously.

In my confusion of suddenly facing so many new unplanted gardening beds, the how-to garden spoke to me again, this time addressing the many virtues of growing perennials. If annuals put all their attention into flowering and setting seed in just one season, herbaceous perennials grow year after year if originally sited in an auspicious location. They put down roots both literally and figuratively. Although it's the rare perennial that sets as many flower heads as the average annual, the individual flowers of a perennial are often (although certainly not always) more subtle and yet somehow more substantial than those of annuals. Irises, delphiniums, and astilbes are substantial perennials. Japanese anemones and dianthus are subtle ones.

It was during the fall of my third gardening season that I started accumulating perennials. As perennials tend to do, the newly planted peonies, oriental poppies, lychnis, and polemonium soon taught me the important lesson of appreciating leaf texture and plant shape as easy equals to the lavishness of their flowers. Over time, I find myself personally favoring flowers on the blue end of the spectrum and round, mounding plants over tall or short ones. Captivated by those two criteria, I convinced myself that the round ball of a crater-lake veronica, with its bluest-of-blue flowers, must be the epitome of flowering perennials. But when that pregnant mound of greenery grew so large that it finally collapsed outward under its own weight, I concluded that its new bird's-nest shape looked "inelegant" and "sloppy" or even "wrong." I fought the sprawl by artfully employing green twine to tie the collapsed bundle back into a mound again, quite proud that the internal string skeleton could hardly be seen at all.

Two years later, while immersed in the springtime task of lassoing the veronica to my own aesthetic agenda, I suddenly recognized that the plant's yearly collapse was exactly the same process individual flowers undergo by opening petals from the center outward. Here was a plant busily engaged in its normal healthy growth cycle, and I wanted to incarcerate it inside a green string prison for committing the crime of aesthetic disobedience. I stopped tying and soon started observing the veronica's outward sprawl as an opportunistic strategy evolved for dropping seeds over a far greater plot of ground than a geometrically perfect mound would ever permit.

As one might guess, this was also the year I developed an appreciation for the sprawling, falling, ground-hugging torus shape. This kindergardener listened attentively to the solicitations of a humble veronica and was soon taught to promote the self-seeding of perennials as a means of clustering groups of plants rather than individual specimens. This newfound sensitivity to the growth dynamics of a crater-lake blue veronica had surely affected my gardening aesthetic. It also gave me my first tantalizing peek at the Mayan compass, which set me on a long, faltering journey leading to greater and greater relinquishment of control over my garden. And acceptance of what was happening of its own accord.

The how-to garden soon pointed me toward unusual perennials, downright Dr. Seuss–looking perennials, choosing such relative rarities as rosy incarvilleas, twirling euphorbias, and spiny everlasting eryngiums over the much more common salvias and rudbeckias. I was increasingly transfixed by formerly unheeded gardening events, perhaps exemplified by the remarkable way the *Alchemilla mollis* focuses a dewdrop right at the center of its thick, perfectly round, blue-green leaves.

So the perennials taught me the essential lesson of seeing far beyond the climax of flower blooming. Over time I learned to appreciate, with equanimity, every aspect of a plant's growing cycle. I began to pay special attention to the moment a perennial first breaks soil, noticing, for instance, that a large grouping of columbines are up and spurting toward the sky long before the platycodons show anything at all. Then the platycodons finally make their anticipated appearance at soil level. They look just like a colony of tiny asparagus. And a full week after that blessed event, I finally notice that one of the plants I had identified as a columbine is actually a thalictrum with columbine-shaped leaves. As another week comes and goes, the columbine remains close to soil level and has started to plump up its stems. Meanwhile, the individual stems and leaves of the columbine-leaved thalictrum have started to look much more delicate than any columbine. Within another week the thalictrum has grown a foot taller than either the columbines or the platycodons.

So it goes throughout the seasons. This recognition of attributes beyond flower and mature shape seemed a sure sign that I had ascended onto another gardening level.

There is a classical approach to landscape gardening that insists we learn our own personal gardening aesthetic after first immersing ourselves in the best of the traditional styles. It is an approach largely borrowed from traditional art education. Students study the theories and techniques utilized by masters like Cézanne and Rembrandt and Picasso before they ever allow themselves to experiment on their own. We draw a better picture and, by inference, plant a better garden *after* we learn the techniques and tools of the masters.

Certainly, it's all useful. All helpful. Had I followed this model, I would have adopted on faith certain plantings utilized by, for instance, landscape architect Russell Page and probably would have learned to appreciate conifers a good ten years before I actually did so. Today those conifers would be ten years fuller and more mature than the trees I finally got around to planting last spring. On the other hand, ten years ago I had not yet discovered the local resource of buried boulders. I had not yet started building terraces. With a front yard of bedrock, I did not yet possess deep enough beds to plant those hypothetical conifers. Ten years ago I would have viewed those conifers as "elements" in my own version of a four-tree garden. And alas, it seems quite certain that they would be long gone by now, sacrificed on the altar of their own exuberant growth.

It is said that the difference between successful people and those who just get by is that successful people tend to fail more often. One important lesson that the classical approach sometimes forgets to mention is that the vast majority of the so-called masters were renegades or outright failures in their own time. They were revolutionaries who believed that relying on too many old-fashioned rules stifles creativity. As that statement pertains to, say, music, I know a local subculture of six-year-olds who, even one year ago at five, loved to *play* music. They continued loving to play music until they started taking violin lessons and their creativity suffocated in favor of a rote recitation of the classical technique.

As that premise relates to gardening, the Japanese garden style, as one example, developed over several hundred years. Its basic principles were constantly being refined and expanded upon by inspired although rebellious gardeners who continually rejected and refurbished the established rules of the time. In other words, straying from anyone's idea of the traditional path does not imply either weakness of tradition or lack of talent. It *is* the tradition. It leads to the continued refinement of one tradition even as it evolves into the next great tradition. Let us heap praise upon all classical gardening traditions. No matter how inappropriate their methods may be when applied to our relationship with place, they remain a source of invaluable free tips from the long-dead masters.

Much of what passes for gardening aesthetics (including my own developing style) is actually a fashion statement masquerading as objectivity. In other words, certain orthodox calls about height, color, texture, and the like have more to do with correctness than truth. They mirror any issue of *Vogue* magazine where the models are supposed to represent the perfect woman, though in fact only a certain stratum of the female population would openly covet that hollow-cheeked, gaunt look.

Reflecting the *Vogue* vision of female perfection, some gardening styles have likewise become institutionalized. There is a good reason for this. Style offers guidance to people unable, for whatever reason, to work things out for themselves. It is, in many ways, the horticultural equivalent of those picture books where children connect the dots and so draw a clever picture. Watching my own children connect the dots with great concentration, I cannot say that the pastime has either helped or hindered their ability to draw on their own. Likewise, following preconceived notions of style provides an easy roadmap leading to a rudimentary sense of place. It neither helps nor hinders the development of a knockout garden.

If any particular style persists for long enough, we start referring to it as a classic. Having stood the test of time, the classics are internally integrative, always historically pertinent, and occasionally beautiful. The redwood deck, for instance, has emerged as a classic gardening element in the United States.

Get enough of these classic gardens started in one locale, and a tradition emerges: the French tradition, the English landscape tradition, the Italian tradition, and so on. If the various classical traditions often reflect a sense of the place they originated (although not necessarily anywhere else), they likewise reflect a strong sense of the lifestyle and fashion tastes of the landed aristocracy of that particular place. The traditional French garden, for example, follows a set of conventions dictating geometrically sheared hedges enclosing great beds of monochromatic flowers. It is in fact a landscape invented for the precise purpose of being viewed from above, from great terraces and bedroom patios, and granting the overall effect of a giant Persian rug covering the floor of one's grand landscaped estate. The French garden thus necessitates a large manor for viewing, a large staff for maintenance, and inevitably a bottomless financial capability to pay for that high maintenance and control.

The English landskip tradition is the direct ancestor of the modern American garden. It is perhaps best exemplified by the work of one Lancelot Brown, better known to history as Capability Brown. Brown meticulously constructed naturalistic-appearing pastoral landscapes (landskips) that presumed to emulate Arcadia, the bucolic Greek paradise garden where centaurs and fauns were said to reside. Brown's constructed view of paradise can be glimpsed in Walt Disney's *Fantasia*, which includes a segment about Arcadia as the visual accompaniment to Beethoven's Pastoral Symphony.

The man's work seems a paradox. This "capability" of his caused Brown to sacrifice great parcels of the natural ecosystem of England—as well as many of the formal gardens constructed during the English Renaissance—in the cause of creating a naturalistic artifact meant to resemble an idealized Greek image of paradise. Brown leveled entire villages just to keep the view around the manor open and naturalistic. But Brown also stands responsible for tree planting on a vast scale. His staff planted one hundred thousand trees on the estate of Lord Donegall alone.

The English landskip tradition has exerted an enormous effect upon twentieth-century Western culture, perhaps best reflected in that exemplar of the modern garden: the clipped lawn. In many respects, the idea of a vast stretch of lawn was splendidly matched to the English countryside and the aristocratic lifestyle from which it originated. The upkeep of the baronial lawn was overseen by a large workforce of gardeners whose fastidious maintenance of acres upon acres of grass was attained entirely by hand, munching herds of sheep, or, much later, by simple hand-driven machines. It has even been argued that the landskip tradition was socially beneficial because it proved to be such a bountiful employer of the otherwise disenfranchised servant class. This high-maintenance task was utterly dependent upon the abundant rainfall, deep soils, and clement temperature variations of the English countryside.

The idea of emulating the garden tradition of one specific culture and place doesn't always translate very well into other cultures and other places. Whereas the lawn was once the highly refined gardening tradition of a few hundred wealthy scions of Empire on the grand scale, it is now the garden cliché of tens of millions of homeowners on a much-reduced scale. Over the past hundred years, the lawn has democratized and humbled itself and finally emerged as the quintessential icon of suburban America. Yet it rarely receives either the traditional high-maintenance hand care or the climatic blessings that did so well to mediate an equilibrium between British culture and the British ecosystem.

If the physical necessities of that original balance have essentially vanished in places like Tucson, Minneapolis, and Orlando, what is retained from the original is its insidious cultural base: the definition of a garden as a place to be controlled. Where place is unfriendly, culture turns more assertive. In places like Spokane, Palm Springs, Houston, and Montreal, achieving the ideal of a beautiful lawn often develops into a matter of poisoning the ecosystem.

Our lawn-tending ways have led to an ecological crisis of some magnitude. The high-nitrogen fertilizer needed to keep any lawn green also pollutes any body of water located downstream. Fifty billion acres of American lawn at an annual maintenance cost of thirty billion dollars[2] demands vast foot-acres of water, which places unendurable stress upon already diminished water supplies across North America. The amount of herbicides utilized to keep the creeping incursion of weeds at bay far outweighs the amounts used even by commercial farming. Because herbicides harm many other organisms in their path—whether they be out-of-sight fish swimming downstream or pets and children who happen to play on the typical lawn's well-poisoned surfaces—the choice of planting a lawn today shares something essential with other ecological irresponsibilities such as refusing to recycle, buying gas-hogging cars, driving off-road vehicles to tour the desert, et cetera, et cetera, ad infinitum. In every case, a once socially acceptable action continues to be fostered in an increasingly overpopulated world and without any thought of its *cumulative* detriment.

There are, of course, other ways to cover up dirt in a suburban front yard without recruiting artificial fertilizers, excessive watering, and herbicidal poison. Discover ground covers. Or cordon off a little parcel of the front yard and plant low-maintenance grasses, which don't demand artificial stimulation. We might also start to regard the lawn the same way many semivegetarians now regard meat: as a condiment rather than as the main course. Surround a much-reduced lawn with flower beds and shrubs. In the process, reinvent yet another English landscaping style known as *the garden room*.

Although my own how-to garden has as yet resisted the temptation of the lawn, it has borrowed on many occasions several conventions from the Japanese gardening tradition. The Japanese developed their elegant style within a temperate and wet climate bestowed with natural stylistic elements (e.g., moss, river-polished rocks, water, and dense evergreens) interpenetrating with vistas of natural features (e.g., mountains and sky). The rules that embody the Japanese style demand a close adherence to shape, shadow, light, reflection, and greenery. Those gardens that mirror the rules most strictly are often very subdued. As in the English landskip tradition, "naturalistic" devices skillfully hide the controlling hand of the gardener. They are planted primarily as a source of deep serenity and peace. And when done well, they often achieve their purpose.

Regard the concept of *shakkei*,[3] which translates literally as "borrowed landscape." An already existent view of a mountain, a pond, perhaps a temple or a waterfall, is incorporated into the general garden design by carefully framing it with trees. In a few exceptional cases, every single tree, herbaceous plant, and manmade addition to the garden is placed not so much to hold one's attention through its own individualistic beauty but rather to lead the eye naturally to the view beyond. Pruning the trees to frame the vista has transformed into a high art form. No sawcuts are ever seen by a visitor's casual glance at the trunk.

Shakkei and the English lawn are both landscape devices, although the former is a perceptual device, whereas the latter is physical. *Shakkei* exists independent of place. The Japanese physical prerequisites of stone, water, and climate need not necessarily be adopted. What is pivotal, instead, is the view itself and the subtle way we go about framing it. The lawn, by contrast, is a physical entity. It demands green grass wherever it grows.

In my own attempt to adapt *shakkei,* I have never fretted very much if the trees are planted in such a way as to make some prototypical Mr. Toyota break out in deep contented grunts. I also find that when the concept of *shakkei* is adopted successfully, the result is so exceedingly subtle that most observers rarely perceive that the plantings were made specifically to blend and focus any particular view. *Shakkei* also serves as its own garden compass. The eye is led to a specific viewpoint and the feet soon follow down that path. The garden and the view interpenetrate to accent a sense of place.

The how-to garden next spoke strongly to me during the winter of my fifth season on the land. The garden was in hibernation, and quite honestly, there was little to enjoy beside the boulders, the wild Oregon grape that frequents so much of the Pacific Northwest, the fir trees, and an exceedingly mossy hillside. Of those things I had planted myself, the bare but evocative Japanese maple proved to be the one notable exception. By now it had spread more outward than up, and a few of the mahogany-colored branches were snaking around one another like braided rope, dispensing a wonderful shape and tint to the otherwise drab winter garden.

One day in early December my family visited the Seattle Zoo, where I found myself more mesmerized by the bunches of luminous lavender berries crowding the branches of a callicarpa bush than by any of the sadly aloof caged animals. These berries were as brilliant as any flower, and yet four inches of snow lay on the ground. It caused me to embark on a study of the relative merits of shrubs and small trees, and to conclude that shrubs are obviously an expression of commitment and longevity in the garden. Flowers may come and go, but shrubs and trees are permanent. Book after book on the subject reinvoked the basic concept that shrubs and small conifers are best thought of as *the bones* of a garden. It is an apt metaphor. Evidently, my garden was telling me that it lacked bones.

The resultant acquisition of several shrubs and trees presented a practical solution to a perennial garden that was consuming entirely too much time and precious water. Any gardener with an unlimited appetite for increased garden area must eventually realize that all those enormously fanciful gardens photographed in so many coffee-table gardening books are predominantly the playthings of the wealthy or the outright obsessive—people who hire other people to manage gardens that have become full-time jobs.

My actual garden area encompassed nearly an acre. Any serious consideration about further expansion hinged on what I have named the three garden constraints of time, money, and environment.

First, time. My career is not farming, gardening, or landscaping. The labor commitment to my gardening avocation was now displaying signs of strain. If I wished to expand yet again, every other part of the entire garden had to become commensurately more self-sufficient. My choice of plants altered drastically: toward the self-sufficient, the long-term, and away from the needy. I sought out plants capable of taking care of themselves without extra pampering from me.

I became a fledgling botanist, noticing that bearded irises and peonies thrive in conditions far drier than we gardeners usually allot them—no doubt a function of their Spanish and Central Asian heritage. I stopped watering them altogether. I noticed those places where sun and trees created shadows during the long hot days of August and planted accordingly. A frost pocket got a different planting. A west-facing rocky outcrop that baked during the summer got something else.

I commenced a garden worthy of winter by acquiring two *Callicarpa* shrubs. Another choice was a *Vibernum tinus*, a shrub possessing the tripartite virtues of shiny evergreen leaves of great merit, shiny metallic blue berries of even greater merit, and clusters of exceedingly fragrant white flowers produced profusely very late in winter. Continuing my love for blue flowers, I now bought several evergreen ceanothus, xeriscaping species capable of thriving on no water at all through the thirsty days of late summer.

The second constraint is money. The purchase of new plants and gardening hardware obviously costs money. I discovered that a $1.98 packet of buddleia seeds proved no more difficult to germinate than radishes, and I soon had more six-inch pots filled with one-foot-tall buddleias than I could ever use myself. They proved wonderful presents for gardening friends, most of whom had never even heard of the plant. Buddleias have the added advantage of attaining up to ten feet in height *and* flowering late during their first season. They put out long racemes of sweetly fragrant flowers during August when not much else is blooming. They attract butterflies better than anything else this side of a bergamot. Certain cultivars seem to possess an ability to attract ants, which don't seem to damage the shrub. I soon planted several in places far away from the house where I could appreciate the endemic ant mounds. I like to think that the buddleias keep the ants happy, in effect communicating a contractual agreement, a coexistence ideogram analogous to my chicken-wire-fence ideogram. Likewise, the buddleias teach me the difficult lesson of how to coexist with ants. The source of all this robust growth, fragrance, color, butterfly feast, and ant retreat starts life as a seed no larger than a particle of dust.

The third constraint is environment. Whatever I choose to plant, I could not permit myself to further strain the limited natural resources, especially a limited water supply. Gardening thus becomes a matter of what we manifest when we have the time, the money, and the natural resources. From then on, the three constraints dictated my own growing style every bit as much as my love for blue flowers.

Another year passed. Ornamental fruit trees were the next season's great discovery. Because ornamentals feed the eye and not the stomach, the nonutilitarian "idea" of them seemed disdainful of my deeply ingrained obeisance to the great American work ethic. In the process of discovering them, I also recognized that apple pie is the yardstick by which we measure traditional American values because apple trees themselves are such halcyon producers. But one day, mostly because of a ridiculously low price, I responded to a local nursery offering *Prunus* (Japanese cherries) and *Malus* (crab apple) species. They now flourish along the rim of my pond like a line of prima ballerinas whose outstanding virtues include striking red bud color followed by profuse pink flower production, interesting bark texture, and an unusual reddish green leaf color in summer and fall. The waxy yellow crab apples that hang from the bare limbs of the Brandywine crab apple have long since become one of the highlights of my winter garden. Crab apples also meet the demands of the third constraint. They never need extra watering no matter how hot and dry the summer gets.

Inexpensive ornamentals hint at a hidden bonus of the second constraint, finances. Because shrubs and trees cost so much, what better reason to study up on all those mysterious crafts utilized by the nursery trade? In fact, learning how to propagate all manner of plants through layering and grafting need not be any more difficult to master than learning to tile a bathroom or setting up a computer database.

Two years ago I received the wonderful gift of a beautiful and relatively expensive mock orange cultivar. I immediately scraped a bit of bark off the soil side of six branch nodules and dropped those branches (still attached to the mother plant) under the dirt with a rock on top to keep them down. Twelve weeks later I had rooted six additional mock oranges. I cut the branches just above the roots and a year later had succeeded at naturalizing mock oranges all over this land. No doubt due to the origination of its wild ancestor in central Oregon, all those naturalized plants now seem much happier in their untended, unamended dirt than the original did in its rich bed of topsoil with weekly watering. Like buddleias, mock oranges are now among the most appreciated gifts I give to others.

Or another easy gift: start lilacs by planting the seed heads gathered from an existing plant. Like buddleias, lilac seeds are no more difficult to germinate than radishes. However, quite unlike radishes, the plants may take seven or eight years to grow large enough to reach flowering size. Then again, any such intimation of the tortoise timetable always proves to be an important gift on its own behalf. The slow passage of time counted from the yearly growth of shrubs and trees pays homage to the fact that the giver knows the recipient is home.

I cannot leave this quirky education of my own garden without mentioning the conifers, the cone bearers, a class of tree that has taken me nearly eight years to learn "how to" admire. The reason for that insensitivity relates directly to place. My own knoll is surrounded by a thick second-growth forest composed predominantly of conifers. Planting conifers directly into the knoll's terraced beds seemed too much like carrying coals to Newcastle.

The change in my attitude came in a flash. I was at a nursery, being shown the location of a shrub, when the proprietor stopped to admire the beauty of a Boulevard cypress just then in the process of opening new needles. This is a slow-growing, columnar-shaped conifer of the *Chamaecyparis* genus that may eventually grow to fifteen feet high and six feet wide. Its bark is a deep red-brown, which provides a striking contrast to the thick, silvery blue needles that seem to corkscrew like a Shirley Temple hairdo. "I've never appreciated conifers," I remarked to the salesman. He looked me over as if I had just announced that I've never appreciated love or beauty, and commented, "I look at conifers as the fur and feather bearers of the plant world. Very sensual stuff."

A customer soon pulled the salesman away, leaving me to wander the aisles on my own. I ended up in the conifer section. Rubbing my palm against the soft bristles of an arborvitae, the feathery plumage of an incense cedar, the hedgehog prickliness of a blue spruce, and the downy softness of an Austrian pine, I was suddenly transformed into a true believer.

I purchased two tiny Boulevard cypresses, two Ellwood cypresses, two blue-green Irish junipers, a yellow-ochre-colored Rheingold arborvitae, a spidery-branched golden conifer known as a *thujopsis*, and the fateful sequoia that soon got planted into a one-tree garden. In terms of form, the first three species will eventually grow into the skyscrapers of the garden, opaque variations on a columnar theme. The next two are more rounded and squat and seem lit up from inside when spied from a distance. The sequoia is, of course, an ambassador to future generations.

As both my garden and I enter middle age, the established beds seem ever more capable of taking care of themselves. I have tried many different gardening fashions, committed several monumental planting blunders, and found myself obsessed with many more categories of plants and landscape devices than either this limited history or the soil is able to nurture. I now find myself looking away from the actual plants and toward the landscape as a unity, although I am also convinced that this projected sense of unity is as much a matter of self-deception—smoke and mirrors—as it is the result of sophisticated planting technique. For example, every place my bedrock knoll drops off toward forest or pond offers a natural cascade of rock outcroppings, moss, lichens, sedum, and wildflowers. A rock gardener in the Japanese style might spend an entire lifetime trying to emulate what those cliffs gather to themselves naturally. But whereas I once considered the cliffs to be "wild," meaning outside my gardening domain, a very slight shift in perception now lets me regard them as exemplars of the well-integrated garden. Yet I have planted nothing on those cliffs besides a few scattered hen-and-chickens. Any more tampering would simply cause one or another of the three constraints (time, money, or resources) to rear its ugly head.

This sensibility for wild areas is an example of the Findhorn notion of always leaving one area in a garden as a natural sanctuary.* Consider it safe ground, sacred ground, and an homage to the biota that preceded the garden. Garden ecologist Forest Shomer asserts that the sanctuary "represents the mystery or unconscious from which non-mental possibilities can emerge and is the resting place of the nature spirits and elementals who don't often take up residence in the control areas of the garden."[4]

This perception of a wild area harmonizing with the cultivated garden now seems the only direction to move toward. It also implies its opposite—that the cultivated garden is capable of being perceived as an integrated extension of the wild environment. In such a manner, the garden offers a heightened perception of nature in microcosm.

•

*Findhorn is the name of both a garden and a community in Scotland famous for growing giant vegetables in sand. Their ideas about organic gardens, and of nature spirits, have deeply affected my own gardening perceptions.

June

The old roses—mostly hybrids developed before the twentieth century—bridge the gap between the wild species roses and the semi-real teas that will hardly grow at all unless grafted onto the rootstock of a wild progenitor. I love the names of the old roses: Nuits de Young, Madame Legras de St. Germaine, Cuisse de Nymphe, Chapeau de Napoleon. These are the alba roses, the gallicas, the bourbons, damasks, noisettes. Now they're making a comeback, and I say hooray. The colors—especially the magentas—are unsurpassed by anything modern. And each flower changes color every day it is open. The flat, quartered shape is so different from the high-centered tea roses of our day.

Their fragrance overwhelms. It offers up a theme as mysterious as plant sentience, as mutable as the weather that alters it. Smelling the rose is as intense an act as wine tasting at an estate on the Rhone; as a five-year-old's birthday party at Baskin-Robbins. I journey outside into a warm, overcast June afternoon and plunge my nose into the old pink-and-cream alba Felicite Parmentier and get inhaled, myself, into deepest rose space.

But how do I describe the smell of old roses—for instance, that wonderful Portland damask Rose de Resht? Or what about that incomparably fragrant alba called the Queen of Denmark? My first inclination is to dredge up fifty-cent adjectives: *magnanimous, rhapsodic, exultant, redolently paradisal.* But these words tell nothing of the experience. They sound suspiciously intellectual and downright pompous while the roses tell neither.

The English language is undeniably rich in describing the visual and the acoustic but fails miserably at describing fragrance. It has been said, for instance, that the scent of the gallica Belle de Crecy whispers of Bach's overture number three. The one called "Air." But what does that tell someone who prefers reggae music? It is the same problem encountered by an English translator of religious scriptures. Sanskrit, for example, is a language rich in mystical nuances, whereas English is not. This failure causes translators of Hindu scriptures to invent silly hyphenated nouns like *such-ness* to explain concepts as plain to any Hindu as eating, sleeping, or laughing. But what is this *such-ness*? Is it just right? Is it something loaded down with a lot of such? No, not precisely.

Perhaps it shares that same sense of immediacy I feel while inhaling the fragrance from the Queen of Denmark. It has been written that the Roman emperor Elagabalus used to throw banquets in which showers of rose petals drifted down on the heads of his guests. The custom was stopped when, on one occasion, so many petals rained down that several dinner guests suffocated. The Queen of Denmark does all of that—and yet this time we live to smell another!

The fragrance of the gallica Charles de Mills holds enough pungent surprises that it occasionally causes me to break out in such happy laughter that I would not trade the plant for any other rose. Some time after this exuberant emotion of mine first surfaced, I read of a centifolia rose introduced in 1810 and called Le Rire Niais. Commenting on this rose, the distinguished rosarian Graham Stuart Thomas wrote, "Why a rose should raise 'a foolish laugh' is beyond my understanding."[1] It is beyond my understanding as well. I chuckle no less.

T. S. Eliot, in *The Wasteland*, translates the Sanskrit word *shantih* as "the peace which passeth understanding." The concept of *shantih* could serve double time describing the intangible mood set by the aroma of any of several old garden roses. The word *passeth* lends something pertinent, even rococo, to the ambience. I dip my face into the very ancient alba rose Celestial and am transported into a Fragonard painting where coy, overdressed lovers dally amid foolish laughter along a garden path strewn with petals while accompanied by a full retinue of cherubs, nymphs, and angels spying on them through an arbor sumptuously draped with this old pillar rose in full bloom.

Then again, *shantih* and Fragonard both lack something essential—perhaps a slight dash of earth, muck, a heaping mound of composted manure "beyond understanding." But Peter Beales, author of the authoritative *Classic Roses*, disagrees with my coarse assessment, preferring to describe the perfume of Celestial as "expensive."[2] Expensive? Does that mean costly? And how does costly differ from the Bach?

Here is where we get carried away by the trap of language, in this case the idea that the fragrance of a rose alludes to high finance or good breeding. I know several teenagers who would understand the fragrance of Celestial far better if we simply declared that it smells *awesome*. Wow! Caramba!! Mama mia, pizzeria!!!

I stop just short of concluding that the rose experts themselves fail most miserably at describing rose fragrance. For instance, that same Queen of Denmark is a very old alba rose, first bred back in the early years of the nineteenth century. The experts assure us that she smells distinctively alba through and through. Nothing else will do to explain her deep secrets. There is, however, some controversy over this authoritative verdict because a few other professional rosarians describe her fragrant charms as "that distinct old rose smell." Caramba!

Rosarian Jon Singer explains the problem of rose fragrance by referring to chemistry. There are thirty-three different named components (and many others still unnamed) making up the concentrated essence of a rose, also known as attar. Imagine if there were thirty-three primary colors instead of just yellow, blue, and red. Add to this the fact that our sense of smell is quite puny compared to our sense of color. Singer adds that "combinations of even a few fragrant materials can be amazingly complicated; with a palette of more than thirty fragrances, the result is difficult to describe in comprehensible terms."[3] That may explain why the moss rose Alfred de Dalmas usually smells like myrrh but once in a while smells like french fries.

If there are, hypothetically, a thousand varieties of rose, who can hope to distinguish between a thousand distinct fragrances? That is why I find no fault when I read in so many rose books that the hybrid perpetual Frau Karl Druschki possesses no fragrance whatsoever. Although the Frau does not have what anyone would refer to as a perfume—either aristocratic or sensual—she does exude a subtle fragrance that leaves one musing about freshness. Let me describe it in comparative terms—not unlike the smell of fresh-mown hay on a windy afternoon in June.

Most of our adjectives for fragrance are comparative: this or that smells like apricots, like honeysuckle, sweetpea-like, orangy. The hybrid musk Cornelia smells like musk. The rambler Dr. van Fleet smells distinctly of apples. And how many times must we read that the perfume of the bourbon Mme. Isaac Pereire is like raspberries? An entire class of roses, the teas, are named for a smell they are said to give off but don't. Which tea is it? Oolong? Orange pekoe? And how ironic that so many of the modern teas have had that luscious quasi-tea scent bred right out of them.

Beyond the rose bed, we say that buddleias smell like lilacs, and most people know what we mean. But no one can say what lilacs smell like. Certain bearded irises smell just like Pez candy. A carnation is said to be spicy but not precisely sharp (I love that idea of a smell being "sharp"). I find that a carnation smells less like allspice or cloves; it is rather sumptuous and soft, something like cinnamon with a pronounced edge of nutmeg. Not much like a gingerbread cookie. More like pumpkin pie made with honey instead of sugar.

And what of the aforementioned Queen of Denmark? She is no musk. No Pez. No raspberry. No pumpkin pie. In the absence of a true language of fragrance, I cannot allude to any other universally known smell and hope to render that scent comprehensible. Neither is her fragrance rhapsodic, munificent, redolent, celestial . . . expensive. All of it is nonsense.

As the Tao boldly suggests, the way that can be spoken is not the way. Or couched in a more accessible context: language sucks immediacy from experience. Philosopher Terence McKenna tells us that a true union with nature is seamless, "unmediated by language, by notions of self and other."[4] On that note, let it be enough to conclude that human beings love to smell the pretty roses. And June is the best time to do so.

The Semi-Real Garden

Someone in my family added plastic water plants to the goldfish bowl. The Mr. Natural who resides in the right side of my brain didn't like the look of it at all, and so I soon requested that whoever did it, please, undo it. My younger daughter, three years old at the time, looked me over as if my sense of aesthetics was the result of some rare Martian disease. She proceeded to climb up on my lap to assure me that a plastic plant is absolutely no different from any of the other plants growing in our garden. "That plant is made out of God, you know," she explained in her most sobering voice while accenting the phrase "you know." "Every plant is made out of God, you know. They're all real plants, you know."

She illuminated this metaphysical thesis by pointing out the window at a gargantuan pink Sarah Bernhardt peony bush growing across the front yard, which was just then starting to unfold its twenty or more massive flower heads. I couldn't help snickering at her choice, which caused her to scrutinize me as if I might be on the verge of offering up a counterargument. Actually, I felt nothing but praise for her choice of Sarah Bernhardt as the corporeal cousin to a plastic water hyacinth. But whereas she insists that both are equally real, I insist—with a bit of irony added for good measure—that they are instead equally semi-real.

Sarah Bernhardt has been so overhybridized that she could never reproduce without the active interference of horticulturalists following abstruse genetic formulas. Ultimately, it means that our five-foot-tall and -wide peony plant doesn't exist anywhere else in nature besides the fawned-over gardens of human beings whose eyes happen to be bigger than their love for what might best be called unadulterated flowers. And though the plant is quite cold hardy, double peonies would far prefer to spend their flowering days in a carefully modulated greenhouse to avoid turning all those shaggy heads to mush at the first sign of a real rain. Moreover, the stems of this so-called real plant won't even support the blooms without some Erector Set arrangement of artificial scaffolding that would shame the great cathedral builders of medieval Europe.

A garden bed full of double peonies offers a flowery parallel to a religious cult held together by a charismatic leader. The cult survives and flourishes through a coercive regimen of propaganda fed by its leader and meant to inflate the purpose of the group by serving up happy, enlightened, and purposeful images. The peony bed survives and flourishes through a constant admixture of luxurious chemical amendments fed by its controlling gardener and meant to inflate the physical size of the flowers. A closer inspection of the cult shows it cannot survive apart from its leader. The members would soon defect without the propaganda. Likewise, hybrid peonies have no existence apart from human gardeners.

Sarah Bernhardt seems always on the verge of defecting. She would assuredly disappear from the face of the Earth as quickly as any false Utopia were she not sustained by the constant intervention of humans who covet flowers found nowhere in nature. My own peony survives—no, she prospers—only as a human desire transformed into a living object. She is a mythical heroine growing inside a semi-real garden, a living creature propagated as much by style and culture as by gene. As geneticist Richard Goldschmidt refers to all such radical mutants, the Sarah Bernhardt peony is "a hopeful monster."[5]

In his *Species Plantarum,* published in 1753, the Swedish botanist Karl Linnaeus crystallized a hierarchal method for naming and classifying biological specimens in terms of their similarity of form or morphology. He called his system *taxonomy;* it includes the kingdoms, phyla, families, genera, species, et cetera, that we all use today. But Linnaeus may have gotten it only half right when he based his system on similarities of morphology. A species' hold on its own existence—the way it is anchored to the natural world—seems as cogent to its classification as the form it takes.

Even as the heirs of Linnaeus assure us that Sarah Bernhardt is more similar to a wild peony than to a wild dahlia, I insist she is as similar to a hybrid dinnerplate dahlia as to a wild peony. Although botanists will eschew my taxonomy as a layman's shenanigan, in fact I believe it can coexist peacefully beside Linnaeus's own. This is no either/or proposition. Linnaeus's morphological taxonomy (and its modern anchoring in genetics) relates to my own proposed existential taxonomy as any horizontal system relates to its vertical analogue: for example, the way hue relates to tint, or the way an all-purpose computer spreadsheet is modified to serve only accountants, only doctors, only lawyers.

If I were the keeper of plant classifications, I would place Sarah Bernhardt in the same semi-real family as all the other Holy Grails of the hybridist's art: the yellow geraniums, the white marigolds, the Day-Glo pansies, the petunias that emulate Persian rugs, incurved florist's chrysanthemums, glitter-flecked tea roses. This is essentially a metaphysical taxonomy, meaning that all the semi-real plants are classified about midway between the plastic water plants and pink plastic flamingos on the far right side of the scale, with all the wildflowers, forest trees, rocks, and mountains crowding the far left. Within this metaphysical taxonomy, a hybrid peony would be found to share as many essential traits with a Jolly Joker purple-and-orange pansy as it currently shares with any of the species *Paeonias*, such as the excellent yet exceedingly unpronounceable *Paeonia mlokosewitschii*.

The aforementioned dinnerplate dahlia offers another example of a semi-real plant. Most members of this eminent family are among the premier flowers of late summer. They don't need much water, and with a generous heaping of compost, the plant can attain the size of a nose tackle in just one summer. But those gardeners who develop an eye and a heart for dahlias will eventually prefer their flowers single or semidouble and not more than four inches wide because the translucent yellow center may be the most distinguished part of the flower. A double-flowering dahlia inevitably conceals this sublime center. But more is at stake here than the aesthetic preferences of a few sophisticated gardeners. In the process of doubling the petals, hybridists have caused the flower to lose most of its basic ability to pollinate.

The ungainly monstrosities of the dahlia world are known as A-size, or dinner-plate, dahlias. They seem the hybridizer's equivalent of a Cadillac hearse. They are oversized and they are lavish. They accomplish through pomp and garishness their agenda of masking the gloomy ambience of extinction. Unlike a hearse, though, they advertise their own extinction. Without hybridists acting as symbiots, they would soon go the way of the ultrasaurus. Dinnerplate dahlias are semi-real. They are the Sarah Bernhardts of the dahlia world. Both plants are members of the semi-real family.

Or regard an entire category of large daylilies known as tetraploids, which possess all the modern horticultural "improvements" such as thicker petals, more saturated colors, and larger flowers. Tetraploids were first introduced through a chemical prank played on normal diploid (two-chromosome) daylily seeds. The seeds are washed in a solution of colchicine, a highly carcinogenic alkaloid. This treatment kills the majority of the seeds. Some others "recover" from this nasty bath and duly germinate into normal daylilies. The process causes fewer of the seeds to acquire an extra set of chromosomes, a trait that, as if by miracle, they pass on to their progeny.[6] Within the metaphysical taxonomy, we place these tortured yet magnificent daylilies a smidgen to the left of hybrid peonies, but only because tetraploid daylilies are, for the most part, capable of reproducing themselves.

Species or wild peonies grow in many parts of Europe and Asia. The flowers are most often some shade of opaque red, with the aforementioned translucent lemon-yellow *Paeonia mlokosewitschii* being the major notable exception. The flower's petals are arranged in a shallow bowl that looks suspiciously like a four-inch-wide buttercup. This resemblance is more than coincidental because the peony is actually a first cousin of the humble buttercup. Linnaeus tells us that both species are members of the *Ranunculus* genus. The ancient Greeks treated the peony as a medicinal herb. According to Homer, the plant was named in honor of the Greek physician Paeon.

The hybridists took over. First it was the Chinese, who over a period of a thousand years upturned and feathered the edges of the blossoms, increased the size of the stamens and the number of petals, and ended up so enthralled by their creation that they borrowed a stylized version of it as one of the major decorative motifs of their civilization. The Japanese got hold of it and focused most of their formidable horticultural talents on increasing the size and shape of the stamens that erupt from the middle of the flower. What they settled on is today referred to as the crested or Japanese-type peony, although, truth be told, much credit for this form must also be given to the Chinese.

The crested peony is justly considered to be one of the masterpieces of flower breeding, a truly wonderful creation, on a par with the alba roses, the Moonbeam coreopsis, the Niobe clematis, the Blackmore and Langdon delphiniums. It is composed of a perfect bowl of buttery-thick single petals in one color surrounding a huge hemisphere of staminodes sprouting in a different color in the center.

For years, the flowers on my only crested peony were semidouble in form, deep velvety strawberry red in color, with a bloodred mound of stamens rising like a medallion from the center. Then, two years ago, about half the flowers on the plant seemed to change course, suddenly blossoming quite single in form and with a striking *yellow* crest sitting in the middle of the bowl. One amateur plant psychologist tried to explain this herbaceous aberration to me as the result of a fancy cultivar root-grafted onto a more hardy rootstock, something on the order of grafting pear trunks onto quince roots. And I'm to blame for the peony's schizophrenia. I must have buried the graft juncture too shallowly, causing the rootstock to sprout a stem.

Another local critic assures me that Chernobyl did it.

I'm not scientific-minded enough to care very much what caused my formerly normal peony to turn schizophrenic without warning, although I certainly stand in rapt admiration of both variations on the crested theme. In my ignorance, I sometimes wonder what would happen if the plant were split in two at the roots. Would each division continue to put out two distinct flower types? Or would I then have two entirely different peonies?

In the metaphysical taxonomy, this peony with the split personality would be placed in the same genus as an equally bizarre clematis plant growing up against the south wall of my house and which blooms only on its east side each July and on its west side each September. Not even the local plant psychologist knows what to make of that one. It also fits in the same genus as a pair of hardy cyclamen once described by the English garden writer Vita Sackville-West:

They smelt delicious in the greenhouse and I carried them triumphantly indoors. All trace of scent disappeared, but that might be attributed to the change of temperature, or moisture in the air, and even a relative lack of light. Two days later, however, the whole room was fragrant, but mark this, the fragrance emanated from only one of the two pots. Next day the situation was reversed: the plant that had been scentless was now doing all that could be wished of it, and the other wasn't.[7]

As with everything else, the Americans and the Europeans—especially the French—developed many exquisite peony forms during the mid to late nineteenth century. Unfortunately, some of the hybridists soon started focusing much of their attention on the sheer breadth and weight of the blooms. And though they have added many excellent cultivars that owe a debt to either the classic Japanese or Chinese form, their most popular creations have been, by far, the ten-inch-wide explosions of pink or red or white flowers that most of us think of today when we hear the name *peony*. Sarah Bernhardt, named after the actress whose very name suggests the sensual effusiveness of late-nineteenth-century France, is considered one of their winners. In all fairness, we do well to admire Sarah's wonderful roundness. Nor can we overlook her talcum-powder fragrance.

Despite my own perhaps overstated acrimony, I actually recommend that everyone grow one double peony *because* it epitomizes all the excesses of the semireal flower world. In the spirit of her own namesake, Sarah is one of the consummate actors of the plant kingdom and, on that merit, a worthy addition to anyone's garden. Even as she infuses a garden with a surfeit of civilized yet jungly, sensual, and even sexual vitality, she remains a tease. Her fertility is a hoax, not unlike that of a champion bodybuilder incapable of bearing children.

I made my peace with this tease of a flower a long time ago. I no longer give her the extra pampering her corpulence craves. She has responded to this weaning process like a trouper. She still manages to produce the largest flowers in the garden, although nowhere near as many as before. My children love Sarah far more than I do, which is the precise reason my younger daughter passed over so many other striking blooms in the border to make her point about divine origins. The joy this little girl gets from the act of picking such mammoth blossoms can only be surpassed in her estimation by talking like a ventriloquist while pinching snapdragons, or fashioning dolls by pulling apart the bottoms of bleeding heart flowers. To my daughter, the semi-real garden is not planted to be admired. Like everything else in her world, this garden is, rather, a place of intense interaction.

I find myself staring at the buds of Sarah Bernhardt with a naughty smile on my face. Flowers are sex organs, and this one seems forever caught in a sexual double entendre. All those extra petals make it virtually impossible for bees and flies to locate the pistils and stamens, let alone pollinate the flower. Yet I may be scandalously wrong about the double peony's ability to reproduce. Within an hour of arranging one of those blushing flowers in a vase, an entire stadium's worth of earwigs falls from within the deepest pink folds of Sarah's skirts to start scampering across the dining room tablecloth.

But whether pollinated by earwigs or not, the seeds produced by this *Playboy* centerfold of a hybrid flower are incapable of producing similarly endowed hybrid progeny. The double peony has instead devised a much more roundabout if not devious reproductive strategy. These huge sex organs—for all intents and purposes, sterile—are the only reason human hybridists continue to lavish so much time propagating the plant artificially. The real business of peony reproduction is carried out by professional plant people dividing the roots to meet the demands of the horticultural marketplace. Sulfur dust is sprayed on the open wound. The roots are laid in a bed of carefully mixed potting soil and left to sprout. When all the stock is sold, the process is repeated over and over again—and for a hundred years already.

Given that context, we do best to consider double peonies and nursery stock wholesalers acting together in a kind of symbiotic sexual dance, not unlike what the clown fish does to coax food from a friendly sea anemone. In this case, which is the fish and which the anemone depends entirely on one's point of view. What is clear, however, is that the Sarah Bernhardt peony endures, while the horticulturalists turn a tidy profit. Like many other relationships, this one is built on sex and money.

The parallels that can be made with inbred sixteenth-century royalty—or perhaps with a contemporary subculture of young men who employ magazine photographs as sexual surrogates—are difficult to resist. Or why not let our imaginations really run rampant and imagine how human sexual organs might evolve if our own species one day developed its own hybridists? Who can disallow the idea that we might sprout something akin to peony flowers, bearded irises, double daffodils, Jolly Joker pansies, to advertise our procreative readiness at the spot singer Bob Seger calls "the fire down below"?

Or has this already occurred? Isn't that what a breast implant achieves? It's a body enhancement meant to advertise increased sexual desirability without also delivering increased fertility. One might wonder if this first seminal step toward hybrid sexual enhancement might one day result in a human race as prone to sterility as the dinnerplate dahlias. In my own fantasy, do I hear the whales, the pandas, and the marbled murrelets of the world letting loose with a rousing hip-hip-hooray?

Why is it that so many pages of gardening catalogs are glutted with the likes of peony-flowering tulips, peony-flowering camellias, peony-flowering dahlias, and perhaps strangest of all, peony-flowering poppies so exceedingly tight-budded that they sometimes cannot even muster the energy to push open all those extra petals? There they sit at the top of their long elegant stem, a golf ball of petals forever locked inside their own calyx; the poppy plant pushes and presses in desperation, not unlike a starving man with a can of spaghetti and no can opener.

It seems that the flower hybridists are currently immersed in the same kind of more-is-better attitude that plagued car designers during the late 1950s, with double flowers as the hybridist's equivalent of a '59 Cadillac. Referring to this trend, one of our most sensitive arbiters of garden taste, Katherine White, has written: "In many pages of the seed catalogues, all blossoming form seems to be disappearing, causing one to look fearfully ahead to the time when our garden beds will be full of great shaggy heads, alike except for color, all just great blobs of bloom."[8]

Harking back to my three-year-old daughter's inductive argument that our perception of reality takes shape from the flowers we cherish, the popular success of double flowers prompts the mind toward large and somewhat troubling thoughts. For instance, what is it about the American, Chinese, and French character that makes citizens of those countries admire (and thus hybridize) great sterile blobs over far more intricate though humble flower forms, as both the British and the Japanese seem to prefer?

In the case of the American character, is this simply the horticultural manifestation of the same preference that caused the American citizenry to elect an actor to the U.S. presidency for two terms because he was a master at avoiding the real issues that faced the country? At the time, this seemed an essential skill for any president to possess, perhaps best demonstrated by the fate of his luckless opponents who are primarily remembered today for asking the American people to face serious problems as they are. In much the same way, the Sarah Bernhardt peony thrives in her overblown mask, while far more subtle and yet fertile peonies are cultivated in few American gardens.

Does the American preference for double flowers offer some explanation as to why during the 1980s our government was so eager to drill oil wells in our disappearing wild spaces rather than embrace better energy efficiency? If this example makes even less sense than the first one, permit me to repeat a postulate evinced from the one-tree garden: that the environmental crisis is a crisis in the way we humans perceive our place within nature. Our penchant for semi-real flowers—or the fact that country fairs award their blue ribbons to the most bloated and, therefore, least tasty vegetables—could offer up the seed of a grand statement about what some might call our national ineptitude to both respect and cherish nature as she is. If it makes some small sense, it signifies that our flower preferences *do* serve as an apt barometer for measuring our sense of place.

For better or worse, call it flower power. The political clout of the phrase can be seen in the photograph of young, long-haired, anti-Vietnam protesters very carefully sticking flowers down the gun barrels of equally young soldiers during the well-attended demonstration to levitate the Pentagon way back in the late 1960s. Despite the fact that no one has ever agreed on whether the Pentagon rose or remained steady that day, the essential message of the image remains as crystal clear now as it was then. Trade guns for roses. My daughter is right after all. Flowers do reflect our view of reality.

Despite the nagging call to conform that Father Time enlists to bridle the once idealistic aspirations of its now middle-aged flower children, there remains some substance to those formerly jubilant and currently nostalgic associations once known as flower power. Citizen exchange groups gobble up airplane seats to every corner of the former Soviet bloc, with a few of the missions focused on the international sharing of nonhybrid seeds and plants. This new rendition of flower power suggests that Western economics has more to offer the Russian people than spitting out American fast-food franchises all over the former Soviet Union. The promoters of this ostensible 1990s version of flower power argue that we may all be in for a rude shock as we turn a corner on the disappearing resource environment of the twenty-first century. Sharing seeds—flowers, trees, grains, and vegetables—across national boundaries and eventually across generations is the only way to ensure genetic diversity.

Genetic diversity is, however, currently being manipulated in its own semi-real direction. We've been hearing for years about all the great things that biotechnology is on the verge of achieving, such as genetically altered plants that resist bugs better and therefore make pesticides defunct. Instead, we may soon get the exact opposite: a slew of new varieties bred specifically to resist ever-stronger chemical doses. Cotton plants are already on the market that have been genetically altered to tolerate a specific herbicide that is known to kill fish and that may cause birth defects in humans. It is also no big surprise to learn that the herbicide in question is produced by the same company that funds the genetic research. Welcome to the semi-real world.

Another much-touted biotech project is developing longer-lasting flowers with so-called novel color traits—for example, true-blue roses. Intriguingly, all attempts have failed so far, although theory indicates it can happen. Sitting alone in my sentient garden, I sometimes wonder if the roses themselves might have conspired against it. Then again, a blue rose! It has its allure, like a highbrow version of the chive-and-sour-cream-flavored potato chips upon which we all occasionally gorge. Or maybe someday we'll choose our vegetable seeds (and vegetable side dishes) by the herbicides they've been bred to thrive on. Now there's a metaphor about a society of semi-real addicts that would chill the heart of even a three-year-old.

As flowers exist wild in nature, they are often a mind-boggling paradox: delicate looking but with an iron constitution. This latter attribute is, of course, the precise reason we refer to so many wildflowers as weeds. But if, as just one example, dandelions didn't pop up uninvited anyplace and everywhere people choose to plant lawns; if they were, instead, rare alpine flowers that bloom only every fourth year on the north face of some precipitously steep mountain meadow located in Upper Baluchistan, they would probably be fawned over and hybridized as much as peonies are today. I'd wager a bet that we would quickly transform the humble and homeless dandelion from being the object of so much herbicidal vengeance into one of the premier "yellows" in the garden. Enthusiastic flower lovers would schedule their vacations to jibe with peak dandelion season, just as they now travel to such public parks as Buchart Gardens on Vancouver Island to view the Himalayan blue poppy or *Meconopsis*. Indeed, the tissue-paper, true-blue saucers of the *Meconopsis* are among the most luminous blooms in the entire flower world and certainly deserve all that recognition. Since a culture's flower preferences do seem to reflect political, technological, and environmental aims and perceptions, it is a very good sign that the delicate *Meconopsis* flower is able to accrue so much more attention than its kissing cousin, the peony-flowering poppy.

The connection that necessarily exists between flower preferences and culture is a subtle one at best. The contemporary cultural predilection for certain adulterated flowers is not some glaring societal wound demanding an immediate campaign to weed out all double flowers and F1 hybrids. We need not write letters to the editor castigating some new neighbor who recently planted a zero-tree garden of double petunias rimming a quarter-acre uninterrupted expanse of green lawn.

As the discussion on the local garden has already suggested, the politics of gardening shares little with traditional politicking, which too often abandons subtlety and neighborliness in favor of polarization and distant governance, leading to that unmistakably masculine if not bullying trait we call coerciveness. Gardening is different from that. It is yielding, sharing, nurturing, humbling. In this case, it is better to flash the community calling card known as gardening and enjoy both the petunias and neighborly enthusiasm. Anything less than cordiality must be viewed as mean-spirited and bigoted. To put it plainly, castigating a neighbor for growing huge, shaggy, multistriped double petunias is not the local equivalent of saving the rain forest.

A better strategy would be to offer a few unfamiliar flower starts to the semi-real gardeners who dwell among us. That neighbor's zero-tree garden openly reflects the hare's pace of American life, which is the prime reason he or she lavishes so much bedding space on the likes of fast-maturing, everblooming, and low-maintenance petunias sticking up like purple whorls along the frosting rim of a greener-than-green lawn. Because such plantings engender a disjointed sense of place, it suddenly takes on added community significance to promote a few unfamiliar flowering perennials—for the precise reason that these plants are neither fast-maturing, everblooming, Day-Glo, nor quite so low maintenance as petunias. Yet all of them are beautiful, which is the main reason they are so worthy of more attention.

Glorious annuals like love-lies-bleeding, lavateras, and the richly fragrant mignonettes languish as sunken treasures waiting to be discovered. As for the perennials, why are the silvery blue sea holly (*Eryngium*), the magenta-trumpeted garden gloxinia (*Incarvillea*), the delicate but stately black cohosh (*Cimicifuga*), the bergamot (*Monarda*), and the absolutely dazzling spurge (*Euphorbia characias wulfenii*) missing from the six-packs of perennials we find at the local nurseries? None of them are difficult to propagate.

Or regard the lovely pincushion architecture of the *Astrantia*. Even in the otherwise exhaustive *Sunset New Western Garden Book*[9]—a study that describes over twelve hundred plants common to gardens of the American West—the *Astrantia* is nowhere to be found. The species is much better known in England, where it is saddled by the wonderful name of masterwort. The erudite British garden writer Stephen Lacey writes about it:

> There is much affection among gardeners for this ancient plant which is so restrained in coloring but sophisticated in design. The tiny florets are arranged like a pin-cushion upon a saucer of bracts, in a pattern of pink, green, and greyish white, and the leaves are dark and finely cut. In the variety, *Margery Fish*, the flowers are larger and cleaner. In a pink setting these white astrantias are delightful, and at Sissinghurst they are massed among martagon lillies beneath the rose '*Maytime*' and the shell pink Escallonia '*Edinensis*.'[10]

Another wonderful British flower book, *Plant Portraits* by Beth Chatto, reminds us that when the dried flowers of the *Astrantia major* are inked and pressed to paper, "the florets lie out like spokes of a wheel, making a very pretty centre rather than a squashy mess."[11] Spoken as only an English gardener could.

My younger daughter and I are standing hand-in-hand at the edge of a garden bed, discussing the virtues of Sarah Bernhardt, whose blossoms seem to be opening even as we watch. Ten pink peony flowers reach up in various stages of bloom; some of them are so huge they look capable of grabbing the little girl and never letting go. For myself, where the double peony makes its home is a garden bed I admire primarily for its siting; it looms up at the end of a dirt path otherwise lined with several businesslike raised beds containing, in sequence, artichokes, potatoes, garlic, asparagus, raspberries, and onions. A sojourner simply doesn't expect it to be there after passing all the rest. And then there it is, brimming over with momentous flowers. This bed is where I have gathered all my semi-real plants.

These include several varieties of bearded irises whose architecture is splendid—three petals rising and three petals falling—and whose blossoms run to the size of two fists. However, it is neither architecture nor even size, but rather *color* that places the bearded irises among the ranks of the semi-real. The flower has explored every nook of the color spectrum, from red through blue through yellow through white, even black. Many of the blooms run to two, sometimes three colors per flower. The hybridists got carried away by the limitless possibilities and soon fashioned red-and-blue ones, brown-and-yellow ones, and even purple-and-white-and-black ones. I have even heard of a green one, although none grows in this bed. That lack is the result of a personal quirk. With the one notable exception of the green hellebore, I regard green flowers to be an abomination. Yet green flowers are no new invention of the hybridists. Paleobotanists tell us that until ten million years ago, all flowers were some shade of green."[12]

Fortunately, the perceptual perils that dog most "mixed colors" do not seem to apply very much to a bed filled with flowers of the stature of these bearded irises. The way they sway together in the breeze on their sturdy scapes makes them look like a herd of herbaceous brontosauruses rising from the composted bed. The only thing more remarkable than these irises' ability to combine so many disparate colors in one bloom—let alone one species—is the names the hybridists have given to the various cultivars. They obviously stretched the thesaurus in their ardor to favor every conceivable variation on the theme of place as paradise. There's Peaceful Waters, Fireside Glow, Broadway, Blazing Saddles, Center Court, Raven's Roost. That last is one of the purple-black ones. There are obviously no Three-Mile Islands, Suburban Malls, Clear-cuts, Ghettos, or Starving Third-World Countries found in this bunch. Nor do we find all the aristocratic French ladies so favored in the naming of old roses.

The irises usually bloom about two weeks before Sarah Bernhardt, although some years the blooms of both species can be seen nodding contentedly beside each other. After the peonies vanish, the lilies soon arrive. The semi-real variety that grows in this same bed is known as the Black Dragon strain, a particularly American adaptation of the already overblown Oriental hybrid lilies. Why it is called a strain and not a variety or a cultivar I do not know. Perhaps it simply strains the bounds of what any flower might achieve on planet Earth.

Black Dragon may be the ultimate two-toned flower. The inside of each petal is a striking white with a yellow throat, while the outside of the same petal is a pronounced maroon. The stems can reach six feet in height, and the flowers are so exceedingly stiff in texture that they might be used secondarily as a bludgeon. Whereas the peony and the bearded iris display their semi-real characteristics in terms of size and color, the Black Dragon travels a different path in eluding subtlety. The lily's fragrance is so ponderously heavy that I sometimes perceive its scent as a visual sensation, watching it waft across the yard on a languid July breeze. The smell could have served as the prototype for the perfume that accompanies my daughter's Barbie doll toilet kit. That also explains why she insists so adamantly that the Black Dragon possesses the very best fragrance in the entire garden.

After the lilies die back, the dahlias of late August finally arrive. Double peonies, bearded irises, and Black Dragon lilies if not actually beautiful are monumental and awesome. The dinnerplate dahlia is simply grotesque, flower power filtered through Marat/Sade, a hideous Godzilla lurking among all the elegant floral brontosauruses. Consider their inclusion in a garden as potentially harboring a semi-real epidemic, a kind of conceptual plague capable of inflicting the dahlia's brute sloppiness upon any plant growing nearby. Imagine next year dinnerplate double peonies four times as large as Sarah grows now, dinnerplate dandelions plundering the width and depth of America. Dinnerplate daughters.

As much as the dinnerplates are sloppy, the so-called B-size dahlias are eminently worthwhile. And the collarette dahlias must be counted among the most wonderfully designed flowers in the entire landscape. Whereas irises vent their semi-real attributes primarily through their ability to mix colors and lilies exhibit a dollhouse fragrance, any dahlia that makes it into the semi-real bed possesses a hard-edged saturation of primary colors far beyond the muster of a real flower. The reds and yellows of the dahlia world are best compared to the reds and yellows found in party balloons, beach towels, downhill skis.

Whereas iris names favor romantic locales and old roses favor French aristocrats, dahlia hybridists like to name their new varieties after just plain folks. There's Frank Holmes, Lauren Michelle, Daniel Edward, and in fact, probably half the population of Canby, Oregon, because so much of the breeding takes place there on the grounds of Swan Island Nursery.

Because dahlias are so exceedingly easy to start from seed, it is worthwhile to collect seed from the hybrids, germinate them the following spring, and then watch what kind of offspring might emerge from such garish parents. Inevitably, next year's batch of dahlias always includes far smaller flowers. Once, I succeeded in raising a few flowers possessed of a remarkable color that can only be called apricot-blue, although that description says very little about what was a translucence as much as a hue.

If this particular garden bed's focus on semi-real plants sometimes makes little sense in regard to my otherwise purist sensibility, I remember thinking at the time of planting that this hidden turn in the path would be the perfect place to group perennials that shared the essential traits of tallness, stalkiness, and heaviness. During that early period in my how-to gardening education, I was quite certain that the bigger the better. Plants possessing massive traits existed at the very top of an imagined hierarchy of herbaceous perennials. I had no idea whatsoever why anyone would even want to grow more humble flowers. Plants such as ground covers eluded me completely. An *Astrantia* didn't stand a chance.

But years after the how-to garden started offering its sage counsel, teaching me to lean toward the subtle and the natural, that semi-real bed still seems to "work." And even if it didn't, I'd probably keep it intact as comic relief, a happy reminder of just how utterly capricious are any gardener's own aesthetic sensibilities. The bed has its own lesson, constantly reminding me that my own so-called sensibility to plants "working together" has very little to do with inherent harmony. If anything, this is the very quality most noticeably lacking in the semi-real bed: whether it be the brief moment when red and blue and white and yellow and tan iris heads are strutting their stuff at odd angles amid the shell pink peonies, and especially during the many months of the year when the iris leaves look on the verge of rotting away without ever actually doing so. But I would no more consider ripping up the bed and starting over again from scratch than I would think of ripping up any other bed on the property.

But as in any garden bed, things die, causing us to add something new, which soon starts crowding out something old. In my case, over time I have added tall willowy species veronicas to counter the hardness of the July lilies. I have added equally tall and yet billowing pure white Japanese anemones to counter the hard yellow dahlias of autumn. Yet I have also remained loyal to the metaphysical taxonomy of the semi-real garden, adding thirty-inch-tall lipstick-red tulips whose individual flowers seem to approach the size of a salad bowl. Their April stature offers an unsubtle reminder about the irises and lilies that follow. Two-tone gladioli have also been added. Their flowery verticality seems to epitomize the semi-real world as well as any of the rest of them, ensuring that this bed retains its semi-real ambience even as my tastes evolve.

There's also the important matter that my two daughters absolutely adore this bed. This is where the *Flowers*, with a capital *F*, grow. Nothing prickly to avoid, nothing too leafy, nothing so tiny and delicate that a child might have to watch where she steps. The lilies smell just like a little girl's play dress-up perfume. The irises look like the kind of flower one might find in a three-year-old's used-up coloring book.

My daughter and I are standing in front of the peony. She has joined me to do the honor of picking three of the largest peony flowers for arranging in an empty vase that currently graces our dining room table. As anyone who has ever done so will quickly attest, picking a ten-inch-wide mound of pink fluffy peony is quite a different experience than picking a calendula, a columbine, a pink, a bachelor's button, or even a six-inch-wide dahlia. For a three-year-old, it's a task containing equal parts wonderment, joy, responsibility, and above all, power.

I lift her up onto one of the granite boulders that contains the bed. She leans over, grabs the nearest stalk with her left hand, and starts pulling with all her might. "Whoa, girl, hold on a minute," I chuckle. "Let's pick the flower and a bit of the stem, but not the whole plant." I guide her right hand to grip the stem just above her left hand, and help her break it cleanly. I offer to hold her flower while she picks the next one. But now she turns adamant about keeping the first flower firmly gripped in her hand. She wants me to pick the other two. I do as she wishes. She studies my own stem-breaking technique and nods her head when the deed is done. Now she insists upon carrying *her own* flower, while I lug the other two hopeful monsters back to the house.

Into the vase they plunge, the center of the table suddenly transformed into a pink mushroom cloud. My daughter looks the arrangement over a moment and then sprints upstairs to her bedroom to return a moment later with a silver Mylar helium balloon clutched in her hand. She tells me to tie the balloon string right around the lip of the vase. For a moment my sense of decorum seems so violated that I want to heave both the vase and the flowers right through the sliding glass door that fronts the dining room. But she looks so sure she's made the right decision. I smile, take the string, and do as she commands. "Yes, I do see what you mean. That makes the flower arrangement complete, doesn't it?" I pick her up off the chair and lead her backward five feet to take in the total effect of this still life of black pottery vase below a cloud of peonies below a silver Mylar balloon.

Once again I am forced to acknowledge that aesthetics is nothing more than articulated personal opinions about how some person feels about beauty and feelings. With that sentiment in tow, I should call up the famous Buchart Gardens, which lies across the strait from our home, and suggest to them that the only reason I don't visit their acres and acres more often than I do is that my kids simply don't last very long gazing at the likes of blue Himalayan poppies, although my wife and I would just as soon stare at them all day long.

Kids want bronze mushrooms, wooden airplanes perched on the top of high poles with propellers that spin in the wind, life-size three-inch-tall gnomes perched in the nooks of rare trees and holding up plant ID tags, plastic geese leading cute squadrons of plastic goslings through the semi-real hybrid tea rose gardens, and especially those colored spherical mirrors that sit on concrete Greek columns and distort the landscape so effectively when you peer into them. A few more spherical mirrors placed here and there, and I can guarantee they'd distort the perception of their garden enough to double their family business.

The composer John Cage once wrote that aesthetics is "anything you can get away with." If so, then how about a hand-carved Little Mermaid languishing on a rock in a reflecting pool with Sebastian the crab sitting on her knee? Place tiny speakers in their mouths so the two of them can sing the theme song from the cartoon four times every hour. I might even suggest they hire my daughter as their artistic consultant. She may not always know what's real, but she certainly knows what she likes.

July

Northwesterners have developed relationships with many different species of local animals. We treat the orca pods as wildlife celebrities; we invent the spotted owl as our symbol of wilderness; we expend vast amounts of money, time, and self-respect trying to get close enough to entice a weighty salmon out of the water. But anyone who digs in the earth in this northwestern corner of the contiguous United States probably ends up relating to slugs more often and more directly than to any other wild animal. Although few of us wish to admit it, slugs are our primary window into the heart of wildness.

Some admit it. Washington State extension agent George Pinyuh, for example, writes that this lowly mollusk should be named the Washington state animal. But what does that mean in practice? Should the gardeners of this fair state stop killing slugs because of some proclamation written by a bunch of political types whose primary aim is winning votes and not healthy lettuce? In fact, slugs seem a far more grounded choice for state animal than, for instance, dreamy-eyed Connecticut choosing the faraway sperm whale for its state totem. What percentage of the people in Connecticut have ever seen a sperm whale? That choice says a lot about Connecticut's global environmental idealism and very little about its regard for the many living creatures who actually co-inhabit that same plot of local real estate.

Then again, what do we Washingtonians have to revere about the slug besides a shared locality? Pinyuh asks us to praise slugs because they serve an important purpose in our lives by providing *an endless source of conversation*. He concludes that if they didn't exist, we'd have to invent them. If that's the best that he can come up with, I say the Connecticut sperm whale makes a lot more sense.

Every gardener acknowledges the place of slugs in his or her gardening experience. But *praise* them? I start out writing to praise slugs and quickly find myself breaking free from my ecological moorings, my words overcome by that dominant image of slime. Slime evokes the monster from the movie *Alien*. It evokes a pathological undertone of sickness and death. Despite the fact that the slugs in our gardens enjoy good health, their presence means that the plants are on the verge of sickness and dying. It doesn't seem to matter that slugs prosper where the soil is alive and healthy. When the slug population is healthy, the garden *feels* sick.

At a Fourth of July picnic full of egg tosses and pie-eating contests, I conduct a little research on the conversational value of this nominated state animal. Sitting on the green grass with some friends enjoying the sun, I casually uncork the subject of what plants slugs like best. The resultant discussion turns into a never-ending tale about local knowledge. One neighbor insists on pansies, although under interrogation she finally admits that she's got an awful lot of pansies. Another neighbor tells us about the time he spotted a banana slug five feet up a magnolia tree munching contentedly on the flower heads. I mention the June morning I chanced upon a slug three feet up the feathery foliage of an asparagus plant, rocking back and forth like a sailor relaxing in a hammock composed of its own slime. The list starts growing. Bearded irises, dahlias, tarragon, any seedling. Lettuce, cabbage, broccoli. The list grows faster than a dahlia in July.

Then there are marigolds. Everyone is smiling now. Yes, that's it. Slugs will go out of their way to get at marigolds. Someone suggests we might all plant a special marigold bed for slugs, something like hanging sacrificial zincs on the underside of a boat to keep the metal fittings from corroding. The slugs would congregate at their red-and-green marigold coffeehouse, leaving the rest of the garden to us. Unfortunately, it doesn't work that way. Slugs reproduce to keep up with a growing food supply. The marigold bed isn't a sacrificial zinc. It's a maternity ward.

One of my neighbors keeps slugs in check by pouring beer in mayonnaise jar lids, which she then places at strategic locations. The little round pools become a slug's variation on the old blues lyric: "If the river was whiskey and I was a diving duck, I'd dive to the bottom and never come up." My neighbor recommends we employ this method very early in the spring. The overwintering slugs drown before reproducing, which keeps the rest of them in check for an entire summer. She recommends a beer brand called Meisterbrau because it's not only inexpensive but also very yeasty. She believes the manufacturers of Meisterbrau must not know what a gold mine they've got. If she owned the brewery, she'd relabel a fair percentage of the suds as organic slug bait and distribute it in gardening centers at twice the price.

Another neighbor ventures out with a flashlight after dark and picks the slugs off plants one by one. That seems to work just dandy for the two local species of large slugs. But what about the little ones, like the pernicious gray garden slug that grows no larger than a grain of rice? By day, it hides deep in the soil and comes out only after dark to mow down every seedling in sight. Carrots are simply impossible to grow when these critters are around. Gray slugs also feast on germinating bean seeds, causing savvy locals to start beans in four-inch pots, which are transplanted into the garden bed only after attaining four inches in height.

But what about slug virtues? Everyone chuckles, looks at their hands, and then laughs a second time. I spout a few homilies about the essential place any wild animal holds within the environment. We all recognize that slugs clean up waste, that they dine on withered tulip stems and grass clippings. Some species even feed on aphids and tent caterpillars. In turn, slugs provide food for snakes, ducks, and frogs. Is it any wonder so many locals feel elation upon spotting a garter snake snooping around the lettuce patch?

But by July the banana slugs are attaining lengths in excess of five inches. Respecting the ecology of place seems to do little to attenuate the frustration of a gardener who's watched an entire second planting of lettuce mowed down overnight. And crowing about slugs among gardeners makes me feel like I'm waving to the crowd of some small logging community from atop the spotted owl float in the Fourth of July parade.

I mention that there are many flower species that slugs go out of their way to avoid. Peonies. No, none of us has ever seen a slug rasping on a peony.

Columbines, daffodils, lilies, bleeding hearts, Jacob's ladder, mums, artemisia, sage, mint, platycodon. Everyone now acknowledges that it would be easy to grow a bountiful flower garden without ever needing to contend with slugs. My pansy-loving neighbor finally admits she would be willing to switch to something else to avoid dealing with slugs.

But no matter which flowers she settles on, vegetables are something else again. Experiments have proven that green is the slug's favorite color. I believe there is no green vegetable that humans eat outside the onion family that a slug won't also eat. Worse still, beer doesn't attract the gray slugs at all. I *have* discovered, however, that gray slugs prefer richly composted soil, and I am often guilty of adding compost to my beds too close to planting time. This year I spread a very hot mix of fresh chicken manure and dry sawdust to the beds very early in March. It worked. The gray slug population was gone by the time I planted my first seedlings three weeks later.

The same George Pinyuh, champion of the slug as the Washington state beast, counsels us to intersperse our crops with quack grass. Yank out the quack grass before it spreads and then let it rot right in the garden bed. Studies have shown that when this persistent weed is killed, it releases a chemical compound into the soil that is fatal to slugs. Unfortunately, this weed is so pervasive and deep-rooted that I wonder if any of its proponents have actually tried to yank it out of the ground. We always get part of the quack grass, but next week the part we left in the soil has spread like a computer virus over the local area network of our garden bed. Planting quack grass won't do. It sounds too much like the U.S. military destroying Vietnam in order to save it.

I have a good friend whose own version of slug prevention shares something essential with people who declare with a straight face that "except for fish and chicken," they are practicing vegetarians. He kids himself that he is a bona fide organic vegetable grower, "except for commercial slug bait." I have tried the stuff myself, although only in a few segregated flower beds. Because poison is poison, I squirted the metaldehyde into those same mayonnaise-lid feeding troughs and then placed the lids at a few strategic locations.

But taking the extra precaution of keeping the poison off the ground is nearly hopeless. Any poor slug who takes the bait soon starts turning its insides outside. The path of the slug's death journey across the soil is soon varnished with a hard, sometimes bubbly, reflective supercoating of slime. Who could have predicted that a two-inch-long animal could possess so much slime? For that matter, who's willing to inform us what's really in the metaldehyde that the slug just spread quite handily across the width and breadth of my flower beds?

And what other living creatures are also at risk? One neighbor declares that the poison attracts dogs and has caused the death of at least one local pet. If so, why is it that almost no commercial pesticides provide a simple label informing its users precisely how long it takes for the poison to break down? Isn't that the most important piece of information? And is this really a sane measure of our disdain for slugs?

I do not know the answer to that, although I do know there are very few gardeners who don't despise the lowly slug. George Pinyuh says we need them for garden conversation. I could live very contentedly without hearing even one more slug joke, not to mention the cutesy slug recipe books found in tourist shops around the Pacific Northwest. I turn the other cheek when one of my neighbors starts telling the so-called hilarious story about the time his dog wolfed down a slug the size of a mortadella grazing his Alpo. He makes it sound as if the sight of it was the most wonderful thing he'd ever experienced.

The Remedy Garden

Many herbs' active ingredients—the chemical substances that define certain plants as herbal remedies in the first place—often play no identifiable role in the actual metabolism of those plants. Yet the sheer abundance of these so-called secondary ingredients makes it difficult to explain their production as a mere coincidence of nature. Some herbalists believe there is only one good explanation for it. Certain plants developed these secondary ingredients to heal the animals who make use of them. As this relationship relates to human beings, the advantage to the plant species is not unlike the symbiotic one enjoyed by the semi-real flowers. Historically, the herbs that healed human beings got themselves cultivated. As long as they kept healing, their evolutionary success was ensured.

As fantastic as this sentient relationship may appear to people who subscribe to a rationalist view of nature, traditional cultures the world over endorse it as a basic lesson in how healing occurs. Traditional healers also maintain that a person's awareness of the herbs he or she uses directly affects the curative capabilities of those herbs. But this link cannot be interpreted as merely psychosomatic. In most premodern cultures, the process of healing is perceived as a vital attunement between healer, patient, herb, and disease. Moreover, herbs work to strengthen the whole system of the body and not just to overcome the symptoms of a disease.

People who rely on locally grown herbs merge their own health with the ecology of home. They grow their own medicine at the place they live. In that manner, herbal healing balances inner ecology with outer ecology. Not coincidentally, the attunement of inner ecology with outer ecology is a key factor in establishing a sense of place.

Modern herbalist David Hoffmann takes the link between health and place a step further. In the same way that an aspirin can be understood as a capsule of chemical components, traditional herbs can be understood as a capsule of planetary life force, what the Hindus call *prana*, what the Chinese refer to as *chi*. In what many would call a clear leap of faith, Hoffmann thus concludes that herbs establish a direct link between a person and the biosphere in the cause of facilitating our own homeostasis.[1] In that sense, herbs provide a bridge that links person to Gaia.

To better understand Hoffmann's assertion, an explanation of the term *Gaia* seems in order. In fact, Gaia relates not only to an understanding of the remedy garden but to all the chapters that follow.

The luminosity of the sun has increased 30 percent over the past billion years. Because heat and light affect chemical processes, one would assume that the percentages of the various gases that constitute the Earth's atmosphere should have also fluctuated by about 30 percent over that same period. Oddly, the percentages of the most common gases have remained remarkably stable—too stable, in fact, for the equilibrium to be a mere coincidence. For instance, oxygen is an extremely volatile substance. Yet it has long accounted for 21 percent of the atmosphere's composition. If there were a bit more oxygen, the organic matter on the planet would have burned up long ago. If there were less, oxygen-breathing organisms could not exist on planet Earth.

British chemist James Lovelock and American biologist Lynn Margulis have proposed the Gaia Hypothesis to account for this atmospheric stability amid so many other changing conditions. The Gaia Hypothesis proposes that the biosphere—the "skin" of the planet composed of all the life in the air, on the surface, and under the soil—actively manipulates the composition of the atmosphere.

Although we usually think of "life" as disparate, disorganized, and noncommunicative, Gaia declares the opposite, that the biosphere is (in Lovelock's own terms) a "self-regulating organism"[2] that controls the chemical composition of the atmosphere for the express purpose of ensuring that life itself remains viable. The biosphere breathes through the cumulative respiration of all the individual life-forms that exist on Earth.

For us to "know" Gaia as a scientific reevaluation of atmospheric chemistry is one thing. Grasping the existential implications of Gaia—for us to "know" all life on Earth (including ourselves) as a functional entity, a self-regulating organism—is quite another.

Perhaps ironically, the concept of the Earth *not* being alive is a fairly new idea that did not gain popular acceptance until the European Enlightenment of the seventeenth and eighteenth centuries. In *The Death of Nature*, ecologist Carolyn Merchant explains that before that time, nearly all human culture believed the Earth was alive. Most cultures were more specific, maintaining that the Earth was a living *female* being, the mother of life. It is our own culture that stands alone by recasting nature as a kind of machine.

It is essential to recognize that none of this is metaphor. In fact, accepting the hypothesis as physical reality demands that we overhaul some of our deepest-held perceptions about the Earth as well as about the human place within the larger community of life. Human beings are, after all, as much a part of Gaia as anything else. Knowledge of our own active participation offers each one of us a philosophical sea change in how we regard our presence here on Earth. Some environmentalists assume, perhaps naively, that an intellectual grasp of Gaia will, on its own, transform the human disposition toward the Earth. Unfortunately, as powerful as the concept is, it is still an abstraction to most of us. It is like going to church to find God but only hearing a sermon about why we *should* believe in God.

But Gaia is perceptual—a feeling and an experience of the Earth—and not just another provocative idea to be added to the growing total of all the abstract ideas we devour on a daily basis. We can grasp the idea of it through an act of intellect, but we can only perceive Gaia by attuning to nature. We need something besides information about Gaia to know Gaia. Therein lies the value of David Hoffmann's assertion that herbal healing balances inner ecology with outer ecology. Balancing inner ecology with outer ecology is a hallmark of Gaia. If Hoffmann is correct, herbal healing as practiced in the remedy garden can provide us with a direct perception of Gaia.

The sentient garden also stirred a seminal perception of Gaia even as it contradicted scientific and cultural orthodoxy. But our perception of the sentient garden is mostly private, and we can enjoy its gifts relatively free from public challenge. The implications of the remedy garden are not only provocative but politically controversial as well. While the subject of herbal remedies makes some people want to be attuned to Gaia, it makes others wish to burn this garden to the ground. It therefore serves us to step lightly down this path, pass through the garden gate slowly, and keep our expectations to a minimum. Once we step inside and examine the powerful plants that grow there, we may find no easy route back to the old medical worldview. Learning to trust the remedy garden means that a trip to the doctor may never be the same again.

The path to the remedy garden first passes through the herb garden. Just about everyone plants a few herbs at some point in their lives. There are people living in tiny studio apartments in Manhattan, miles and miles above and beyond the nearest patch of dirt, who still manage to grow parsley, chives, and cilantro on a sunny windowsill. That sprouting greenery may be the only direct connection to gardening, not to mention dirt, that these city dwellers ever get to enjoy—pocket paradise planted on a bolted-shut windowsill on the ninety-ninth floor. Then again, what's a burrito without fresh cilantro?

Beyond the city gates, and wherever green thumbs flex themselves, herb gardens are often designed differently than either vegetable gardens or flower gardens. For instance, a vegetable garden works best as a straightforward plant factory: rectangular beds carefully subdivided into long straight rows, each row fastidiously tended to maximize food production and minimize labor.

A flower garden is also different, usually tipped more toward the aesthetic harmony of the planting as a whole and less toward any aspiration for efficiency. Flower beds seem to work best when they avoid straight lines and angles. Unless one is growing flowers as a crop for market, or unless our eccentric garden statement has us marching along the beds inspecting the troops, flowers do not seem to evoke as much when set in straight geometric patterns.

We do best to leave straight rows and massive geometric plantings of flowers to eighteenth-century French manors and/or civic displays. For example, the U.S.-Canadian border crossing just south of Vancouver, B.C., favors beddings of red begonias, white petunias, and blue ageratums laid out to represent monumental U.S. and Canadian flags. Patriotism marries geometry while the bedding plants seem mostly to serve as bridesmaids. The customs agencies seem caught making a vain statement about the nonarbitrariness of national boundaries: *borrowing* flowers in an attempt to grant some small part of every government's futile wish that the vegetation and physical features of this fair planet really do follow the straight lines cartographers draw on maps. Such linear/presentational gardens seem to work best viewed from the balcony of an eighteenth-century manse. Or through the windshield of an automobile caught in traffic.

The English cottage garden style eschews straight lines. It utilizes vast groupings of flowers (and few semi-real flowers) projecting upward and drooping downward and especially reaching outward as if the plants were in the final stages of erasing any sign of human intentionality. Landscape architects have even been known to contrive a number of curves in a formerly straight garden path just to keep the mood intimate, the goal mysterious, the perambulation tempo slow, the long view nonexistent, and the short view ever-changing. This laissez-faire, disheveled look is, as one might expect, one of the most difficult design concepts to attain. A successful cottage garden necessitates prodigious plant knowledge, quasi-militaristic discipline, and backbreaking labor—all of it employed in the paradoxical service of invoking the studied abandonment we might encounter in an idealized woodland meadow. The less the hand of the gardener is evident, the better it seems to be.

An herb garden is usually a far more casual affair than either a vegetable garden or flower garden. It may be the herbs themselves that refuse too much attention on the gardener's part. Unlike vegetables and flowers, most herbs (although certainly not all) care little whether the soil is shallow or deep, rich or poor. As a general rule of thumb, herbs also prefer it far drier than either vegetables or flowers, which in practice translates to a lot less pampering and a more environment-friendly planting. As with a flower garden, the general look of the herb garden is geared more toward the aesthetic than the practical. Many of the best herb gardens seem on the verge of a studied wildness that would be the envy of any English cottage gardener. However, this state of affairs often has less to do with the careful hand of a gardener and more to do with the fact that so many herb species tend to express their vitality by spreading over an amount of space far in excess of what even the most farsighted gardener believed possible just a few short months earlier. Herbs achieve all that herbaceous mass on a soil-and-water allotment that would wither most vegetables.

There is much evidence that the earliest gardens were not pleasure gardens—pocket paradises running rampant with wondrous flowers and fulsome vegetables—but rather herb gardens. In fact, most of the *decorative* plants in the famous gardens of antiquity were planted and prized primarily for their healing powers, secondarily for their value as spices, and only thirdly for their aesthetic value.[3]

In other words, the original herb garden was always a remedy garden: the place where medicine grew. Consequently, the first gardeners were also the first pharmacists. The gardens of the Egyptian queen Hatshepsut were sited around plantings of the myrrh tree and chock-full of the medicinal plants of her time. Roots from various healing herbs were found mummified in her tomb. The famous hospital gardens of the medieval Arab world foreshadowed the ubiquitous physic gardens of Western Europe in the sixteenth century. Both were remedy gardens. The first botanical garden in all of Europe was started by a pharmacist, Luca Ghini, in Renaissance Bologna.[4] Ghini's garden was a remedy garden. Of course most herb gardens today no longer do service as remedy gardens. But if herbs no longer accrue such power, one may well ask why so many of us bother to plant a separate area to contain the so-called herbs.

When I was short on space, I used to incorporate a few dill or basil plants into the vegetable garden. Other herbs are commonly sold as ornamental flowers. Calendula, for instance, is commonly retailed as an ornamental annual. Despite its obvious flowery connotations, calendula is also one of the very oldest and most effective pharmaceutical herbs in cultivation, long used to heal burns, bruises, and skin inflammations. Even today it is the active ingredient in many commercial brands of skin cream.

When we grow calendula, it is the flower tops we seek to harvest. Pick them as they blossom. Or, if we wish, we might follow this twelfth-century directive for harvesting calendula: "Wait until the moon is in the sign of Virgo but not when Jupiter is in the ascendent."[5] As arcane as this instruction may sound, it actually offers the good advice of forgoing the harvest of the earliest blooms and waiting until July or even later when the essential alkaloids of the calendula are at their greatest concentration. To make a tincture, we may no longer wish to soak a handful of the flowers in a half quart of whiskey for five or six weeks as certain herb books recommend.[6] That would make us smell soused all the time, not to mention that alcohol tends to dry out the skin. Substitute vegetable oil with just a dash of white vinegar added. Rub it into the skin as needed. A dose is five to twenty drops.

Eventually any compulsive gardener starts visualizing some little corner of the garden to collect all the herbs in one place. Long before I ever tried to answer my own question of why build an herb garden, I confronted another simple question: What is an herb? *Rodale's Illustrated Encyclopedia of Herbs* takes several stabs at comprehensive definitions, although, taken together, they seem to obfuscate the distinctiveness of herbs in a futile attempt to distinguish herbs from spices. According to Rodale, leaves are herbs, whereas seeds, roots, fruits, flowers, and bark are spices. Herbs are grown in temperate regions, whereas spices are tropical. Herbs are green and subtle of taste, while spices tend to be brown, black, or red, with dramatic, pungent flavors.[7]

Unfortunately, this definition would have us believing that the calendula flower and the echinacea root are spices and not herbs, as are dill seeds and rose hips. Not a chance, although I cannot say precisely why. In fact, there is no easy way to correct Rodale's mistaken identity except by donning a Dr. Seuss hat and declaring that herbs can be spicy and spices can be herbal. Only herbs may *not* be spicy. And spices may *not* be herbal.

Rodale goes on to say that an herb is simply a plant or plant part valued for its medicinal, savory, or aromatic qualities.[8] Obviously, this definition includes a broad spectrum of plants including trees, shrubs, and flowers. Henry Beston, he of Cape Cod's outermost house, wrote in *Herbs and the Earth* that an herb "has not come down to us as a purely decorative thing. [Nor is it] use which has kept the great herbs alive, but beauty and use together."[9] If it's beauty we primarily seek, then what we plant is an herb garden. If it's utility we seek, we are either cooks or healers, or both.

Like the idea of semi-real flowers, the idea of herbs may be better understood by classifying the plants in question in a vertical "herbal" taxonomy instead of Linnaeus's horizontal model. However, quite unlike the semi-real flowers, herbs are as real, as ancient, and as self-sufficient as any plant might be—the Mississippi Delta blues of the plant world. That simile is also meant to suggest that like country blues, growing an herb garden is an acquired taste. Yet there are very few herb gardens that contain nothing but "official" herbs. My own makes space for montbretias, dianthus, and even a plum tree. It contains a few semi-real daffodils.

An herb garden is also an herb museum, which goes a long way toward explaining why so many gardeners gather their herb plants in one location. The decision to commence digging demands a curator's perspective as much as a horticultural passion. However, a plant collector is sometimes a distinct breed from a gardener. The collector is more interested in the growth of his or her collection—the history, the subtleties of identification and nomenclature—whereas the gardener finds simple pleasure when immersed in the process of digging soil and participating in the passage of the seasons. A collector, whether of bottle caps, baseball cards, or herbs, experiences the sublime in categories and availability, by discovering something rare, or by sharing something especially choice with another avid collector. Even as an herb may also be a spice, so most gardeners are, to a certain extent, collectors. Rarely does anyone besides a collector (or a serious herbal healer) bother to plant such quaintly historical and weedy-looking herbs as eyebright, skullcap, and selfheal.

A collector of herbs is not necessarily an herbal healer. Likewise, an herb garden is not necessarily a remedy garden. An example may better clarify the distinction. Horehound is commonly found alongside parsley or oregano in the herb section of many nurseries. Its accessibility suggests that many gardeners seek it for their own private herb museums. But horehound is by no means conventionally beautiful. Still, it has the look of an herb; its leaves possess that lovely blue-green, bumpy fuzziness common to so many aromatic plants. When the leaves are crushed, it also displays the medicinal fragrance of an herb.

The plant's very name has an evocative ring to it, strongly suggesting a curative history. Yet despite that name's undeniable potential as a subject for punning, horehound is not named after a bordello dog. It is rather the Egyptian sky god Horus, who is said to arbitrate the curative power of the plant. The Greeks used horehound for curing dog bites. Folk legend tells us that because *Horus's hound* remedy causes vomiting in strong doses, it also possesses an added ability to break evil spells, just as the vomiting did in the movie *The Exorcist*.[10]

But the current demand for horehound is hardly remedial. Few herb gardeners tap the medicinal properties of the herb, although they often tap its parallel value as a historical conversation piece. The allure of the plant is predicated entirely upon its look, its aroma, its link to Egyptian mythology, and perhaps to the fact that it was a major ingredient in children's cold medicine until the 1960s. Once horehound is planted, very few herb gardeners ever bother to take the next step of gathering the leaves, drying them, and then steeping them in hot water when their children get congested.

Most contemporary herb gardens exist as remedy *museums* and not as remedy *gardens*. No matter; constructing an herb museum can still be a worthwhile task. This is a symbolic garden, a semantic garden, a historical garden. A walk through it often evokes images of the Middle Ages: a time when medical technology referred primarily to mortars and pestles; when housewives and monks and pre-feminist "witches" browsed the garden paths on any bright sunny morning gathering dewy sheaves of aromatic plants, pinching a leaf here, a flower bud there, searching out the raw material for daily potions, decoctions, elixirs, and infusions. It is in this capacity that the very names of the aforementioned eyebright, skullcap, and selfheal start to accrue much power. The more we walk inside the herb garden, the more we come to recognize that this same medieval garden is the direct antecedent of a late-twentieth-century browse down the straight aisles of a drugstore trying to decide whether to buy the twelve-hour cold capsule with eight preventatives or the six-hour cold tablet with twelve preventatives.

Planting a special herb garden also solves the very practical issue of where to grow plants—like mint, lemon balm, borage, and horseradish—that need to be segregated because they would just as soon overtake everything else in sight. I confess to a bizarre spectator's delight watching the very invasive lemon balm slug it out with the equally invasive apple mint planted in the same narrow bed five years ago. Their strategies are entirely different. The lemon balm germinates hundreds of seeds in every unaccounted-for crevice, whereas the apple mint sends up whole plants directly from nodes on its far-reaching root system. Although most humans don't usually regard plants as being especially dynamic, a gardener's attention to detail reveals these two very fragrant species constantly making incursions across their common boundary like two slow-motion shoguns locked in battle.

Late one fall I cleared a rather large corner of my yard where the bedrock sits just a few inches below the soil surface. I then commenced the seemingly endless process of mortaring rocks together to define my own herb garden. I was intent on building a remedy museum and a garden of aromas. Five years into the project, the museum has turned into an elaborate series of terraces and beds tumbling down a gradual slope. All the completed beds are connected by the quintessential feature of any proper herb garden: a skinny walkway made skinnier still by exceedingly aromatic plants crowding the edges of the path.

My own herbal walkway winds and slithers among the oddly mortared, stone-traced beds like the proverbial crooked man's version of a Minoan maze—jogging slightly left then right then left, all within the space of ten feet; under a grape arbor here, around a Japanese maple there, and alongside the horehound, the French lavender, the Greek oregano, the catnip, the echinacea, the valerian, the wormwood, et cetera, and so forth. By fall, with the fennel and the dill and the sage five feet tall and droopy, a person cannot walk that crooked path without starting to smell like a pickle. The path eventually meanders around a gigantic glacially deposited boulder properly called an *erratic*—a term that does double duty as an apt description of my design strategy. This boulder also serves as the domicile for a rather Promethean brown lizard who keeps the children mesmerized every time it ventures out to feed. The lizard pays its way by doing a fair job of keeping the bugs and slugs at bay.

Spying that oversized lizard darting between the cicely and the anise toward its den under the glacial erratic, I sometimes conjure up an entire salad bowl of associations, both surrealistic and medieval. For example, consider that valerian, source of the drug Valium, is a powerful sedative. And the name *sage* derives from the Latin for "salvation." The ancients associated sage with immortality and, specifically, clary sage with clarity of sight. Stir in a large dose of whimsy and, *voilà*, imagine that clary-eyed wizard, lizard king of the valerian patch, casting a magic spell over my two virgin daughters that causes them to sleep forever. It is no accident that I also grow horehound, which, we now know, the ancients used to break magic spells.

Perceiving the herb garden through whimsical eyes produces an interesting side effect. Even as we try to understand and feel how ancient laypeople may have related to the herbs in their lives, we may also imagine how the healers themselves first acquired the essential skill of equating a certain herb with a specific malady. What caused these first doctors to chew on the bark of the willow tree and know intuitively that here was a cure for headache? In fact, whoever did so discovered the active ingredient in aspirin.

Certainly there had to have been an aspect of trial and error, which occasionally led to deadly results as well as complete cures. Yet without any other remedies with which to compare it, even a minor cure, an occasional cure, rekindled the patient's lingering hopes even temporarily and thus came to be appreciated. Nor can we discount the strong possibility of attunement: that preindustrial human beings may have been much more sensitized to such herb-induced alterations in the normal course of any illness, no matter how minor; thus even the hint of a cure might have been capable of stimulating the body to heal itself. Some modern herbalists believe precognition played a part as well. The best ancient healers worked through visioning, perceiving *in advance* the ways a new plant would affect their patients.[11]

Some modern herbalists take a cue from the sentient garden when they forthrightly assert that an herb is far more than just a chemical agent. It is an active participant in the healing process, a kind of botanical guide leading the human body and mind back toward homeostatic balance. Kathleen Harrison McKenna, a researcher of psychotropic healing, talks of witnessing a traditional Amazonian shaman attuning to the symbiotic powers of any unknown plant.[12] Within the gates of the sentient garden, it may have always been the plant itself that whispered the healing secrets of its alkaloids.

A well-developed oral tradition ensured the transmission of herbal knowledge down through the generations. Likewise, healing was considered to be a very desirable skill in any society. A person able to cure another accrued much personal power, and the education of an herbal healer had as much to do with philosophy and politics as it did with gardening or plant identification. To know the properties of herbs and minerals, the causes of rain and drought and the mystery of life and death—all such things must have excited the wonder of early philosophers and stimulated them to find solutions to problems that were doubtless often thrust on their attention in the most practical form by the importunate demands of their clients, who expected them not merely to understand but to regulate the great processes of nature for the good of humanity.[13]

Granted, such relationships between nature, healers, their societies, their patients, and their remedies are for the most part long gone. Yet some aspects of this relationship do still exist, although they are now covert. Where they exist, they are often part of the vast medical underground called alternative healing. As far as the medical establishment is concerned, stubborn old notions about entranced shamans, about the garden as a pharmacy, about ancient healing methods founded on herbal cures like "chaste tree" and "false unicorn root" and "eyebright," about healers spending years developing their own specialized powers to attune to plants, are now generally believed to be at best patently romantic and at worst medically frivolous. However, the brisk sales of herb books demonstrate that a large minority still harbors a very modern longing to retain and incorporate into their own lives at least a scrap of this ancient lore.

Over time, any gardener who collects herbs also begins to accrue a basic understanding of what it could mean to be an herbalist. Whenever we research the history, the active ingredients, and the cures attributed to the new plants added to the herb garden, we are also drawing one step closer to an ancient system of knowledge. We find ourselves able to distinguish at a whiff the difference between French and English lavender. Or we garner simple satisfaction over the evocative manner in which the common names of the species roll off the tongue: southernwood and rue and woodruff and Good-King-Henry. We may savor the opportunity to inform our strolling guests that the Pied Piper of Hamelin may have used more than music to lure the rats out of town. Legend suggests that he also employed valerian (which smells like dirty socks and tastes like the proverbial bitter herb), known to intoxicate both cats and rats.[14]

Or regard lovage, which begs to be punned as a dietary amendment combining roughage with love. Lovage is a very large and rather rank perennial herb that looks, smells, and even tastes a bit like overglandulized celery. But who uses it these days? The best I can imagine is some one-hundred-year-old black woman from the Mississippi Delta exchanging lovage recipes with a one-hundred-year-old great-grandmother just off the boat from Croatia. And almost no one else in earshot has a clue to what they are referring to when they repeat the word *lovage* over and over again. Yet for most of human history the pungent root of the lovage was considered a first-rate diuretic as well as a cure for rheumatism and jaundice. Even today, some Europeans still use it to cure stomachaches and kidney problems.

If it all sounds a bit too quaint or even silly, then also realize that modern medicine, in its sometimes maladroit role as cultural arbiter of postmodern reasonableness, also agrees that lovage works quite well as a diuretic. In other words, whether you make your obeisance to the American Medical Association or naturopathy or even the wicked witch in *Snow White*—if you drink lovage tea, you can bet the bank it is going to get a rise from your bladder. The powers of lovage offer just one reason why a full one-quarter of all prescriptions dispensed in the United States today contain active agents derived directly from plants. On that same note, the distinguished pharmacognosist (pharmacological historian) Norman Farnsworth wrote of traditional Chinese herbal medicine, "Could it have survived for 3,000 years if the entire populace was being served placebo medications?"[15]

Who can say for sure when the passive curiosity of the herb collector gives way to the participatory relationship that exists between herb and herbalist? In my case, careful research led to careful experimentation. In such a manner, remedy museums eventually transform into remedy gardens. Now, years later, I am happy to use (and recommend) some of the same woebegone herbs to cure some of my own family's ills.

No, not the foxglove, which is one of the most common and most beautiful garden flowers yet which also contains digitalis, a heart stimulant capable of causing lasting harm when not administered properly. And no, not annual poppies, the source of the poppy seeds found in cookies but also the source of opium, morphine, and heroin. Ironically, though it is illegal to harvest the freshly flowered poppy seed case, it is not currently illegal to grow it. It must reseed itself prolifically since the white, red, or pink flowers grow to profusion in a fair percentage of the gardens within a hundred miles of my house. And no, not the artemisia called wormwood, which can be the source of much admiration for the feathery gray texture its leaves impart to any garden. It is the active ingredient in absinthe, the intoxicating brew that Van Gogh was allegedly imbibing when he thought it was the ultimate good-sense gesture to grab a razor and cut off his own ear. There are several other artemisias I would recommend over wormwood, including southernwood, mugwort, and especially the cultivar called Powis Castle.

While some people believe passionately in herbal healing, many others just as passionately employ the word *quackery* as a catchall phrase to describe any such "unprofessional" medicine. Never the twain shall meet. That is the reason almost every book about herbal remedies includes a disclaimer to serve as a judicious response to the Food and Drug Administration, the malpractice industry, and of course the American Medical Association. For instance, the authors of the Smithsonian book that quotes Dr. Farnsworth merely discuss the use of herbal remedies *as an example* of why we need to preserve the ecosystem in the anthropocentric cause of conserving unknown resources. Yet they still feel a need to prominently display this no-nonsense warning:

> It is dangerous, possibly even fatal to employ self-dosage or to experiment upon one's self with local plants. Many herb teas have not been scientifically investigated.[16]

Rodale's Illustrated Encyclopedia of Herbs is far less shrill, couching its disclaimer this way:

> This book is intended as a reference volume only, not as a medical manual or a guide to self-treatment. We caution you not to attempt diagnosis or embark upon self-treatment of serious illness without competent professional assistance. The information presented here is not intended to substitute for any treatment that may have been prescribed by your physician.[17]

Strong words and good advice, although, strangely, our society demands no similar disclaimers at the beginning of books about wine, cars, or even handguns. For that matter, given the amount of horrific knowledge that continues to accumulate about universal pesticide and herbicide use, about chicken meat laced with antibiotics, and about hormones in cow's milk causing some ten-year-old girls to sprout breasts three years before their minds are able to deal with them, it seems the height of irony that our society does not consider putting health disclaimers on just about everything connected with grocery store produce. The fact that disclaimers appear specifically in so many herb books points quite emphatically to the current litigious nature of the healing business.

Whenever an herbalist sets out to promote herbal remedies publicly, he or she becomes painfully aware of the possibility of arousing the wrath of the medical establishment. Unfortunately, this professional concern sometimes seems suspiciously like a medical version of 1950s-style McCarthyism. The roots of that wrath run far deeper than this particular book was ever meant to dig.

Does this chapter demand a disclaimer similar to the above examples? In fact, both disclaimers imply a lack of common sense and a fear of litigation as much as they voice a genuine concern for the health of their readers. One might wonder if common sense has vanished along with shamanism. Are people that dumb? Will they read about Van Gogh and dash off to the local nursery while also making a quick detour to the drugstore to buy razor blades? The external use of calendula on one's skin does not also counsel the internal imbibing of digitalis or the abuse of cocaine. In fact, an all-inclusive disclaimer implies something insidious—that the *preparation* of calendula skin cream involves a taboo knowledge conventionally regarded to be the exclusive domain of medical doctors, pharmacists, and especially drug companies. Yet disclaimers do have their value. They serve to warn the curious to keep such plants as garden hellebores, foxgloves, and lobelias out of the mouths of the ignorant and the very young.

On that note, this chapter's disclaimer reads:

> Only thoughtful people, careful people, should study, grow, and
> take herbal remedies. Know thyself.

If this discussion of the disclaimer seems long-winded, there has been a definite purpose to it. With the subject of the disclaimer finally out of the way, I must confess that my remedy museum has long since completed its transformation into a full-fledged remedy garden.

For instance, everyone in my family swallows a capsule of powdered echinacea, cayenne, and goldenseal at the very first sign of a cold or a flu. We favor several other herbal remedies as well, but this one seems the exemplar upon which my argument for the medicinal utility of herbs seems best hung. Here's the rub: our echinacea/cayenne/goldenseal caps have always exerted a very positive effect on the general healing process. We find that a dose enacts veritable wonders during the early stages of an ailment, but that it accomplishes almost nothing once the cold or flu has grabbed hold. There must be something to it. These three herbs have been used—either together or apart—by human beings as an immune-system stimulant for thousands of years.

I'm no expert. I cannot state with any degree of authority what these herbal ingredients actually do once they percolate through my colon. Some will hear this confession and conclude that in my admitted ignorance of the chemistry involved, I have no business putting any strong potion in my body, let alone promoting in print that others try it as well. To that I would argue that I promote nothing besides good health. Each of us must find our own healthy balance between inner ecology and outer ecology.

The cayenne (*Capsicum frutescens*) makes the body sweat. A fresh root from the purple coneflower (*Echinacea purpurea*) tastes slightly sour and yet strangely salty, although not from any salt contained within the root. It is as if the active principle within the root were mining the salt from all the various points in one's body and depositing it precisely on the back of one's tongue. The goldenseal is less direct still. It is probably the best known of the three, and possibly the most toxic of the three, being known to cause stomach ulcers if imbibed to excess. In moderation, it seems to linger in the body, acting directly upon the mucous membranes.[18]

The most revealing—and perhaps the most revolutionary—aspect of this remedy is the fact that we do not use it *only* at the first sign of cold or flu. Instead, we take smaller doses on a fairly regular basis. Our immune systems must evidently remain in a state of homeostasis, because we definitely suffer fewer colds each winter than we did before we started the regimen.

This so-called preventative relationship that develops between medicine and patient encompasses a dynamic that is quite foreign to our own Western, allopathic (cause-and-effect) brand of medicine. Although we tend to think of modern medicine as *the* medicine—and though many medical practitioners openly promote their profession as if it were the one true faith and not just a specific healing philosophy based on a specific body of knowledge—allopathy encompasses only one of many potential healing philosophies. In the most general terms, Western allopathic philosophy focuses its awesome technological and chemical weaponry on battling symptoms and killing organisms. It cures illness, which is quite a different objective than encouraging and stimulating health.

I do not offer up this nutshell description of Western medicine as a belittlement. The curing of disease is one of the great achievements of our civilization, and Western medicine is still the only worthwhile place to turn when (for a few examples) one needs a polio shot, a cure for pneumonia, or emergency treatment for severe trauma. However, much of the rest of the world, including the entire indigenous world, views the allopathic approach of *the* medicine as a rather specific and sometimes shortsighted approach to the question of health. They distinguish the symptomatic approach of Western allopathy from holistic and often herbally based *preventative* medicine.

Most preventative practitioners would, in fact, openly encourage the regular imbibing of cayenne, goldenseal, and echinacea capsules as a means of building up the body's resistance to disease.[19] That the keepers of allopathy tend not to agree with this thesis is perhaps typified by the Smithsonian book's somewhat arrogant disclaimer that "many herb teas have not been scientifically investigated," which strongly implies that there is no clear value to *any* herbal tea (although they may have been used generally for ten thousand years or more) until such time as allopathy concurs.

Too many doctors would prefer to click their tongues and roll their eyes at the very mention of herbal home remedies. How can I, a layman, possibly know the proper dose of echinacea? For that matter, what does the obscure word *attunement* have to do with healing? In fact, any swallower of herbal capsules or herbal tonics is well aware that some health professionals believe we'd all feel exactly the same way taking a placebo of equal parts belly-button lint and goldfish urine while running far less chance of hurting ourselves. I don't know. I do know that I don't get so many colds each winter.

Some of the doctors who object the most to some poor soul first growing herbs and then preparing and finally using herbal remedies (not to mention recommending them to others) seem not to care a whit whether the likes of powdered echinacea and cayenne are actually helpful or not helpful. In certain cases, that blind disdain leaves the cynical impression that the most intolerant among the M.D.s are reacting to the fact that herbalists simply grow what cures them without first handing out a hundred dollars an hour to find out what it is that ails them. They seem to believe that the main effect of herbal remedies is a thumb to the nose in response to centralized medical authority. Home remedies thus make a political statement despite themselves, offering a *local*, homegrown, herbal cure for what ails us. They reconnect the healing process to an attunement with the Earth and thus, in their own little way, goose the dominant centralized health care system of the United States.

It seems fatuous to dismiss the remedial value of certain herbs because someone possessed of a little gardening knowledge and an independent mind can grow herbs in his or her own backyard. There is no point in dismissing herbal remedies because that grower may then discreetly dispense his or her herbs to family and friends. There is no point in dismissing herbs because their active ingredients, their strengths and weaknesses, and even their effects and side effects cannot be as precisely determined as those of their carefully tested pharmaceutical counterparts. And lastly, there is no point in dismissing herbs because their distribution cannot be controlled by a centralized body of professionals.

In fact, there is little point in overlaying the contemporary symptomatic medical point of view on top of the less causal, preventative treatments offered by certain herbs. With so much conflicting information to sort out, and so many entrenched worldviews at stake, who can hope to know precisely what heals and what merely feels like healing? Is there any point in comparing meadowsweet with aspirin? Maybe so, but only because both contain salicylic acid as their active ingredient. Is there any point in comparing clary sage with over-the-counter eyedrops, burdock with calamine lotion, or even marijuana with corn whiskey? The best retort might be: choose your weapon. And don't break the law unless you are prepared to change it.

The opposite stance is also shortsighted. To utilize *only* herbs to the exclusion of drugs—as if the term *organic* or *herbal* were a panacea in and of itself—seems a case of cutting off one's nose to spite one's face. Is there any point in comparing, for instance, the preventative echinacea with the symptomatic tetracycline? Or put another way, sometimes we need to send in the peace corps sooner, and other times we need to send in the militia later. In fact, given an imperfect world, both processes have their place. An ongoing regimen of the preventative echinacea may make the far more severe symptomatic tetracycline less likely to be needed. But when a life-threatening infection is diagnosed, put the echinacea aside and call a doctor. On the other hand, there is a fast-emerging counterculture of cancer victims who are reaching for herbal treatments like chaparral after their chemotherapy has failed to cure them.

The mind-set that favors herbal remedies is often the same mind-set that cringes over all the contemporary, dysfunctional, and fear-inducing medical baggage of malpractice insurance, litigation, doctors' salaries, and the bloated advertising budgets of drug companies. If it is ever possible to strip all of that baggage away, we may eventually uncover one fundamental theme that connects herbalists to the M.D.s: that taking care and assuming responsibility means there is eminent value to herbs and drugs.

The anticentralized, local, and Gaian aspects of home remedies turn herbal healing into a subject pertinent to any discussion about a sense of place. The medicines prescribed by the medical establishment are overwhelmingly devoid of place. They have been synthesized at centralized chemical laboratories and administered by a centrally certified group of health professionals. These medicines are largely generic, meaning that the combination of ingredients is geared to treat the largest number of possible patients. "Custom" doses cost commensurately more.

Yet almost all of our professional medical remedies have been accessible to the society for less than fifty years. Because their distribution—not to mention their very existence—is inextricably bound to contemporary technological civilization, one may rightly wonder how we all might continue curing ourselves should this highly centralized juggernaut falter. Though it may seem like cultural heresy to even suggest such a scenario, exigencies of environment, politics, and resource availability veritably ensure that our culture is in for some major alterations to its centralized structure over the next fifty years. It seems eminently plausible that all our high-priced medical technology may not always be quite as accessible (or even desirable) as it is today. In fact, current pricing strategies for certain drugs already make herbal alternatives seem viable as the obvious local solution.

It is for precisely these reasons that farsighted caretakers of the local—for instance, the bioregionalists—have started collecting and disseminating information about curative herbs. It is one reason they also grow the plants of our herbal heritage. They are networking the herbal equivalent of the well-known "seed savers," that established international community of gardeners and farmers dedicated to nurturing genetic diversity in food seeds by growing *heirloom* food crops that have been cast aside by farmers in favor of chemically dependent monocrops distributed by centralized seed companies.

The nonprofit group Botanical Dimensions is just one group that offers an exhaustive database containing much traditional lore surrounding the healing virtues of plants. Their preserve in Hawaii is a kind of medicinal farm, a vast repository of many thousands of the plants used for centuries by the indigenous *curanderos* of tropical regions around the planet. Who can say for sure that some *medical* disaster akin to the Irish potato famine (or the much more recent corn die-offs) does not wait in the wings for all those who have bet their lives on the remedies of a centralized medical establishment tied to centralized drug companies that distribute their high-tech synthetic products through transportation modes based entirely on centralized petroleum access?

A remedy garden offers more to its practitioners than a sharp hook for hanging social pronouncements about our overcentralized medical system. It is more than a survivalist's hedge on the bet of what to stock in the after-the-apocalypse futuristic pharmacy. It is more than an atavistic bridge leading backward to a very spotty seventeenth-century pharmacy. It is more than a drug museum, more than a smelly-rooted collection of plants once upon a time collected by people called peasants for the primary purpose of making the human body puke and fart and piss, to use the Shakespearean vernacular. By the way, to stimulate those same Anglo-Saxonized conditions, one might seek out (in order) an herbal emetic like hops, a carminative like allspice, or a diuretic like the wonderfully euphonic-sounding pipsissewa.

An herb garden is also a wonderful provider of fresh herbs for the table. My family grows two crops of basil each summer in a special pampered bed that receives more water and soil amendments than the rest of the herb garden combined. We regard our basil crop as one of the home runs of gardening. And although there's a veritable baseball team of choices out there, including such exotically fragrant items as cinnamon basil, anise basil, and even the visually stunning purple basil, we opt for the old standby: sweet Genovese basil.

Our aim is to harvest the leaves, bring them in the house, and immediately start blending them with extra-virgin olive oil; we freeze the resultant green mud in twenty or more half-pint containers. We defrost a container each week all winter and into the spring. We mix up the green mud with sunflower seeds, Parmesan cheese, and garlic grown in our own yard. Presto: a pesto a week over the entire year. It's important *not* to freeze the cheese, the seeds, or the fresh garlic.

We also grow saffron, the real saffron, which is the long red stigmata of a handsomely purple, autumn-blooming crocus. Bought in bulk at the retail level, saffron currently costs over forty-five hundred dollars a pound,[20] although given the backbreaking labor it takes to gather so many stigmata by hand, it hardly seems worth the effort. Tens of thousands of stigmata are placed under pressure in a special kiln. This causes the saffron to dry into thick cakes that are used for commerce. I bought three dozen saffron corms (a corm is somewhat similar to a bulb in appearance, although it is actually able to dig itself deeper into the soil) because I sought the flowers that bloom in mid to late fall, at a time when little else is blossoming in the herb garden. Crocuses don't demand much care, and they are quite content to have other plants growing on top of them all summer long. By late October of the second season, I noticed that there were far more plants growing than I had started originally.

Mostly on a whim, I collected the stigmata—three to each flower. I dropped the rich red-orange threads onto a paper towel and then placed the towel on a windowsill out of the direct sun for a week. When the dried stigmata had shrunk to a third their original size, I stored them in a glass vial and placed it on the spice rack. Once again, presto! Unless you plan to dine on paella every week, a hundred saffron threads will readily serve your needs. It adds a uniquely earthy flavor to a meal. That amount should last until next year's harvest when the natural division of corms will ensure an even larger crop.

Another favored herb is the agastache, or anise hyssop. The leaves are a deep green with a decidedly purple cast to them. The smell is utterly exquisite, and even in a garden with many other licorice-based fragrances the agastache stands out for its aromatic depth. Some of the plants combine the best fragrant traits of chocolate and root beer; others seem more of a blend of vanilla and cloves; while still others smell like licorice blended with the sweetest cinnamon. My favorite old roses pale by comparison. No wonder agastache is a key ingredient in some liquors and perfumes. My kids treat the agastache shrub as a kind of candy store. They break off leaves all summer long, popping them into their mouths for a tingly taste they prefer over mint LifeSavers. All that praise for the plant's fragrance, and yet the flowers are the most beautiful blue-purple, bottlebrush spires in the entire garden. They dry splendidly for winter wreaths.

One caveat: Although many nurseries label the plant as anise hyssop, agastache is no variant of the garden hyssop also found in nurseries. Garden hyssop is a much stronger-smelling, medicinal herb once used "as a most violent purgative" in the words of the famous seventeenth-century herbalist Nicholas Culpeper. The volatile oil in garden hyssop is so decidedly overpowering that its leaves were once strewn about the floors of hospitals to mask the odor of dying. By contrast, agastache is sweet, lovely, and intoxicating.

As one might suspect, my herb garden grows expansive. If your own space is limited but you'd like to grow a few herbs, then by all means start an herb garden in a spot with poor soil. There's no need to truck in topsoil, no need to deprive those nutrient-needy flowers of their already limited garden real estate. Define the basic shape of the herb bed, till it to the depth of a garden fork, and deposit a few large rocks for effect. Start out by planting a couple of chive plants, a Greek oregano, maybe a French lavender, perhaps a bergamot for the bees and butterflies it attracts. Definitely add a Russian sage (*Perovskia*) and an agastache if you can find either one.

Here's a final herbal tip for gourmet cooks: If you cook Thai food but can't find a steady supply of lemongrass, go to an Asian market and buy some fresh lemongrass with the roots still attached. Plant them right in the ground under the same conditions you'd plant basil. Step back and watch them grow. Northern gardeners should bring the plants inside the house in October and watch them thrive as houseplants. If you are unable to locate lemongrass with the roots still attached, try planting the hardy lemon thyme. It makes a fair substitute and a wonderful ornamental besides.

And get yourself a good herb book, or you're still missing half the fun of starting an herb museum. Several are mentioned in the notes to this chapter. *Rodale's Illustrated Encyclopedia of Herbs* and *The Herb Book* by John Lust are among the best. Give a copy to your favorite doctor.

August

The raspberries and blackberries have set an especially heavy crop this year. The holly tree has more berries than ever. The juncos are feeding in the trees, eating up the madrona berries much earlier than normal. The first dews of late summer illuminate the spiderwebs that have suddenly appeared everywhere we look. There are more woolly bear caterpillars than usual, and the yellow jackets seem to be building their nests in the ground rather than in the eaves of our house. The cat's orange coat doesn't usually get this thick until December. The apples ripened a good two weeks earlier than normal, and we started eating them by the middle of the month. Even the grass seems a darker green this summer.

According to one of the Foxfire books and my more down-home neighbors, all of these signs strongly indicate that we're in for a long, cold winter. Since August is when I plant the winter vegetable garden, this year I've decided to start the process ten days earlier than usual—on the first day of August.

For next winter I'm focusing on just those varieties of greens that have already proven they can withstand a week or more of twenty-degree weather. These include two mainstays for winter salads: a Japanese mustard green with thick feathery leaves, called mizuna, and the nutty-flavored, European corn salad. Both vegetables defy the cold, even seem to grow more vigorous after a week of hard freeze. Corn salad is the slightly more cold hardy of the two. Shaped like a miniature Bibb-type lettuce, it may be the only leafy plant that actually tastes better after sitting frozen under a layer of snow for a week. I've started two hundred corn salads, mostly because the plants are picked whole, and sixty mizunas, whose outer leaves are harvested.

I also favor a few varieties of root crops selected for their thick leaves. These include the glossy, sweet-flavored white-green leaves of the Lutz beet and the radish-flavored Shogoin turnip. Along with a planting of a dozen purply Russian kale and a dozen red-on-green rhubarb chards, a homegrown salad in January looks as colorful as a July salad full of nasturtium flowers and purple cabbage.

There are also leeks. Bulblets from last year's crop usually attain an inch in diameter by mid-February; and they have become a favorite of late winter stir-fries. Lastly, I've started two dozen four-inch pots of a lettuce variety known as Winterkeeper. We plant the lettuce in early August and harvest the outer leaves in October and November. The plants go into remission in January, although as the weather warms up again in March, they start to grow again. They provide the first lettuce of the new season.

I always let the strongest mizuna and corn salad plants go to seed. By early May, I've harvesting enough seed to satisfy my own needs for next winter. I pass around envelopes of the extra seed to those neighbors who marvel at the verdancy of my winter garden. I figure if I keep selecting seed from the most hardy plants, over a few more years, I'll eventually have a crop of winter vegetables able to take the worst that winter is able to mete out.

The Predator's Garden

Where I live, on an island in Puget Sound, the winter clouds will soon hang so low in a leaden sky that they will seem an element of the ground as much as of the atmosphere. Any reprieve in the cover always seems a function of the Earth acting like a snake, gradually shaking itself out of an old, used-up skin, rather than of the sky suddenly relaxing its tight grip. Despite Puget Sound's somewhat unjustified rainy reputation, two weeks of nonstop cloud cover can never be equated with actual rainfall. During the dry winter of 1987, the clouds arrived, as usual, in mid-November. But we received little more rainfall that winter than did Southern California.

I have become attuned to these seasonal changes of local weather since I first took up gardening. I can remember that 1985 and 1990 were cold winters; 1991 was so warm that the dogwoods never dropped their leaves; 1983 and 1986 were dark winters. In a dark winter the default blanket of clouds does not break for ten or even twenty days at a time. If I live to be ninety, I'll look like an old, weather-beaten peasant leaning on a rake. I'll be the guy the newspaper interviews for local color when a drastic storm occurs. I can hear myself now: "Why, that storm can't hold a candle to the winter of '87 . . ." I don't regard such a self-image as merely quaint. Local knowledge is a treasure. Knowing the history of local weather is as essential to a culture's sense of place as is knowing the history of local soil. Our elder gardeners are often the people most capable of mining memory in the cause of maintaining a history of the passing seasons.

When the clouds of late fall finally clear out, it's like winning the lottery but even better because nobody loses. One evening when we least expect it, the clouds split asunder. With the Earth's warm insulation gone, winter rushes in; the Northwest coast's prevalent thirty-three-degree weather immediately plummets an automatic five to ten degrees. The family wakes up in the orange light of 7:00 A.M. to the chatter of juncos and finches searching for seeds over the rich carpet of green winter mosses. Their songs disorient. We close our eyes a moment to be transported to a warm June morning bursting with columbines and roses. Open our eyes and find ourselves back in the February world, all crystalline moss and glowing gossamer spiderwebs. My daughters run outside to examine the frost heaves as if they were an outright treasure, something far more precious than the less accessible but more common trumpeter swans and bald eagles that fly overhead every day at this time of year.

I know that the best February display in my own front yard will occur at ground level. All the juicy and overblown harbingers of the cultivated human spring—the hyacinth, daffodil, Galanthus, crocus, to name but a few—will be well along on their seasonal cycle. These imported cultivars seem especially rowdy celebrants of the end of winter. They peek up through the loam as if seeking some externalized verification of their own earthly existence. Is it time? Is it time? In fact, the accelerating growth of the bulbs over the next few weeks predicts the weather far better than any mere human weather forecaster. Nonetheless, I can still be found out in the garden on bended knees pleading with them to push their luck a little less exuberantly. "Be careful," I warn the crocus, "you may think it's time, but this isn't Central Asia or Spain or wherever it is you call home. It's still winter."

But the cultivars never listen. By the first week in March, all these immigrants have rumbled to full attention—expanding, churning, kicking away the topsoil in wave upon wave of athletic thrust. Yet surprise of surprises: everything flourishes. And in that rarest of climatic events, when the March mercury drops below twenty degrees, the cultivars seem to bear it, although they grow slightly more passive, patiently awaiting the turn back to spring.

Contrasting the disoriented exuberance of the cultivated bulbs with the far more conservative growth pattern of the natives, we learn something significant about the link between plants and climate. The natives may be far less ostentatious, but they are far more tenacious than the cultivars. They live and flourish in the wild, expanding into vast groves without any outside coaxing from the likes of human beings bearing bags of bonemeal. The natural flowers of this neighborhood—the skunk cabbage, shooting star, coral root, stork's bill, chocolate lily, hairy cat's ear, Oregon grape—have not shown much of anything above ground in late February. They seem to have accrued a special wisdom of place garnered through millennia of growing and dying, thrusting and waiting: all of that cumulative and quite mutable experience we know as evolution.

Then one remarkable day everything in the garden, wild and tame alike, seems to agree that it has warmed up for good. I learn about this unanimity by paying special attention to one particular wildflower: the calypso orchid that flourishes in the deepest part of the forest. When the little pink flowers start to open, we might as well bet the bank there will not be any more frosts.

Now the plants push, flex, ram, impel upward and ever outward. If this verbiage seems overtly sexual, then visualize the vulnerable and tender cup of a chocolate lily receiving a hairy bumblebee, or a bed of asparagus thrusting their tips through the steamy black humus of a sunny April afternoon. Is it any wonder that the Turks used the "wanton" tulip as a sex augury? Red petals offered a declaration of true love; yellow signified hopeless love; and a black center caused the heart to burn from unabated passion.[1] Such a surety of influences makes me wonder what the medieval seers would have made of my own Appeldoorn tulips that show red, yellow, and black in each flower.

This burgeoning garden is a neighborhood of which I am one neighbor, one hardworking component of the whole. I provide nutrients in the form of compost; a watershed in the form of minicatchments; weeding in the form of abundant mulching and no artificial poisons. For their own part, the flowers provide eye-popping displays of beauty. The vegetables provide fresh food for our table nearly twelve months a year. The herb garden provides emollients, purgatives, teas, and rich flavors. The trees and berries provide a veritable paradise of fruits.

This description of the relationship between gardener and garden also makes it abundantly clear that we gardeners are the predominant predators of our own garden. Then again, predation is a vital component of any peaceable kingdom one might name. Where beings live, there is always sustenance and sacrifice, living and dying, give and take. If the plants have a religion, it is probably the Mayan sect that constructs sacred memorials to the cycles of the seasons. As the seasons provide one to the next, so gardens and gardeners both reciprocate by providing a healthful continuity to the growth and withering of the seasons.

For the local blacktail deer, February is the cruelest month. The deer's known stores of young tree shoots and other browse material are nearly exhausted. Everything that grows wild is betwixt and between, meaning there is not very much to eat. But there's more to this than meets the eye. To fully understand the browsing habits of a deer is also to recognize the winter strategy of the herbaceous native plants. I may have gotten it wrong when I concluded that the natives evolved to remain underground as a hedge against the danger of late frosts. That may certainly be one reason for the strategy, but equally important is the fact that by February the local deer are ravenously hungry. The native plants have evolved a sense of place that includes an ability to fend off deer attacks.

So the plants have schemed up a botanical version of price-fixing. They agree to remain underground until all of them are ready to rise as one. For example, if the wild camas flowers followed the profligate example of the imported tulips and pushed through the earth in February instead of late April, they would be deernipped to the quick—and probably be quite extinct by now. But by April the world is exploding into leaf and bud, offering abundant browse to sustain a healthy deer population. Naturally, every wild plant that chooses to remain succulent or leafy all winter long—for instance, the Oregon grape and the wild rose—also possesses a formidable armor of needlelike thorns. Anything less vicious is fair game.

Until I started a garden, I never considered the deer to be a predator simply because I did not consider plants as prey. As a transplanted city dweller, I imagined the sighting of a deer from my own living room window as the blessing of a rural lifestyle. Were I a nongardener, no doubt it would still be so. However, this ardent planter now gazes upon his front yard with an entirely different set of eyes. For example, the wild rose has concocted as awesome a defense as any fleet-footed impala on the African plain. Likewise, the deer appears as ruthless as any tyrannosaurus. In this case, *ruthless* is defined as an exasperated gardener's synonym for *hungry*.

It took the local deer exactly two winters to discover this garden full to the brim with nonnative fruit tree saplings and foolhardy nonnative bulbs poking their succulent greenery four inches or more above ground by mid-February. I watched one of these early forays, quite transfixed, from behind the blind of my living room window. The small female would have made an effective role model for Eve, gesturing tentatively as if she were unwilling to believe that this vegetative Eden held no hidden devils waiting to lunge at her should she make the wrong move. She stared at a young plum sapling in careful apprehension for nearly a minute, then finally grabbed hold of a branch with her teeth, ripped off the bark, and immediately jerked her head up high to survey the scene as she chewed. She gobbled it down and immediately took a single step back before cocking her ears forward.

Something spooked her. It might have been the fact that the exposed-bedrock yard offers no cover. Or that the smell of wood smoke sometimes lingers on the knoll at this time of year. A brightly lit house also implied the potentially deadly threat of a nearby dog, although we don't have one. Perhaps she finally spied me spying her from behind that otherworld of glass. Or was it some fundamental intuitive distrust of this uncommon winter feast laid out before her senses? Here was a magical kingdom beyond her imagination to grasp, a situation simply too foreign, all full of prune-plum cambium, thick hyacinth leaves, and gargantuan raspberry canes. The deer seems a creature whose every sense seeks after mistrust. She dashed into the woods and was gone.

From that point on, I inspected my kingdom every single morning right into June. As far as I could tell, she never returned. Was this predation a onetime occurrence? I should have known better.

The next year commenced my long-held dream of attempting to grow food through all twelve months of the year. The concept of winter gardening in a climate that hovers around freezing for three months demands careful planning of the beds, a genuine compulsion, and a thorough knowledge of what to plant and when. As one example, cole crops like broccoli thrive in the lengthening days of early spring, whereas other coles, like Chinese cabbage and certain cauliflowers, seem to prefer the shortening days of fall.[2] I discovered the special plants that thrive in cold conditions: the corn salad bred in France, tyfon from Holland, mizuna from Japan, red kale from eastern Europe, and especially the myriad forms of cold-hardy greens bred over centuries in China including choy sum, green-in-the-snow, and kai choy. I started keeping three beds in Jerusalem artichoke tubers, potatoes, and parsnips. All three offer up their bounty during the coldest days in January and in fact seem to grow sweeter as the days grow colder. My hard work was paying off.

All you need is love . . . *and* organic gardens. It was my interest in winter gardening that led me to believe that in organic gardening lies the salvation of the world. Herein lies the single most meaningful and accessible step any of us can take to end the hegemony of the centralized technological fix that has become so central to our lives and so debilitating to our ecosystem. Even a city dweller can grow something in a window box. And if not, let every one of us support organically grown produce as the ultimate good cause for the environment.

I learned to sing the praises of the lowly earthworm, who neutralizes the soil, builds enriched topsoil from its castings, provides oxygen to the roots of growing plants, and recycles as much as thirty tons of topsoil per acre back to the surface each year.[3] So, also, I learned that 2.7 *million* pounds of earthworm-eradicating pesticide is spread on this American land every single day.[4] Consequently, a world full of bountiful organic gardens may be the most realistic way to put the pesticide companies out of business permanently. A home garden needs no transport, no elaborate distribution system. It thus offers a viable self-realized means to contain petroleum overconsumption.

I learned that twenty vegetarians could be fed on the same acreage needed to feed one human meat eater.[5] Even milk came under my scrutiny. Although the American Dairy Council assures us that cow's milk is nature's most perfect food, in fact it is the most perfect food for no one besides a baby cow, which has four stomachs, doubles its weight in forty-seven days, and is destined to weigh three hundred pounds within a year.[6] For reasons such as these, I rejected store-bought produce almost too boisterously, while transmuting my organic message into a harbinger of doom. I warned my nongardening friends that those Mexican-raised tomatoes were also a repository for carcinogenic pesticides. And while some of them either joined their own local co-op or immediately took up gardening for themselves, others found my language akin to the rantings of the preacher in Hawthorne's *Scarlet Letter*. It took a while before I learned to temper my comments.

Still, my family grew healthy. This occurred not only because freshly grown produce contains more vitamins and minerals and less junk-food fats and chemicals but also because of what Wendell Berry described so well:

> It may take a bit of effort to realize that among modern achievements, perhaps the most characteristic is the obsolescence of the human body—but it is true. Jogging and other forms of artificial exercise do not restore the usefulness of the body, but are simply ways of assenting to its uselessness; the body is a diverting pet, like one's chihuahua, and must be taken out for air and exercise. A garden gives the body the dignity of working in its own support. It is a way of rejoining the human race.[7]

One day it dawned on me that I was like a sober ant diligently working in *preparation* for an utter breakdown of society. Should the petroleum industry collapse, should the trucks, ships, and planes that deliver food to market be exploded out of commission, should any or all of us be called upon to fend for ourselves, then my family would still be able to set a healthy and sustaining table in perpetuity. I rejected the use of hybrid seed in favor of open-pollinated types, a measure that makes good sense as a means to add one more degree of independence from a food distribution system I could no longer trust.

I found myself not only accepting this disturbing state of affairs but in fact arrogantly thumbing my nose at it, daring it to come. I went ahead and expanded the bed of Jerusalem artichokes because this crop shows almost nothing above ground from late fall until mid-spring. In other words, the tubers grow deep enough to escape the initial onslaught of, you guessed it . . . nuclear fallout. Should the apocalypse come, I would be prepared for the worst. Go ahead, let the roving gangs of *Mad Max* food pirates do their worst. They would never find my little larder of Jerusalem artichokes. Yes, it is true. I thought those bizarre thoughts.

There I stood, prepared for the worst. However, I was not prepared at all for the realpolitik as represented by the February onslaught of that delicate female blacktail deer. By now I was starting to think of her as just another garden pest, a four-legged Japanese beetle. Unlike any beetle, however, she possessed the strategy-forming mind of a smart mammal and had carefully scoped out the scene before determining that no dog lived on the premises. Furthermore, no human had yet challenged her with guns, arrows, slingshots, rocks, or any of the other projectiles favored by such as I in combating an incursion by such as she. During the course of that year she devised an ingenious browsing strategy based on the on/off status of my own house lights. Like the Japanese at Pearl Harbor, she attacked as we slept.

The second year's raids commenced in late February. The three deer (she had upped the ante by giving birth to two fawns) destroyed four beds of chard, kale, lettuce, cauliflower, and cabbage in a single night. When I inspected the damage the next morning, for the first time in my life I was moved to conceptualize the implications of owning and shooting a shotgun. Luckily, the urge toward this Rambo solution to my problems soon passed.

Over the next several weeks I spent well over a hundred dollars building a seven-foot-tall fence around my vegetable patch. I went so far as to string chicken wire under the ground to keep out the local rabbits and rats just in case they got any ideas. I then went ahead and replanted two entire beds of radishes, kale, and broccoli. But a hailstorm, a week-long freeze at twenty degrees, and winds in excess of fifty miles per hour soon leveled all my young starts. No winter garden that year.

Although I solved the problem of protecting the vegetables, I still had a long way to go to safeguard the many smaller beds that proliferate on my eccentrically landscaped property. My property? Is that what it was? Had I become so vain as to disregard the irony implicit in that contrived term *property*? Here was a legal human term used to describe a skin-deep layer of earth measured and plotted onto a map by a pencil-wielding human surveyor; all of these territorial graphics generated for the primary purpose of adding my so-called claim (that which somebody else might call their town, their nation, their planet) to the local tax register. Yet we all do it: transmute a sense of place into an object, turn our deep-seated aspiration for reinhabitation into a financial arrangement that necessarily obscures a potentially sacred relationship to the land.

On a deeper level, I realized that the possessive pronoun *my*—as it relates to the noun *property*—is possessive only as it applies to human beings crediting the land of other human beings. In fact, the two words offer a provocative statement about our human sense of place in a wildlife-depleted world. The deer and her kin never read the tax register. They did not honor the plat lines. They trespassed. They broke the law. The three of them continued to ravish just about everything not set behind that seven-foot-high fence. They ate *my* tulips, *my* sweet william, *my* brussels sprouts. *I* was outraged. *I* wished *I* could make all deer extinct within the boundary of *my property*. That the deer did not and could not recognize such terms of possessiveness offers an exceedingly simple explanation for the extinction of species in a world overpopulated by human beings. I came close to reenacting the long-term human folly of destroying an environment in the hopes of saving it.

But there was hope for both me and the deer. I noticed a pattern to her predation. One night this mouth on four legs bounded up the rocky knoll I call home and banqueted her way through an unfenced bed of yellow-and-red Juan tulips rimmed with sweet william and primroses. Someone in her entourage obviously enjoyed the repast because they all returned the very next night to continue browsing through another tulip and sweet william bed. What was it about these specific plants? I had to find out.

The next morning I picked one of the erect tulip leaves and turned it over in my hand. It was a substantial thing, pea green in color and, surprisingly, far more succulent than the kale, which was considered the prize green of my February garden. Feeling a bit like Alice trying to decide whether or not the mushroom would make her larger or smaller, I went ahead and bit into the leaf. It was sweet and savory at the same time, perhaps a bit stringy, but essentially as tasty as anything I grew for winter salad greens. Next came the primrose leaf, which physically resembled a miniature romaine. It was tasteless. I was less sure about the sweet william. The cherry-red, lance-shaped leaves looked like nothing else endemic to the human diet. But curiosity prevailed. One bite proved to me that it was as bitter as it looked.

Except for a few staggered commando raids, the deer party stayed away from my garden for another whole year.

I came to expect her arrival sometime during that next winter. Not to be disappointed, at 10:00 P.M. on one clear evening, I opened the door to let the cat out only to come face-to-face with my garden's February persecutor. She stood in the moonlight quite alone, not more than twenty feet away, staring at me through huge doey eyes from the perimeter of the primrose bed. We watched each other for what seemed a full minute. What was it about this beautiful animal that made me so unwilling to share a few meager greens during the coldest time of the year? As I pondered this essential question of control, the deer grew accustomed to my presence. Did she sense my own hesitation? Possibly so, because she began to test it by munching through the last of *my* sweet william. Something snapped. I bolted from the porch like a banshee, determined to jump that deer if I could only catch her. Catch her? Before I had even reached the steps of my front porch she was a hundred yards down the hill and gracefully loping over the four-foot-high brush into the forest.

I stood there in the cold night air and, for the first time in this adversarial relationship, felt a glimmer of genuine admiration for the beast. The night was warmer than usual, a hopeful sign that spring was indeed nearby. I had a hunch that as soon as the normal forest growth rejuvenated itself, I would not see my adversary, except infrequently, until next February.

I sat down on the top step to surmise the options. I could selectively plant only those flower species undesirable to the taste buds of a deer. Daffodils, delphiniums, irises, and annual poppies are just a few of the plants that no deer in my yard has ever chomped on. Or I could disregard the deer's predation, plant whatever strikes my fancy, and in effect permit her to decide which plants would survive to blossom and which would become deer fodder. Or I could scare the deer away from my gardens permanently. A resolute dog would accomplish that in no time. I myself could become the resolute party, standing by my front door with matches in one hand and a cherry bomb in the other, waiting diligently for the deer to appear, at which point I would light a firecracker and loft it like a grenade at the feet of my herbivorous challenger.

Or I could take a hint from any of several traditional cultures, as well as the more starry-eyed of my friends, and attempt to "talk" to the deer: reason with her, ask her politely to please refrain from eating my cultivated beds, explaining in plain language how much pleasure those blossoms always bring to my family and friends. Why not strike a bargain, offer to plant a special bed of tulips in exchange for leaving the rest to me?

I chose the dog.

And so commenced a campaign to ease in the idea of a new canine family member with both wife and daughters. I started looking at my neighbors' dogs in an entirely new way, weighing which pedigree best served a household with two young children. One day I got so far as putting on my jacket in anticipation of a trip down to the local pound. But at that point, car keys in hand, I finally relented. Reward a dog for barking at man and beast? A dog whose job it was to help me reenact the human folly of destroying an environment in the hopes of saving it? A dog whose sole purpose in life amounted to protecting tulips from a little deer during the few months of the year when the woods offered little for her to eat? What about the other months?

Good question, if one that not enough of my neighbors ever seem to ask themselves. Stories circulate around town about individual dogs who have been trained to keep deer out of gardens. They skulk off at midnight to form packs, reverting to their feral ancestry, hamstringing already half-starved deer before finally tearing them to pieces. It seems a classic case of pets reflecting the wild monster within ourselves, doing the dirty work, inadvertently generating a savage metaphor about how we humans exploit and devour nature—the big bad human masquerading as the big bad wolf.

I soon learned there is an ongoing local controversy about the right of local farmers to shoot and kill these roving dogs that were never trained to tell the difference between a wild fawn and a ranch lamb. "Hey mister, that dead dog was somebody else's property"—which leads to the evolutionary non sequitur and legal quandary of what is worth more under the law, a lamb killed by a dog, or a dog killed by a farmer? The dead deer, of course, has no standing whatsoever. A few neighbors also expressed the bizarre idea that any deer accrues more value dead than alive. Some of them went so far as to declare—by deed if not by self-incriminating word—that certain animals like deer and ducks (that which they euphemistically refer to as game) are best met with a loaded shotgun, and whether it officially be "in season" or not.

Another pertinent issue surfaced. The deer are overpopulating this neighborhood as a result of their natural predators in this part of the world—especially the cougars—having all been killed off. One neighbor made the point that dogs who kill deer are actually serving as nature's attempt to right the balance between long-gone wild predators and overpopulating prey. Although I found myself agreeing with him that we did not want to reintroduce mountain lions to the neighborhood, his justification of letting dogs kill the deer seemed an abomination. I had no easy answer to his stated problem of overpopulating deer in a world that is likewise overpopulated by human beings. A strictly enforced hunting season seems to do the job as well as we might hope for in an unnatural situation.

I concluded that a dog was no longer an option. Instead, to appease what was fast becoming the death throes of my own anxiety, I went out and bought a single firecracker. For the next four nights in a row I systematically rose from my chair at half-hour intervals just to whip open the front door with matches in one hand and an appropriately named jade garden salute in the other. When my wife asked what on earth I was doing, I replied, "Hahaha, only wanted to give the deer a good scare."

But clutching this miniature rocket in my hand, I also felt discomfort. I had voided the deer from my own definition of neighborhood. Whether we employ nuclear bombs, dogs, or jade garden salutes, violent solutions are less fundamentally a manifestation of our power than of our anxiety. In this case, a compulsive desire on my part to re-create the peaceful alternative lifestyle regurgitates itself as an undeniable statement about interspecies war. Kill for peace.

The deer reacted accordingly. She vanished altogether. Nor was there any sign that she had surreptitiously snuck into the yard during the wee hours. At first, with my sense of credulity stretched to the breaking point, I wondered if I had inadvertently and quite unconsciously tapped into the original plan number four: that of discussing the issue mind-to-mind. Might my own stubborn fury be interpreted as an example of what the psychics call *focused attention*? My linear education made this supposition as difficult for me to swallow as a bowlful of sweet william leaves. On a practical level, it made no sense because everything so far seemed like a classic case of *mis*communication. With the current situation beyond my comprehension, I relented by spending the next evening immersed in a video of *Platoon*. That's when the deer returned. She ambled through a distasteful daffodil bed before commencing her task of granting my sweet williams a crew cut fit for a training camp recruit.

Is it possible that she somehow *knew* I was too busy watching *Platoon* and so would not reach for the jade garden salute? In fact, whether the deer possessed the tactical stealth of a Scarlet Pimpernel, or whether instead she simply conjured up the illusion of stealth, no matter. Either way, it changed the course of our relationship. I relented. Fireworks seemed as invalid a response to a hungry deer as growing Jerusalem artichokes is to fending off nuclear fallout.

The special parameter of this story is not so much that the deer was stealthy, intelligent, or even possibly telepathic. Rather, the relationship itself had evolved to include interspecies *neighborliness*—an essential feature of any sense of place. For over three years, my own specist and selfish point of view forbade me from giving the deer its due as a key member of the same ecosystem upon which I had built my home. Now, something changed. Hurting the deer started to accrue some of the same attributes as a baseball fan's shouting to kill the umpire. But when we kill the umpire, we kill the game. When we kill the deer, we destroy the neighborhood. When we work too hard to build our world outside the loop of nature, we lose sight of a fundamental ability to see the loop for what it is: the central glorious fact of our existence. Likewise, the flourishing relationship between gardener and deer seemed to offer a key, affording a deeper entry into that same natural system to which I had long sought admission as a planter of flowers, trees, and vegetables. Is it possible? The role of the little doe had metamorphosed from a devious thief to an arbiter of ecology.

Lest anyone doubt it, the truth is foxy stuff. It intervenes in several contradictory forms at the same moment. In this case, the deer returned and returned and returned. Like the toniest New York café, my yard had been "discovered." So it seemed one thing to revel in the deer's attention as a precious gift from a gifted being and quite another thing to deduce some working method for nurturing a garden of unfenced flowers within the very same ecosystem utilized by a hungry herbivore and her spanking new fawn. She had given birth again.

As I mentioned earlier, the deer never touched certain plants. For instance, she avoided any flowers in the *Ranunculus* genus, including such ornamentals as anemones, delphiniums, peonies, and columbines, to name a few of the better-known species. Neither would she eat rhododendrons, marigolds, poppies, lilies, tomatoes, potatoes, garlic, artichokes, asparagus, onions—in fact, a veritable country garden full of flowers and vegetables. This observation provided a glimpse into a more farsighted strategy for replanting the few ravaged beds. For example, because the potato plant served as a forbidden fruit (I got very queasy when I nibbled the edge of a leaf), I planted the potatoes *outside* the garden fence. I wondered what would happen if I surrounded my young and still-vulnerable plum trees with the nearly pharmaceutical aroma of a bed of self-seeding poppies and wormwood. And for no good reason at all, I started dividing the tulips and replanting them along the perimeter of the forest. Growing along the deer path, a few of those tulips still make it to flower. Perhaps it is the sign of a tough cultivar transforming into a tougher native.

What I had stumbled upon were the first tentative stages of what is properly known as a *permaculture* garden. This is a method of horticulture that favors the permanent approach to a flourishing garden with a minimum of artificial primping by a human overseer. We eliminate the use of all poisons, artificial fertilizers, and violence as a means of inducing plants to do our bidding. We eschew the horrific commercial practice of eliminating every living thing that grows over, on, or under the soil and then laying a coating of some petroleum-based chemical before planting just one variety of one crop, which can only be kept alive by spraying more pesticides and more herbicides that taint everything that depends on the land for years to come.

Permaculture insists we plant fewer hybrids, not as a hedge against nuclear winter but because these infertile athletes of the flower world are not actually self-perpetuating. Instead, we favor annuals that reseed themselves and perennials that do not need special pampering. We mold the garden to fit the contours of the land rather than exhausting huge amounts of time and money to excavate a garden plot prone to erosion or perform other high-maintenance exertions. We educate ourselves to the microclimates of the garden, planting the squashes where the sun shines and the gooseberries where they'll get some shade. Because the garden grows itself, permaculture emerges as a gardening method fit to feed the seventh generation. I envision a hopeful Utopian image: my own great-great-great-great-great-grandchildren gardening one day alongside the progeny of that deer in the shadow of a giant sequoia tree.

And last January, with apples overflowing the winter larder, I went so far as to lay an entire bushel of half-turned banana apples beside one of the deer's favored paths. I snickered to think she might also get a bit inebriated from eating too many. She found them within forty-eight hours and ate every last one, which led me to acknowledge that this surreptitious deer had been browsing the knoll more often than the evidence suggested.

One naturalist neighbor offered a counterpoint to this purported benevolence, opposing the gift as my own inadvertent attempt to tame the deer, to turn her into a dependent. I disagreed. To lay a gift at the feet of a wild animal once a year seemed more an act of coevolution than of coercing subservience. I preferred to treat my gift as the contemporary counterpart to a belief of the Huichols of Mexico, who revered the deer as a harbinger of abundance. Or the ancient Chinese, who honored the deer as a teacher of communication within the supernatural realms. I reinvented myself as the conceptual heir to the many shamanic peoples who recognized the deer as a possessor of grace and compassion,[8] a creature who merited a yearly gift giving. In fact, these were all the same attributes that had coevolved in our own relationship.

Perhaps coincidentally, it is mid-February as I tell this tale about the deer in my life. It has been a brutal month after an otherwise mild winter. The area was hit with a storm two weeks ago that brought zero-degree temperatures and ninety-mile-per-hour winds. As usual, the tulips, the daffodils, the irises, all had a few inches of greenery thrusting above ground when the storm struck. Now two weeks later, the edges of their leaves are obviously frostbitten, although they have started to grow again. And my winter garden? Until the storm hit, it had seemed a miracle that provided parsnips, Jerusalem artichokes, kale, cabbage, beets, and even some romaine lettuce as late as the end of January.

But winter gardening must remain the ultimate challenge for at least one more year. Almost every vegetable within my seven-foot fence succumbed to the cold. Only the leeks and parsnips seem to have made it. And as always, the Jerusalem artichokes growing outside the fence have produced more tubers than any of us could possibly eat. My fantasies of doom are diminishing. This spring I plan to cut that bed in half.

I sit at the word processor this morning in an attempt to put the cap on this chapter. By noon I had saved the file, left the computer humming, and walked into the kitchen to fix some lunch. A woodpecker, a jewel of a creature saddled with the zany name of red-breasted sapsucker, contentedly knocked its head back and forth against a Douglas fir just outside the kitchen window. I watched this strange variation on the universal theme of working for a living only to have some movement at the opposite end of the yard steal my attention. Two deer stood browsing across the northwest slope of the knoll. These were newcomers, a male and a female, and, at least at this distance, appeared larger than the little doe. I guessed that they might be her twins, now grown up and already educated to ravish my garden on their own behalf. I also noted how unperturbed the deer seemed to be in the face of that raucous drumroll knocked out by the woodpecker. By contrast, when I started to wash the dishes just to keep busy as I watched, I dropped a serving spoon into the sink. The clatter brought the two deer to full attention, despite the muffling barrier of a double-pane window, six inches of fiberglass insulation, and fifty yards' distance.

A half hour later the deer still browsed, although they also seemed to be spending an inordinate amount of time licking each other's face. They wandered up onto the top of the hill, seeming to shrink to normal size as they approached my own eye-level vantage point. To be honest about it, I can no longer be certain that this "new" female is not actually my old friend seen for the very first time by the bright light of noon.

Deer are said to *browse*. They do not forage, nor do they graze. They take a few steps this way and that, drop their head, and almost blindly bite whatever looks promising directly in front of their face. Then they lift their head quickly, scan the lay of the land, cock their ears, eventually take a few more steps, drop their head again, and grab hold of another bite. These deer are munching on grass, madrona leaves, and even the first tender growth from a patch of *my* Canterbury bells. They step right up to my plum tree, take a whiff of the Irish Spring soap hung up as deer repellent on one of the branches, snort, and quickly move back to the Canterbury bells. I have not made so much as a twitch. Next they stop to fully savor two or three licks from the inside of each other's huge ears. Is it love or is it grooming? Or perhaps it is just salt that they crave.

Now the male spots me through the window. Yes, he is looking directly at me. I freeze. He moves sideways to me and cocks his ears stiffly. I keep staring into his eyes. The female keeps licking his ears. The male widens his eyes and then freezes as if uncertain what to do next. He bolts. She bolts. Clomp, clomp, clomp, they bounce across the rocky moss of the knoll and down the hill. Gone. The woodpecker keeps on knocking. Knock-knock-knock . . .

September

An expanding human population puts more and more strain on a limited water supply. This is not only a national and international problem—somebody else's problem—but a local problem as well. It's your problem. My problem.

Continued garden expansion strained my already stressed well. My family needed an alternative water source. A pond made sense. Actually, it made so much sense that four nearby neighbors decided to have their own dug at the same time. My wife and I fretted over the expense. Fifty dollars an hour for a bulldozer was a meaningful consideration. We decided to go ahead with it, waited for September when the water table is at its yearly lowest. We chose a spot next to an orchard, a place where few established trees grew. There would be less to destroy.

Watching the bulldozer push down the few trees that held the spot was a sobering experience. The metal beast seemed invented for the sole purpose of grinding live earth into dead ground. Flattening it, neutering it, clearing the land in preparation for whatever desire we may have in store for it.

We tried our best to base our decisions about the life and death of plants on an individual basis. We established a hierarchy. Saving the three largest trees, all Douglas firs, received top priority. A highly ornamental madrona possessed of a glowing red bark and shiny evergreen leaves got more consideration than a few Douglas firs of the same size. On the second day of clearing, a white fir slowly emerged into the light as the dense shrubbery in front of it got flattened. We felt like the first human beings to set eyes upon the world's most perfect Christmas tree. Thumbs up, which also necessitated that we push the pond thirty feet to the north of the original site. Willows and ocean spray got little consideration; the task of annihilation was somehow made easier when we started calling them scrub. Thumbs down. Plowed under.

As the site was cleared, the shape of the eventual pond came into focus. Just as we had balked at spending too much money and felling too much forest, so we now balked at stepping over our own property line. My next-door neighbor came to see what all the fuss was about. He was likewise concerned but finally commented that if our soon-to-be-dug hole stepped a few feet over the line, it simply meant more waterfront for him.

The actual digging process followed a recipe. The dozer operator first piled the topsoil in one area. When the dozer hit blue clay three feet down, he started pushing it out of the hole and shaping it and tamping it into a dam on the downward side. At fourteen feet deep he still hadn't found the bottom of that blue clay deposit. It was a good sign. Our new hole would definitely hold water. The topsoil was now molded over the top of the clay dam like frosting on a cake. He told me to plant the dam in clover. It would keep the steep sides from eroding.

In four days we had ourselves a fifteen-hundred-dollar hole a hundred feet long by fifty feet wide. The dozer operator told us not to worry if it didn't fill up during the first winter of rains because it was sure to fill up after two winters. Another neighbor dropped by and praised our new pond as a fine real estate investment. With a body of water so close to the house, our fire insurance rates were also bound to drop. We stood at the rim and stared into the blue mud of our wise investment. Even as dollar bills jumped from my hand into the dozer operator's pockets, so they seemed to be jumping back into my hand again. I passed out the beers. We drank and laughed until dinnertime.

The night the hole was finished, I gathered some firewood into a tepee shape at the deepest part of the clay bottom, stuck sparklers in the mud all around its perimeter, and then lit a bonfire to consecrate our new pond. It was a family celebration. But also our family apology. We welcomed the hole even as we mourned the dead trees. Drums and rattles were handed out. We made some noise. My elder daughter, at four, led the dance. She jumped around the flames chanting the made-up phrase "so-na, so-na, so-na" over and over again.

We sang the names of the plants that would benefit from this new source of water: the apples, the apricots, the native elderberries, the wild currants, the clover. My wife and I discussed how we might cultivate a pond environment free of algae and leeches. We decided to stock crayfish and goldfish. I asked how the leeches would find our pond. She answered that they arrived on the legs of ducks.

Over the next wet winter, herons, mallards, mergansers, even some Canada geese, visited our increasingly wet hole in the ground. By May the pond was eight feet deep. We had planted two endangered American chestnuts along the outer rim of the dam. We planted rugosa roses, homegrown mock oranges, native dog-woods, Siberian irises, a gunnera bog plant with six-foot-wide leaves. The goldfish were already having their first babies. They were also taking care of the mosquito larvae. We swam in our pond nearly every day that first hot July.

The Sacred Garden

My first experience of the sacred garden occurred in a place few people would identify as a garden. Located two hundred miles southeast of the magnetic north pole, the area was part of a High Arctic wilderness far beyond the ken of human residents. Yet the deep insights about soil, flowers, and the circle of life that I acquired there transformed the way I experience gardening. It led to the writing of this book about learning a sense of place through gardening. Like Dorothy in *The Wizard of Oz*, I had to venture very far, indeed, to learn that there is no place like home.

I was in the Canadian High Arctic, scouting a location for a film about vanishing beluga whales, polar bears, and other lost and emergent interspecies relationships. Out on the land, living under the midnight sun, I soon found myself as transfixed by the constant presence of the brightly luminous arctic wildflowers as by anything the bears or the whales offered.

The predominant geology was a broken-up shale as thin as potato chips. With no soil to speak of, the tiny plants that thrived on this brittle, dry, crumbly earth lay scattered about in splendid isolation from one another. Sometimes fifty yards or more of bare ground lay between each diminutive plant. But every so often, while crunching around in the potato-chip barrens, I would stumble upon a veritable eruption of flowers growing together so exuberantly as to create their own significant hummock. So much relative fertility focused upon one particular spot in an otherwise homogenous wasteland seemed an anomaly to me. I started searching around for a pattern or a reason to explain it. But I never found, for instance, some significant trickle of fresh water running just below the top layer of shale. I never found anything at all.

These randomly placed hummocks of vegetative exuberance were the most remarkable rock gardens I have ever seen. Ivory-colored saxifrages, moss campions, alpine poppies, and smoky-waving cotton grass huddled like jewels in the shale. Hundred-year-old willows composed of quite a bit more root than trunk, and utterly contorted by the weather, spread across fifty square feet of ground, although never more than four inches tall and never thicker than a pencil. Bloodred mosses were rimmed in Day-Glo golden mosses rimmed in vivid green mosses and everywhere speckled with inch-tall, beige staghorn fungus. I was especially charmed by a grape-sized white balloon of a flower possessing velvety purple stripes running down its sides and later identified as an arctic campion.

Every day something new came into bloom, while something old went to seed.

All day long and all night long the sun circled the horizon, never setting, and thus never ceasing to cast exaggerated shadows in the unique manner it assumes in those climes of twenty-four-hour daylight. The filtering effects caused by the varying positions of the sun also altered the colors of the landscape so predictably that I developed a nearly astronomical sensibility to the plants—as if the sun and the flowers were two aspects of the same cosmology. When the monochromatic ochre moss of noon started shimmering as if lit up by a golden light from inside, I figured it must be about 6:00 P.M. When the same scene looked chartreuse, I guessed it must be midnight. And when it took on a nearly monochromatic gray-green cast, it had to be 3:00 A.M.

One afternoon I took a long walk along a gravel beach with my Inuit guide, Simon, and his twelve-year-old son, Norman. After a few miles we came upon the carcass of a musk-ox. The skeleton lay in one pile, while a semidecayed, although odorless, mass of hair and flesh lay a bit farther up the slope. Simon bent down to examine the hair pile: sniffed at it, turned it over with his hands, and finally stood up and smiled. He explained in halting English that the herd had been attacked by wolves two years previously, driven from the security of the plateau down to the very edge of the open saltwater bay, which almost certainly forced the musk-oxen to first give up their defensive circle of sharp horns facing outward and then, finally, to bolt. He explained this tactic as "a great wolf trick, huh? Hahaha" that finally left this two-year-old calf unprotected. The animal was probably killed at the edge of the water and then dragged a hundred feet up the slope of the gravel beach where it was consumed. The wolves returned to the carcass at least one more time, which caused the skeleton to now lay in a different pile than the offal.

He then informed me that it would take about ten years for this mound of flesh and hair to decompose into a hummock capable of supporting plants. His matter-of-fact answer to my unasked question about the placement of all those glorious gardens startled me for its simplicity. There was nothing arbitrary about it. Instead, these wonderful rock gardens contained a very precise record of predation within this sparse environment over the last several hundred years.

My perception of the pretty little flower beds altered accordingly. That moss over there? Did it mark the place where a caribou was overtaken by polar bears a hundred years ago? Or perhaps it was formed five thousand years ago when a beluga whale stranded at a moment in time when the beach itself washed a hundred feet higher up the slope than it does now. Were the remains of the carcass slowly consumed by blowfly larvae? And was there a natural progression of plant types germinating in the rich debris, something along the lines of fireweed preceding salal preceding red cedar in the place I call home? When I asked him about it, Simon shrugged his shoulders. His gesture declared to me that, after all, he was an Inuit hunter and not a gardener.

Strange feelings about time and timelessness soon arose in me. I started hiking the land in search of more hummocks. Larger hummocks. Brighter hummocks. I found one whose center contained a very angry jaeger sitting on eggs. Another one held a network of lemming tunnels. I would sometimes sit down at the edges of a hummock, take off my hiking boots, and tickle my feet on the luxurious moss. In fact, the polar landscape ceased being bleak the moment I sat down in it. It verified my hunch that we gardeners are shortsighted at best, and anthropocentric at worst, when we define any garden as "the control of nature by man."

Occasionally, I lay down right in the center of a hummock and inevitably perceived myself as one more primeval pile of mammal remains. I'd close my eyes, listen to the unceasing wind, and hold my breath as if practicing some exotic yoga of place meant to resurrect all the cataclysmic secrets strewn across an epochal scale. Though I obviously sought some understanding about the place, I didn't know quite what it was. The more connected I got, the more alive I felt. And the less I was able to verbalize it.

I lay there on a little hummock of arctic poppies wrapped in several layers of polypropylene and Gore-Tex and imagined myself not as an outsider trying to absorb something of the spirit of the place but as a co-creative participant in that same process. How would I interact with this protracted gardening process if I lived here? Nothing came readily to mind until I imagined building soil. I would find a suitable spot on the gravel and then wait patiently for a polar bear to arrive and exact the coup de grace. I envisioned my relatively hairless carcass eaten up by a large predator. The undigestible parts would be excreted on the spot, that scat later consumed by ravens and finally excreted a second time over a much larger area.

Five years afterward, little flowers would start sprouting wherever raven droppings settled. Where my phosphorus- and calcium-rich skeleton finally found its rest eventually grew an entire hummock, probably with dimensions slightly larger than my own current frame, say seven feet long and three feet wide. If my bones were deposited on a slope, that hummock would probably spread across the ground disproportionate to my own original shape, somewhat like the way a shadow clings to a slope. All water-borne nutrients would succumb to gravity, my former self finally transformed into a soil garden: my organic compounds seeping into the ground, slithering down trails in the potato-chip shale while the long deep roots of plants locate the rich soup from ever-greater distances. The mosses and the fungi and the ground willows and the many varieties of colorful flowers would alter my shape once again to twice or three times its original dimensions.

I stopped to examine the balloon flowers and saw myself as a shape shifter. I watched a parasitic jaeger diving for fish and wondered if one of its heirs might someday build its nest within a miniature willow thicket grown up around my bones. But when might that be? A hundred years after my demise? And in a thousand years? How many generations of arctic birds would I have succored in this, the most severe of planet Earth's gardening collaborations?

If these morbid images seem unnecessarily melodramatic, I must add that it was a real emotion abetted by the fact that there were so many polar bears in the immediate vicinity. I was a prey animal in a land full of predators, and it caused me to constantly scan the ice floes and whirl about to check my rear. In fact, this singular sensation of always being on guard against predation has long remained the strongest memory of camping on that little bay.

I lived in that place in the presence of the sacred. But what I actually felt there, experienced there—an unnameable sensation which I now name a sacred sense of place—seems as far removed from the actual telling of this story as the capability of a disk of computer software is removed from a cursory examination of its ones-and-zeros code.

Mircea Eliade writes that premodern societies viewed the world from two angles: the profane and the sacred. First, all things in nature are profane, meaning that they are material, substantial. The profane world is disorganized, chaotic, and therefore usually uncontrollable and even menacing. As unmanageable as the profane world seems to get, its peril is balanced by the existence of a fixed and stable sacred world.[1] Within the sacred world everything possesses a spiritual essence, a soul, an order, and an intrinsic connection to the larger web of life. Tapping into the sacred world also offers believers the best chance of neutralizing many of the worst hazards thrown up by the profane world. The medieval view of heaven and hell, and the Oriental view of yin and yang, might be understood as two familiar adaptations of this very ancient way of perceiving the universe.

Sacred places were utilized by many indigenous cultures for coming into close contact with the sacred. These places connected people directly to the eternal, the mythical. A sacred place could occur in the landscape. It might be a holy mountain, a grove of trees, or an unusual rock formation. But it might also be man-made. For some cultures, home itself was regarded as a sacred space. In any case, the sacred space was an ideal space. But it was never regarded as a mere invention of the intellect. This was no social design like Utopia, no abstract plan for paradise, no nowhere garden. A sacred place was a real place, and people often visited it. Visiting a sacred place lent a distinct sense of order to the geography of home.

Our own culture tends to utilize the techniques of science to access a place. We measure the size of a locale, inventory its ecology, calculate its mineral composition, grant it a certain monetary value—in so many ways quantify a place's relationship to society. As often as not, the process of quantification leads to control and exploitation. We might even stretch a point and regard it as a nonsacred technique for neutralizing the chaos of the profane world.

Favoring these methodologies of access, our culture tends to repress non-utilitarian relationships to place. It was for this reason that Eliade characterized modern society as "nonreligious," in the sense that it has desacralized and de-mythologized the world. Although we today may intellectually comprehend the two realms of the sacred and the profane just as well as any indigenous man or woman, we do not know how to live their way. Writing about this dilemma, cultural commentator Witold Rybczynski concludes that for us, there can only be profane space and profane time.[2] The reasons are as complex as culture itself, although anyone taught to regard land as property to buy and sell is much more prone to treat nature as an object.

Sacred places are not accessed for the purpose of "understanding" as science hopes to understand nature. Land is not an almanac of numbers waiting to be compiled. Nor are sacred places accessed for their material benefits. Traditional peoples utilized sacred places instead to access the holy, the eternal, the infinite. The sacred sense of place might be best explained as a kind of physical umbilical located at a specific site that connected people directly to the mystical order of the universe. This form of access led not to knowledge or to fortune but to communion: a sense of spiritual participation with the very process of living.

Likewise, the concept of sacred time was utilized in the form of recurring rituals and ceremonies that reintegrated human beings with the eternal. Sacred time has nothing to do with clocks. Sacred time might even be construed as the duration in which time has no meaning.

This sense of the sacred was seamlessly integrated into all aspects of the lives of traditional peoples. A person immersed in a sacred life not only *comprehended* the sacred as a wellspring of order and meaning but ate it, trod upon it, breathed it. We are, by contrast, largely the children of a materialistic worldview that attempts to provide a parallel sense of order and meaning to our lives by withholding a sacred worldview.

That may be the primary reason that the modern English language is currently so meager in words describing the spiritual bond that connects people to place. This book, for instance, has named the relationship *a sense of place*, although certainly the word *sense*, by itself, offers very little acknowledgment of the sacred. We Westerners tend to use the words *sacred* and *spiritual* either tenuously or at least restively. Here are two words that are meant to signify a human being's most profound relationship to the universe, yet we seem to have gone out of our way to obfuscate our own personal perception of it by adding an opaque layer of theological connotations.

Modern religions build churches, synagogues, and mosques to mark the place where spirit resides. Most of us end up believing that it is the building (and to a lesser extent the community of like-minded believers) that makes a place fit for prayer, and not a place's intrinsic natural essence.[3] Most modern religions encourage little or no sense of place because their beliefs were formulated to be expressed anywhere and everywhere. Historically, this Western sense of religious ubiquity has long been wed to the exclusivist belief that Christianity is the only true faith. Together, the two ideas offer a prime rationale for evangelism. They go far to explain the West's century-old putsch to destroy native traditions even as we reeducate indigenous people to our own profane relationship to nature.

Perhaps the best that Judaism or Christianity can offer in the way of a sacred sense of place is the concept of a spiritual pilgrimage to sites like Lourdes or Fatima where miracles are said to have occurred. Once a holy site is validated as sacred, its original natural context is just as often destroyed. This clearly indicates that it was never the actual dirt and plants that were sacred but rather the visitation by God or Mary.

Now that the concept of Gaia is slowly gathering momentum in scientific circles, more people are becoming aware that our culture has no spiritual foundation to explain what this ingrained relationship to nature could signify for each of us individually. Neither Judaism nor Christianity teaches us that nature is alive and capable of interceding in our lives in a positive, spiritually enhancing manner. We have never been taught what it might mean for us to commune with trees, to treat other species as peers with rights, to relate to mountains as animate, to live in balance with the air, to feel the pulse of the ocean in our own blood. We have never experienced a sense of give-and-take with the soil and the rocks. Perhaps tragically, until the environmental crisis began to stare us right in the face, we were never given any incentive whatsoever to adopt a societal ethic focused on natural balance. Techniques to hear nature better are precisely what a sacred sense of place offers us.

In an address entitled "A Basic Call to Consciousness" delivered at the United Nations Conference on Indigenous Peoples held in 1977, representatives from the Iroquois Nation attempted to put the Judeo-Christian "placeless" view of the sacred into context by declaring that "the majority of the world does not find its roots in Western Culture or tradition. The majority of the world finds its roots in the Natural World, and it is the Natural World, and the traditions of the Natural World, which must prevail."[4]

Since the days of Rousseau it has been fashionable for natural philosophers, and later environmentalists, to promote Native American spirituality. Proponents argue that this is the worldview most capable of leading us in our dire need to rediscover nature as a source of the sacred. Detractors are likewise quick to point out that so-called pagan societies were woefully ignorant about how the world actually worked. The ethics that developed from the Native American spiritual worldview were essentially flawed because the spirituality itself was steeped in ignorance.

All of the above may be true. On the other hand, anyone seeking a prototype upon which to develop a modern *sacred* sense of place can find no better example than the spiritual worldview lived by, for instance, the Lakota, the Okanagan, or the Inuit. Environmental psychologist James Swan writes: "In Western Society, if one talks to God, it is called prayer, but if God talks back to someone it is symptomatic of psychosis. In contrast, among the Inuit and other shamanic cultures, if spiritual voices do not come to one's mental ears then one is considered mentally ill."[5]

These same Inuit also believed that God was one with the land and the creatures who dwelled thereon. Intriguingly, they had no sense of any special natural areas set aside purely for preservation or recreational opportunities. The English word *park*, for instance, is translated into Inuktuk as "a place where white people play." Other languages and other cultures do just as well as Inuit's Inuktuk. For instance, the Sanskrit word *svaha* connotes a sacred place, or more precisely "the place within a place," where the spirit of nature is said to reside within a person. Likewise, *svaha* echoes the purpose of the Mayan compass. In that same Iroquois address, Western political ideals about freedom and liberation are depicted as woefully anthropocentric in their scope. They are thus incredibly vain as an expression about how to best live life on Earth. "The people who are living on this planet need to break from the concept of human liberation, and begin to see liberation as something that needs to be extended to the whole of the Natural World . . . the liberation of all things that support Life—the air, the water, the trees—all the things that support the sacred web of Life."[6]

The Anishinabeg people of Canada have a word, *pimaatisiiwin*, vaguely translated as "the good life" and meant to pinpoint the sensibilities a people acquire through the continuous inhabitation of a place. As Anishinabeg spokesperson Winona LaDuke has written, "*Pimaatisiiwin* is what we are to strive for, as individuals, as families, as communities. Implicit in *pimaatisiiwin* are two basic tenets: cyclical thinking and reciprocal relations."[7] Cyclical thinking perceives of the world "working" in terms of a natural order of birth and rebirth: what we sometimes refer to as the feminine aspects of moon, tides, and seasons. Thinking cyclically, whatever one does today will always "come around" again, in the cycle of time. The second tenet, reciprocal relations, defines "the responsibilities inherent between a people and the ecosystem."[8] The Anishinabeg believe the plants, the animals, the soil, the stones, are all animate, all have a "standing" of their own within the extended community.

Speaking at a conference of scientists and social theorists, Jeannette Armstrong, representing the Okanagan of eastern Washington, reminded her audience that the human race means different things to different people.

> The way we talk about ourselves as Okanagan people is difficult to replicate in English. Our word for people, for humanity, is difficult to say without talking about a connection to the land. The Okanagan word for ourselves means [the ones who are dream and land together]. . . It means that we are part of the land. We

are torn from the land. We are a piece of the land. Before anything else, we are the living, dreaming, Earth pieces.[9]

The Lakota of the northern Plains have a term, *wakonda*, variously translated as a divine object, "the life force," and other times as the process manifested to invoke that life force: "making medicine." Its second meaning is vaguely analogous to our modern sense of prayer, although it seems to involve a bit more than simply supplicating their God, more than repeating certain set words and phrases. The Lakota make medicine by taking sweats, smoking herbs, sitting squarely on the ground, and conducting specific ceremonies at specific locales. Making medicine at certain places has the ability to heal us in particular ways by linking us directly to the healing spirit of a place. Like the Okanagan, the Lakota view themselves as pieces of Earth. The act of healing a person, either oneself or someone else, is ultimately regarded as the same act as healing the Earth. The two cannot occur separately.

Not only is "making medicine" a quite different process than offering prayer to a God who lives everywhere (and thus nowhere in particular), making medicine is also something very different from what doctors do to us. We do not expect our doctors to pray for us; we might complain if they prescribed pilgrimages to heal us. Nor does any medical school teach its doctors that they are healing the planet through the healing of individuals. Healing a place, an ecosystem, a habitat, is the job of biologists, ecologists, land managers. None of us expects these professional stewards of place to take responsibility for healing the people who reside there.

The English concept of God provides us with nothing commensurate to *pimaatisiiwin* or to "making medicine." Dolores LaChapelle writes that even *Wakan Tanka*, often translated as a Lakota God known as the Great Spirit, was never comprehended as a "god" or even a "spirit" in the Western sense of the words. The Lakota Bob Bunge translates it as "that which flows through all things."[10] This sense of a sacred flow or field seems much closer to the conviction expressed in the chapter on the remedy garden by the modern herbalist David Hoffmann, who views healing herbs as capable of drawing a person into the circulatory system of Gaia. In such a manner, Hoffmann himself might be considered a new kind of gardener: a sacred gardener.

The Lakota were nomads and hunters, not gardeners. They foraged their vegetables and their herbs. Then again, the act of foraging has already been described as perhaps the essential aspect of any paradise garden—that state of grace described as walking around a locale simply picking whatever it is we want to eat in the moment. In terms of the sometimes upside-down conceptual themes of this book, we might thus regard the foraging (but nongardening) Lakota as preeminent paradise gardeners.

There is more to this than meets the eye. "Making medicine," for the Lakota, sometimes refers to making a pilgrimage to a specific plot of ground in the cause of health. An active relationship to place promotes curing. In such a manner, we might regard these Lakota nongardeners as remedy gardeners. Or consider that the act of nurturing place in the cause of a place's *own* health is the ultimate goal of both *pimaatisiiwin* and the one-tree gardener.

In the ancient Chinese geomancy known as *feng shui*, the land is said to shape the people who live upon it. Literally meaning "wind-water," *feng shui* might be understood as the Chinese version of the Lakota's "making medicine": the healing art of harmonizing *chi*—the life force of the land and atmosphere—with the *chi*, the life force of humanity.[11] Practitioners of *feng shui* assert that fertile soil breeds healthy people, unhealthy people live on poor soil, people who live on loamy soil grow fat, while sandy-soiled inhabitants grow thin. Practitioners of *feng shui* were conservationists long before conservation was fashionable.[12] The advice they gave concerning the soil makes it clear that they were also gardeners.

Feng shui also teaches that people possess two souls. The *shen* soul is associated with the heavens; the *kewi* soul relates to the Earth. We exist precisely at the intersection, the middle ground, between heaven and Earth. This leads to yet another idea that distinguishes many sacred traditions from Western religion: heaven and Earth are equally sacred. Neither is profane. The sacred equanimity between heaven and Earth offers an essential lesson for modern culture. For instance, reinterpreting the current environmental crisis through the lens of *feng shui*, we understand it as the just consequence of a people who placed too much emphasis on apotheosizing a heavenly disembodied soul, which caused them to lose their earthly soul in the process.

In the discussion of the local garden, Michael Pollan suggested that gardening offers an *environmental* middle ground between the lawn and the forest. The garden is the place we meet nature halfway.[13] *Feng shui* proposes that the garden offers a *sacred* middle ground as well. It lies at the middle ground where the Earth meets heaven—in other words, wherever human souls are found.

While the drive we utilize to build our world is noticeably lacking an expression of the sacred, the environment upon which we build our world is in dire straits. *Feng shui* counsels that the two realities exist in a cause-and-effect relationship. Then again, most of us have no interest in remolding our lifestyle to the nonscientific agrarian ideals offered by *feng shui*. Few of us are interested in basing our lives, our homes, our communities, to reflect the primitive lifestyle of the preconquest Lakota, Okanagan, or Anishinabeg.

Some would argue that our culture *must* return to these "other ways" or face certain environmental collapse. I would attenuate this idea. We don't have to live as the preconquest Indians did. We couldn't if we wanted to. But recognizing that our consumptive culture cannot continue "as is" bodes for a fundamental transformation in lifestyle. A new societal lifestyle lies in wait just over the horizon. It will manifest depending on our choices concerning consumption. The most important choice may not be precisely about what specific products and technologies we decide to curtail or not curtail. It goes deeper than that: points directly at the issue of our perception of the sacred. Do we or do we not embrace the sacred within nature? The result of that choice may well emerge as the great clarifying issue of the next half century.

A new philosophy called *deep ecology* has recently ascended from within the greater environmental movement. Deep ecology attempts to redefine a person's, a community's, a nation's, and a species' ecological relationship to the planet as a sacred relationship. Many deep ecologists declare that the best thing we human beings can do for the natural environment is to first repair the immediate damage and then learn to leave the remaining wilderness alone. They believe that our species will never solve its environmental problems until we likewise learn to recognize and honor the sacred in nature. In other words, a revitalized sense of the sacred is the only lasting environmental remedy. Nothing else besides a sacred sense of place will ever break the back of the destructive causality.

So far, this chapter's premise of learning to experience the Earth as sacred is not that different from the platform espoused by the deep ecology movement. But deep ecologists anoint *wilderness* as the only true fount of the sacred. There is, however, a perceptual danger in pigeonholing our experience of the sacred by exalting exotic environments—whether it's a special church, a synagogue, or southeastern Utah.

Perhaps unintentionally, when deep ecologists exalt wilderness to the exclusion of the rest of the world, they tend to limit an apperception of the sacred to a small cadre of wilderness aficionados. By denying the equally sacred potential of the "middle ground" that lies at the center of all our lives, they limit their very important message to a wilderness priesthood. The whole world needs to experience the sacred places in nature. But this is not meant to imply that the human race would be negligent or nearsighted to treat the remaining wild areas as cathedrals of planet Earth. As described in some detail at the beginning of this chapter, my own arctic experience of wilderness led me to crystallize an idea of rediscovering a sense of place inside the garden. Indeed, wilderness is profound. The message of deep ecology is likewise profound, even though, in this one way, it limits itself by exalting wilderness to the exclusion of other places.

How else might we re-vision a sacred relationship to the Earth from out of the center of a profane culture? I would suggest that an enhanced sense of place offers a very clear path leading toward a reinvestiture of the sacred in our lives. And the garden, the sacred garden, is what we already have at our disposal to rebuild this ancient path. The environmental crisis *is* a crisis in perception. A sacred perception of the garden might lead to new insights about cities, suburbs, and farms—all the places human beings actually dwell. It is one essential tool in remolding culture to embrace the sacred on a daily basis.

The sacred garden is the place we go to contemplate our own two souls of heaven and Earth. In the process of doing so, we cultivate a sense of the sacred in our lives. Although we may plant flowers and vegetables there, the sacred garden is better understood as the place we plant our feet. It could be a quiet corner we visit to sit and admire a tree. In that sense of *sitting*, and not necessarily *doing*, people like the nongardening Lakota emerge as our mentors in the cultivation of the sacred garden.

Obviously, our deepest ideas about the garden need much alteration if they are to serve us in such an exalted way. Such a depiction of a garden not bound to digging soil, planting flowers, and harvesting fruits and vegetables goes far beyond the classic European view of what a garden is. Then again, the Japanese raked garden has little to do with digging, planting, and harvesting, and yet no one would suggest that the Zen monks who tend it are not gardeners.

At any rate, of all the gardens in this book, the sacred garden may have the least to do with the traditional European garden. It is certainly not about the control of nature for aesthetic purposes. Nor does it follow any specific garden design. To know it we may first need to discover the place where gardening intersects with *pimaatisiiwin*, intersects with "making medicine," with *svaha, feng shui,* and all the other ideas human beings have accumulated throughout history to express a sacred relationship to place.

If there is to be a deep ecology, there must also be a deep gardening. It involves deep hoeing, deep digging, deep planting, deep harvesting, deep sitting, deep listening . . . deep interacting with natural processes. Deep gardening happens in the sacred garden.

These sentiments should be familiar by now because we have already visited this garden under another guise. The sentient garden earlier demonstrated that a garden need not be passive, the mere recipient of our labors, a controllable object waiting to be assembled. It is, instead, active, a thing capable of assembling. It possesses a co-creative, interpenetrating aspect that dynamically links human beings to place. Because the sentient garden is a place where "voices come to one's mental ears," it flirts with the mystical even as it endorses what the Inuit refer to as health. Just knowing it makes medicine.

Many gardeners already recognize "flirting with the mystical" as a common experience of gardening. The sacred garden transforms this flirtation into the precious gift of unconditional love.

Discursive prose is best suited for transmitting images, ideas, stories, and facts, whereas the cusp where a person meets the sacred is infinite and eternal. Faith does not originate in the brain or in the mind's eye, but in the heart. Relying on words to describe spiritual matters—no matter how beautifully expressed—disengages the sacred from its extra-experiential center. Our sense of the sacred is corrupted in the process.

We writers try hard to explain the unexplainable, which may explain why so many essays about the sacred end up sounding like mush. As I myself learned while trying to describe the elusive fragrance of an alba rose, the language of "such-ness" simply doesn't cut it.

A language of riddles and innuendo may serve better. Regard the sacred garden as the ultimate nowhere garden that can be found anywhere once we know how to experience it. The sacred garden is also a remedy garden, although it does not necessarily grow the herbs of our well-being. Well-being pours forth no matter what grows inside its beds. The sacred garden is also a soil garden that grows food, not so much for the belly as for the soul. Or consider it a semi-real garden whose only ornament is a Mayan compass pointing simultaneously out toward the flowers *and* in toward the gardener. It is a local garden that makes us feel at home wherever we may be at any moment. The sacred garden is all these gardens. So it is a sentient garden that tells and retells the compassionate story of humanity's wounded perception of Gaia. And with that invocation of Gaia, we are once again confronted with an unconventional garden that is no metaphor.

As the inadequate language of the sacred insists, this garden is also none of the above. On that note, take a leap of faith with me.

The sacred garden is four-dimensional: not just a place but also a time. Or stated precisely, the sacred garden emerges when a sense of place is wed to a sense of the timeless. The one-tree garden, resplendent in its sequoia-tree imagery of the generations, offers a good prototype for creating a sacred garden. Temporal charisma, first explained in that context, is a key attribute of any sacred garden. Let's explore the signs.

Old roses—the gallicas, damasks, albas, centifolias, Chinas, as well as their close progeny—also possess temporal charisma. Like angels and sequoia trees, they seem to live forever. A gardener cognizant of an old rose's complex lineage develops a sense of interacting with the eternal. A visit to Appomattox Courthouse in Virginia reveals an old China rose known as Old Blush growing by the doorway. A Mathew Brady photograph of Lee surrendering to Grant at the courthouse in 1865 displays the exact same plant growing there.[14] There is an old rose growing in Germany reputedly planted a thousand years ago by Charlemagne himself.

There is something else at play here besides extended age. Many old roses are the happy result of chance pollinations. The original parents of some of the choicest of the old cultivars have never been identified, and in many cases the parent plants are extinct. That is why so many old roses can only be propagated from cuttings. Rooting a cutting from an old rose is one of life's most mysterious rituals. A gardener snips off a branch with two or three joints. He or she sets it in a peaty soil and keeps it moist at all times. With luck, roots will sprout, leaves will erupt from a joint. The lineage is extended one more generation.

But the rose we root today is not just a *descendant* of some old cherished flower that Napoleon wore in his buttonhole or Richard III wore in his cloak or even Cleopatra wore in her tunic. No birds, no bees, no seed, was ever involved. That new rose is not precisely a baby. It's not even a new plant. It is, rather, a clone—an actual piece of the original plant. In such a manner it lends to the gardener a deep sense of continuity with all the other rose gardeners throughout history who took their own cuttings, got the branch to root, and then passed on their successes to loved ones, friends, and customers. Knowing this process for what it is can be a very humbling experience and a spiritual resource that offers an invaluable lesson in grounding. These semi-real old roses link our own garden with every other garden that ever grew them. I would offer that this is a sacred connection.

Historian Keith Thomas has written that the notion of a garden as spiritual resource is deeply embedded in the human psyche. During the late eighteenth century, it led to the so-called garden cemetery movement. One of its spokespeople, the poet William Wordsworth, maintained that urban cemeteries were inadequate, "for the want of the soothing influences of nature." Wordsworth's now forgotten contemporary, the poet John Edwards, urged that the dead be buried in rural areas—not because urban cemeteries posed a health hazard for the living, but because they were spiritually inadequate to the souls of the departed.[15]

A Haida carver approached a tree with reverence, made an offering of cornmeal, and asked its permission to cut off a branch—in effect inviting the tree's spirit to be present in the carving process.[16] This holy relationship between plant and human is by no means confined to North America. Traditional shamans in many different cultures kept a sacred tree as the axis upon which to mind-journey to the worlds above and below. The groves we associate with the Druids of ancient England illustrate a sacred view of plant life that extended over thousands of years.

The Egyptian god Osiris was closely associated with the growing of wheat. Religious holidays, including the Christian Easter and the Jewish Sukkoth, originated as ritual observances of the spring planting and fall harvest. In such a manner, every religion in the world gathers a significant part of its *original* symbology from a recognition of the sacred garden.

Each of these examples also demonstrates that the sacred garden exists only as we relate to it and not as any specific garden design. One does not ring up a landscape architect to order a sacred garden. That explains its relationship to the nowhere garden. Should we locate it, we find that it draws us into itself. We are one aspect of its wholeness, which prompts an overwhelming sense of integration. At the moment of recognition, we may realize that we exist as its only reified aspect. The main task of any sacred gardener is supplying human awareness to the garden. In that manner, the sacred garden is the cosmologist's *anthropic principle* brought back down to Earth again and planted along with all the other seeds and cuttings.

Mircea Eliade made the strong case that we live in a profane time. Our window to the sacred is much reduced. Likewise, many writers, social critics, environmentalists, and philosophers are now suggesting that the survival of civilization is dependent upon a reinvestiture of the sacred within our lives. Yet imagining any passage from the profane to the sacred seems fraught with peril. Should some idealistic future administration in Washington, D.C., or Tokyo or Paris or Moscow suddenly pass programs to reinvest its people's relationship to nature with a sacred quality, it would cause a drastic alteration in all resource-dependent activities. Society might come to a halt, founded as it is upon a profane motif: a quantitative, unbalanced, consumer-oriented relationship to the Earth. If so, then how do we begin the transformation without also destroying ourselves in the process?

In some quarters, even to propose opening that sacred window onto nature causes fear and reaction. Jobs would be sacrificed, lifestyles altered, religions compromised, even lives ended. Some of us would rather sacrifice the last spotted owl, cut down the last ancient forest, if such an act bolsters that old lifestyle for just a few more years. Contrarily, the signs of nature's demise are everywhere. We know we must throw open the window. And though some of us may not survive if we do, all of us may not survive if we don't. The dangers are real. Some argue that we face them or perish.

The path leading into the sacred garden travels much less dangerous terrain. It takes the opposite tack: imposing change not from outside and above, but from inside and from the soil right under our feet. We make the changes ourselves because we come to understand that they are life enhancing. Gardeners already love their gardens; a growing minority of them already treat their gardens with a deep and abiding respect. Perceiving the sacred garden thus emerges as a first gentle step in a greater reinvestiture of the sacred in nature. Regard it as the elementary school, the primer, the playground. But although it is a gentle path, it also has its danger. Like so many of the garden paths we have trod in this book, once we pass through the gates of the sacred garden, we may eventually find ourselves getting sucked into the center of a cyclone. There is no turning back.

It can be difficult to achieve a sacred relationship to the Earth living on a suburban or urban plot. There is simply less chance of feeling suspended within a protective bubble apart from the hubbub. The profane scenery is simply too close at hand. At best, we enjoy a brief interlude away from the incessant ticking of the social clock. The Japanese recognized this problem centuries ago, which is precisely the reason they invented the concept of *shakkei*, or borrowed landscape. That which we cannot hide, we do better to incorporate. By doing so, we attenuate the grating presence of the hubbub. It becomes an integral aspect of the garden's overall aesthetic. Unfortunately, unless *shakkei* is employed with great artistry, it can work in the other direction as well, compromising whatever restive powers a garden already has.

Despite this single artful device, we might justly conclude that the sacred garden is more often large and luxuriant, something more on the lines of the grand four-tree gardens of the English aristocracy. This is, of course, the garden type upon which we already base our contemporary ideal. Unfortunately, acknowledging this state of affairs also implies that the sacred garden can only be actualized by the wealthy. It is the rich man's plaything and not the sacred expression of his own day laborers. We live in a culture that sanctifies expressions of wealth, which offers a good reason why the rich man's garden has emerged as our ideal. But the sacred garden is more a relationship than it is an ideal or even a place. It possesses no special set of physical attributes. Nor does it become more sacred when we invest it with more labor. More money.

Some might believe, just as incorrectly, that the gardener's primary job within a sacred garden is doing nothing. This is not true. There can be no idle passing of time. The sacred garden exists as the gardener's own deep contemplation and loss of individual self. Although these acts are perhaps the least physically strenuous of any gardening labors, they demand more focus and more attentiveness than any other task in our lives. The distinguished Buddhist teacher Thich Nhat Han has developed a spiritual practice he calls *walking meditation*, which sometimes involves working up a sweat. In such a manner, gardeners have their gardening meditation. It includes deep digging, deep weeding, deep planting, sitting, interacting, et cetera.

Experiencing the sacred garden that cannot be designed or constructed is a difficult undertaking. Are there books to guide us? In fact, whereas the sentient garden had almost no literature devoted to its scope and potential, the sacred garden fares much better. The great horticulturist Luther Burbank made no secret of the fact that he used love and transcendence as the underlying modus operandi for his highly successful plant experimentation and development.[17] There are many Jewish commentaries on the sacred garden, none of them more beautifully written than those by the Ukrainian Rabbi Nahman of Bratslav. In the persuasive example excerpted below, he begins with a statement about a *sentient garden* singing to God. And yet, when we hear it as such, it is at that precise moment that the sacred garden emerges:

> *Every blade of grass sings poetry to God*
> *without ulterior motives or alien thoughts—*
> *without consideration of reward.*
> *How good and lovely it is then,*
> *when one is able to hear this song of the grasses.*
> *It is therefore a precious thing*

To conduct oneself with piety
When strolling among them.[18]

In contrast to this exultation, the unbounded gusto that leaps from the pages of so many gardening books seems merely enthusiastic. Yet many modern gardening books also allude to the contemplative sense of timelessness one encounters while walking the gardener's path. The fact that so few of them come right out and use the word *sacred* probably says more about our culture's current discomfit over labeling so-called nonreligious activities as spiritual than about the underlying feelings.

One recent book that confronts this issue openly is *To Honor the Earth*, whose author, Dorothy Maclean, is best known as one of the founders of the famous Findhorn Garden in northern Scotland. Her book contains a number of poetic channelings from nature and garden spirits. Whatever one may believe or disbelieve about the phenomenon known as channeling, the reflections she presents offer a powerful statement about the relationship known as the sacred garden. For instance, Maclean's horse chestnut spirit offers this: "When you grow gardens without awareness of the divine life as expressed through our kingdoms, you cut yourself off from a large part of life." The southernwood declares: "Our patterns, as expressed in the plant world, come through in perfection because they issue forth from a still center." And finally this from the fruit tree: "Nothing is worth doing unless it is done with joy; in any action, motives other than love and joy spoil the results. Could you imagine a flower growing as a duty and then sweetening the hearts of its beholders?"[19]

If the sacred garden seems so undeniably elusive—nearly Taoist in the contradictions implicit within its explication—how can any of us ever hope to design a landscape that meaningfully nurtures the sacred relationship? I have searched for a personal formula. In my quest to explore the relationship called the sacred garden, I was illogically drawn to the strange otherworldly bog plant known as *Gunnera manicata*. Gunnera is by no means beautiful in the traditional sense of plant beauty. In fact, it might have served as the prototype for the singing plant in *The*

Little Shop of Horrors, the one that keeps crying, "Feed me, I'm hungry." Its green, prickly leaves can measure over six feet across, each of them rising from the ground from its own thick stem, which is covered with quite lethal-looking shiny white thorns. The leaves look like giant hands, each one partially cupped, reaching up to the sky as if actively supplicating for sunlight and rain. The flower looks like a cross between a pineapple and a pinecone.

This gunnera is no pretty charmer like a rose or a Japanese maple. But it stops people in their tracks, serving as the garden's equivalent of a teacher of Zen picking up a stick and whacking a student across the back of the neck, while shouting at them to live in the present. Visitors to my garden may be thinking or talking about anything else. When they come upon the gunnera, they stop talking and simply stare, doing their best to take the measure of this unfamiliar giant.

The result is the same awe people reserve for large animals, old-growth forests, and long views. Like orcas, the gunnera may seem a bit menacing by virtue of its size and weaponry, although the disorientation it causes is quickly ameliorated by an indefinable sense that here lives a creature as fully realized and approachable by human beings as the natural world has to offer. One guest commented that those giant and veined upturned leaves looked as if they might be trying to communicate with us through a gunnera's version of sign language. With no trunk to speak of, the gunnera seems as if the Earth itself has sprouted hands.

The gunnera grows from the steep bank of a pond. Its leaves hang over the water attended by huge orange, feathery goldfish who often luxuriate in its shade. Each summer I place a single lawn chair in front of this one-gunnera garden. Some visitors sit down and soon get lost. I hear sighs break the stillness of the pondside silence. I have watched as visitors refocus their eyes and drop the set musculature of their faces, as if unconsciously signaling that they are no longer clinging tightly to the inside of their own thoughts. The gunnera and the pond and the goldfish have successfully conspired to roust their spirit out of its cranial hiding place and relocated it, if just for a moment, at the place where their own feet touch the ground. Only innuendo can explain it. That place, and not the place where the gunnera sprouts, is the center of the sacred garden.

Therein lies the reason that only indirectly am I the gardener of that place. I may have filled the pond with goldfish. I planted the gunnera. I surrounded it with Siberian irises and bamboo. I put out the lawn chair. Yet I have little to do with the sense of the sacred that arises there. In good Taoist fashion, I conclude that the gunnera offers nothing but an example. As such, it is possibly a distraction from any true comprehension of the sacred garden. As the Tao teaches: "The whole world says that my way is vast and resembles nothing. It is because it is vast that it resembles nothing. If it resembled anything, it would, long before now, have become small."[20]

October

Like most everyone else, plant retailers charge what the market bears. Nothing else can explain the lack of relationship between the ease of propagating certain plants and the retail cost of those same plants.

Take bamboo. It should be among the less expensive woody plants, at least in the Pacific Northwest. It can double or even triple the size of its shooting roots in just one season. Granted, it sometimes takes a couple of years to grow roots big enough to bring to market. With the help of a stout saw, one root can easily be divided into several pieces.

It is not perishable. A landscaper friend dug up several clumps of timber bamboo in August one year as a gift for my garden. But then she forgot about them. They sat bare root in her dark garage for four months. When I asked what had happened to them, she gasped, apologized profusely, and sent them off by mail the next day. It was a cold snowy December afternoon when I planted the clumps in the frozen ground. Yet they all survived and had attained a height of four feet by the following autumn.

For both these reasons, one would expect the price of bamboo to be more in line with tree peonies, sequoias, daphnes, or any of several other shrubs and trees that are not the world's most in-demand plants, yet which are not especially difficult to propagate. These others can be acquired for under twenty dollars, and occasionally half that. Bamboo rarely costs less than thirty dollars a root.

I cast no blame on retailers. In fact my own theory about the economics of bamboo retailing is more pro than anti nurseries. I like to believe that nursery managers price the plant so high as an altruistic gesture to protect the environment. Bamboo is one of the most invasive plants in nature. If a species like the giant timber bamboo were as cheap and as readily available as rhododendrons at the local chain stores, the United States could conceivably lose all its beautifully diverse urban forests faster than you can say *Phyllostachys bambusoides.* If retailers start to promote bamboo as they now do rhodies and roses, forest lovers might do well to picket the government to take drastic steps to save the giant pandas, which are, of course, the only creatures besides Zen monks that thrive in bamboo forests. Pandas will keep the bamboo in check.

I have always regarded nurseries as plant museums without an admission charge. My own knowledgeable gardening family piles out of the car and starts browsing the displays the same way we do at the aquarium. Every so often we pause in front of some shrub or tree and ask each other where would we plant this gem on the off chance we could afford it. If agreement on siting is reached, then, more out of curiosity than anything else, I nonchalantly steal a peek at the price tag. Forty dollars for a sixteen-inch maple sapling? No, impossible—many species of maple can be propagated by simply sticking a cut-off branch in wet peat moss. Someone must have put the decimal point in the wrong place. It's got to be four dollars. In fact, the price staring back at me seems just about as arbitrary as the bloat that passes for the price of an average painting in the average art gallery. I end up shaking my head and corralling my family back to browsing mode.

I am not unaware that this head-shaking routine also indicates that I'm long overdue in admitting that the days of the nickel pack of chewing gum are gone forever. Few people are getting rich in the nursery business.

The analogy of a nursery being some kind of freebie museum for plants is self-delusory because I never make it back to the car without buying several new plants. Perhaps a few more lobelias to plug up those holes in the patio boxes, or a must-buy pot of agrimony for my herb museum. The clever nursery owners cultivate the look and feel of free admission, while they end up laughing all the way to the bank. I watch my agrimony grow over the months and years, and feel just as contented as they do. By the way, during the Middle Ages agrimony was once mixed with pounded frogs and human blood as a cure for internal hemorrhaging.

I struck out a few years ago trying to find bare-root chestnuts in the local nurseries. Then I saw them for sale in one of those unsolicited plant catalogs that tend to describe every single item in exactly the same overblown superlatives. You know the one I'm talking about. "Wow!" "The best ever!" "Unbelievable harvests!!" Staring me in the face was a cartoonlike drawing of a huge, rounded, perfectly shaped chestnut tree loaded down with enough nuts to refresh anybody's memory of Fred Astaire and Ginger Rogers strolling down Park Avenue during any Christmas in the 1930s. The company wanted eight bucks for two trees. WOW! Now that was a low price. I called in my order immediately. I should have known better.

What arrived in the mail three months later might be kindly described as two sticks with little strings of roots sticking out of one end. I accorded those two meager sticks a treatment perhaps better reserved for baby condors or Queen Elizabeth's grandchildren; and one of them surprised me by putting out two leaves at the end of the summer. The other one was dead on arrival. Unfortunately, chestnuts demand two trees to produce nuts, so nearly a year after I placed my initial order, I called the mail-order house, described the death, and was tickled pink when they quickly agreed to send another stick. I received that third stick, lovingly stuck it in the ground, and then watched it wither away. Meanwhile, after two full years in the ground, the single living stick had four leaves. Some deal. Eight bucks for three trees with a total of four leaves after two years.

I visited a local nursery the next October and was nonplussed to find a whole row of six-foot-tall, exquisitely healthy and beautifully branching chestnut saplings for a mere twenty-nine dollars apiece. That's the reason I shall always choose to shop for trees in a nursery rather than through a catalog. You see what you get, and you get what you pay for.

October is the best month for bargain hunting. Plant retailers are trying to get rid of inventory before winter settles in. Anything in a one-gallon pot is better sold at a discount than relocated into a bigger pot (at a bigger price) and then stored over the entire winter.

I sometimes fantasize stumbling upon the secondhand-store version of a nursery.

The Weed Garden

Crabgrass may have been humanity's first grain crop. The Stone Age lake dwellers in Switzerland grew it. It has been a staple since prehistoric times in India, and in parts of Africa it is still used as the basis for porridge and bread. Native Americans did not eat it. As strange as it may seem to any mower of lawns, crabgrass is not indigenous to the Western Hemisphere. It did not appear in the United States until it was introduced by the U.S. Patent Office in 1849 as a promising new forage crop for livestock. The government referred to it as "foxtail millet," a translation of the name given it by the Chinese, who for centuries regarded it as an important food source.[1]

One hundred and fifty years later, the tenacious little monocot has naturalized across the width and breadth of this fair land. Today, when we regard crabgrass at all, it is as the number one weed pest of the suburban lawn. It may be the hands-down winner in nurturing the explosive growth of the North American herbicide industry.

As this thumbnail history of human-crabgrass relations is meant to demonstrate, humanity's weed problem supports a theory repeated many times throughout this book: that the environmental crisis is a crisis in perception.

Holistic-minded organic gardeners have always considered weeding to be an integral part of the gardening experience. Nonholistic gardeners disagree. They view weeding as an irksome task somehow separate from the "real" gardening work of planting, watering, and especially enjoying a tidy landscape. Holistic-minded gardeners shake their heads. Paying close attention to weeds teaches gardeners many things, for instance, humility in the face of nature's own insistent schedule. To them, there can be no separation. To imply there is seems a function of flawed perception—the result of viewing a garden as an object rather than a process.

The fairly recent advent of chemical herbicides has done little to alter either of these two variations on the one theme of human-weed relations. Holistic-minded organic gardeners avoid herbicides; their relationship to weeds has remained largely unchanged by the availability of the latest chemical fixes. They remain contented with, or at least resigned to, the daily task of dealing with weeds.

Meanwhile nonorganic gardeners grab up the herbicides that have become readily available over the past half century. They spray some of them on the garden and some more of them on the lawn. The process rids the yard of weeds while it expunges the gardener's annoyance over weeding. These nonorganic gardeners are quick to point out that a commitment to herbicides means less garden time wasted in weeding. The garden looks tidier, sooner.

Organic gardeners shake their heads. They repeat again that the process of weeding is inherent; it is not separate from the rest of the gardening process. Whether we weed thirty minutes and sit thirty minutes, or spread herbicides for twenty minutes and sit for forty minutes, we've still spent an hour inside the garden. Speaking of time, weeding forces human beings to slow down. That's good. Our clock-watching, nature-unheeding society can only benefit by learning to bend to nature's time.

Herbicide users point out that chemical use has its own advantages. A single gardener can manage a larger plot. Herbicides also permit greater yields. Organic gardeners shake their heads. To them, a garden is as big or small as a person can manage without getting annoyed. The very idea that garden efficiency increases as herbicide and chemical fertilizer usage increases has always seemed a marketing hoax. It's been disproven many times, as in the Chinese organic gardens that yield nine times more than an inorganic American farm. Organic gardeners assert that herbicides mostly fulfill a discontented consumer's yearning to employ new technology to replace the old.

So far neither side has even mentioned the poisonous effect that herbicide use has on the garden and the environment. That subject has been detailed so eloquently, and so many times, from Rachel Carson's *Silent Spring* to Louis Reggenstein's *America the Poisoned*, that it need not be dredged up again except as a brief statement about vexation: if the annoyance felt by nonholistic gardeners toward weeds seems about the same as it always was, the expression of that annoyance has changed mightily. Before herbicides, a gardener's discontent rarely led to poisoned soil, groundwater, earthworms, birds, pets, and, to a lesser extent, its human users. Now we all live with it.

There is still time to change our ways. We might consider resolving the problem of weeding by sidestepping herbicides in favor of a simple perceptual solution. For instance, we could deal with crabgrass's intractable "weediness" by giving it back its old Eastern European name of manna grits, a descriptive title suggesting the high esteem granted it by the Polish, Czech, Slovak, and Hungarian immigrants who ate it as a staple food and who stand most guilty for planting it everywhere they settled in North America. The concept seems breathtaking if not implausible: solving the dangerous herbicide problem that is currently spreading through suburbs all across America by employing public relations. Let's reintroduce manna grits back into the American diet.

But that's a dreamer's solution.

Depending on our creationist preference, either God or nature makes plants. But only a human being can make a weed. I reach that biblical conclusion because weeds are nothing else but plants that spring up where human beings do not want them. Often, weeds are the plants that originally evolved to fill the minor role of colonizing bare ground after fires, landslides, and floods. According to historian Alfred Crosby, all such plants "found themselves wonderfully preadapted to spread across the expanses stripped clean by the Neolithic farmer's plow or sickle."[2]

The invention of weeds probably occurred in the ancient Middle East in synchrony with the parallel invention of agriculture. The cultivation of wheat and barley in particular favored the laying bare of the soil twice a year, once before planting and once after harvesting. Wherever soil is laid bare, certain wild plants are always going to fill the void.

Already adapted to direct sunlight and disturbed soil, many weeds soon added a tolerance for compacted soil caused by boots, hooves, and wheels. Some of them, like the thistle, may have even adapted themselves to the brand-new human endeavor known as weeding. Adaptation continued unabated for four thousand years, the evolved weeds spreading as agriculture also spread across Asia and Europe. Over time some of the plants first regarded as weeds began to gain recognition as both low-maintenance foodstuffs and potent healing remedies. Dandelions and chickweed provided an easy source of greens. Along with mullein and tansy, they soon became mainstays of old-world remedy gardens.

Then came the European age of discovery. The stage was set for a botanical conquest probably unlike anything else in the history of life on Earth. These same Eurasian native plants—so tenacious and so admirably adapted to cleared ground—conquered the Americas and Australia as swiftly and completely as did their migrant human counterparts. The Europeans burned and plowed the earth wherever they conquered, completing the task of colonial inhabitation in a mere tick of the ecological clock. Jungle was turned into sugarcane plantations, prairie transformed to wheat fields, temperate forests into subsistence gardens.

The Eurasian weeds had a four-thousand-year head start over the natives at moving into the human-made environment. Innocent native flora, in the Americas as well as in Australia, never had time to adapt. By the time that certain fields were left fallow to be reclaimed by nature, the conquest was already complete. The native plants couldn't compete in their own changed land. That is the reason so many reclaimed areas of our country are today dominated by introduced plants.

The deed is done. Many wild plants that ten thousand years ago filled the small niche of quickly germinating on churned-up ground now reside in just about every other area of the globe possessed of similar climate and soil. Botanists even have a name for the global conquest by weeds. They refer to the result of that conquest— the homogenization of ecosystems—as the *emergent global ecology*. The needs of the dandelion, for instance, jibe admirably with the artificial ecological niche known as the cultivated lawn, which is why we today call it a weed. European thistles thrive all over America. The most common hedgerow tree in my own rural neighborhood is the introduced hawthorn. It is locally considered a weed.

Many American natives, including goldenrod and Oregon grape, were introduced to England and soon popped up in gardens as treasured ornamentals. Today, the British still treasure these imported species, while American gardeners will have little to do with them. One person's weed is another's specimen plant. Who cherishes what remains an issue of smoke and mirrors.

There were no dandelions, no Queen Anne's lace, no chickweed, no shepherd's purse, no groundsel, no nettles, no plantain, no mullein, no henbane, no tumbleweed—the list goes on and on—growing in the United States at the time of the European conquest. Intriguingly, almost every single one of the above-mentioned "weeds" was introduced *purposefully* by colonialists who carried the utilitarian seeds of their homeland in their bags, satchels, baskets, and trunks. Many maligned plants, including most of those mentioned above, have spread widely after transfer, usually as a result of introduction to gardens as ornamentals or food plants. Queen Anne's lace, for instance, is nothing more than a cultivated carrot gone feral.

Evidence suggests that nearly every one of a hundred and twenty different species of thistle presently growing wild in the United States was introduced by Europeans. The Puritan John Josselyn wrote of visiting an Indian village in New England in 1637. He found many of the indigenes suffering from "a stuffing of the lungs," which he duly cured with a well-known tonic of the age he prepared himself using a coveted store of imported thistles.[3]

The bane of my own property is the biennial bull thistle. It starts life as an aerodynamic white fluff not unlike a dandelion parasol. It catches the slightest breeze and rides the updrafts as elegantly as a raptor. Depending on wind conditions, the seed may land miles or even hundreds of miles away from the mother plant.

But that's just the start of the survival strategy of this wonder plant. Long before the bull thistle displays much of anything above ground, it has already sunk a long fleshy taproot deep into the earth. This taproot drills through compacted clay that I am unable to break up with a shovel. As anyone who's ever tried to eradicate a thistle by cutting its leaves or stalk soon finds out, this taproot sends up a greater spread of leaves each time the visible stem is cut back. Cut it back a few times, and the taproot might even split, sending up two plants within a week or two. I have to cut mine back four or five times before the root finally gives up the ghost.

Left to grow, the taproot soon sends up a dense whorl of leaves not unlike a bull's-eye target made out of pincushions. The edges of each leaf possess what is perhaps the thistle's best-known characteristic—its needlelike thorns. The gray-green prickly whorl of leaves grows outward rather than upward during the first summer of the plant's life. As if an insidious adaptation to lawn mower blades, the plant eventually achieves a two-foot spread although it rarely attains more than an inch in height. This yearling can hide all summer long in a field of four-inch-tall clover, proving the hypothesis that certain weeds have adapted splendidly to the ever-present threat of human weeding. It might never be seen at all until the clover dies back in the fall. But step on it barefoot, and this landmine of an introduced medicinal herb is guaranteed to cause a painful wound.

During the second season of the bull thistle's life, the plant sends up a glorious three-foot stalk of symmetrical foot-long leaves, which looks positively luminous when sunlight reflects off the translucent thorns. At the very center of this growing gray-green pincushion of leaves now emerges a shaving brush of a pink-purple flower protected by its own armor of sharp in-pointing needles. The genes of this clever flower do not restrict the blooming period to any precise week or month during the season. It therefore becomes quite useless for a farmer to designate a specific time of the summer to picking off all the flower heads. A bull thistle can bloom (and thus go to seed) anytime between late spring and frost.

Let us now repeat the strategies of this humble albeit Promethean plant. The airborne seeds make localized eradication virtually impossible. The thorns make it impossible to grab a hold on the plant to rip it out. The thorns also keep insects and slugs from preying on the succulent leaves. The taproot ensures that even if we grab hold of the plant, some small piece of root remains behind which may split into two thistles. The plant's ability to flower anytime means that neither spring flood, summer drought, September frost, nor especially a human weeder is going to impede its ability to set at least a few seeds during the course of a year. There is even some evidence that thistle seeds can lay ungerminated for years on the forest floor, as if biding their time in anticipation of the violent soil disturbances that occur only where human beings reside.

Given all this persistence, we are confronted by an especially wry parable about the state of human vanity in the face of raw nature to learn that it is "against the law" in thirty-seven states to allow a closely related species, the Canada thistle, to grow on one's land.[4] Can anyone doubt that the spiny fugitive happens to flourish everywhere the climate suits it? If only the spotted owl, the snail darter, and the Amazonian rain forest were so tenacious.

From an ecological perspective, the most perfidious weed accrues as many virtues as shortcomings. The seed of the bull thistle is a favorite food of the goldfinch, and the sight and sound of this gay yellow songbird lifts the human spirit anytime and any season. The red admiral butterfly favors the plant as a fortress nursery. It lays its eggs at the axis of the spiny leaves, where marauding ants cannot navigate the stems. Neither cattle nor deer are masochistic enough to nibble on the eggs inadvertently.

But it is the thistle's taproot that provides the plant's greatest utility to Mother Nature. Because the plant thrives where not much else will grow, we might regard the bull thistle as one of nature's foremost tools for fighting soil erosion. While my own land was a wild scrub forest, there were no thistles. As I mentioned in a previous chapter, one summer a bulldozer was brought in to level a small play area and dig a pond, tearing up a half acre in the process. The prickly immigrants soon moved in, favoring a clay dam that had been tamped down by the heavy bulldozer treads. I soon realized I couldn't have provided a more perfect thistle environment if the dam had been designed and cultivated only to encourage thistles. The first thistles germinated on the clay within a month. Those long taproots quickly sank themselves through a foot or more of compacted clay, breaking up the surface and preparing it for the less hardy plants that would inevitably follow. They held the sides of the dam in place until the winter-planted perennial clover (another European introduction) germinated the next spring.

The land I call home is too gnarly for a lawn mower. Instead, I "weedeat" the grounds five or six times each summer. I first don a dust mask to keep the grass pollen and gas fumes out of my nasal passages. Then I put on protective glasses to keep the twigs and dismembered slug bodies from flying into my eyes. I use earplugs because the whine of the machine is so loud. I wear old clothes because no matter how careful I am, everything about me, including shoes and shirts and hair, smells like gasoline after an hour's workout. When the job is done, when the engine has finally been stilled, my hands and my arms feel like ginger ale for another half hour. The case could thus be made that I am as much a casualty of the process as the thistles, quack grass, and Oregon grape.

I have never met a woman who enjoys weedeating, although I suppose there are some who do. Without meaning to sound sexist about it, I have observed that the women gardeners I know love to dig, plant, hand-weed—all nurturing tasks— but regard any yard maintenance dependent on the internal combustion engine to be a man's job. I do not deny that the machine is both smelly and noisy. I enjoy it nonetheless. Some pop psychologists might explain my enjoyment as the male's dark-sided instinct for conquest. This explanation has the ring of truth about it. Then again, weedeating makes me feel like just another weed busy molding a niche to fit its ecological desires. If weeds can recompose the land with such unbounded exuberance, why can't I?

Weedeating is different from lawn mowing. I regard it as lawn mowing for the individualist hunter/gatherer, a suburban warrior's version of weed maintenance. A weedeater operator targets individual plants one at a time, draws a bead on the quarry like a Jivaro hunter aiming a blowgun at a gamebird. Like a blowgunner displaying his prowess, I feel a certain pride at my hand-to-eye dexterity. When I'm focused, I am able to sever all the chickweed surrounding a patch of pole beans without so much as grazing a bean plant. I secretly compare this acquired adroitness to the light touch a guitar player employs to coax melodies from the strings. Am I the only one who views weedeating and guitar playing as parallel art forms? Whirrrr goes the rotating string blade. One more blackberry plant artfully severed at the root.

If weedeating seems a task fit for Jivaro hunters and B. B. King, lawn mowing seems a cross between Zen meditation and a parade-ground drill. Put on your ear mufflers and let your mind drift off into a cosmic blither even as your legs goose-step around the yard. But there's nothing artful or dexterous about it. The task offers the same nonrelationship to individual plants that a bombardier expresses to his individual victims when he pushes a red button to drop a bomb out of the belly of an airplane.

Granted, it's too bad that lawn mowers and weedeaters make so much noise. Too bad the fancy electric versions are useless in a big yard. But how else can we maintain a yard? Do we employ a herd of sheep, sometimes referred to as locusts on four hooves? Do we hire a congregation of servants with scythes as did the nineteenth-century English aristocrats who are responsible in the first place for popularizing the concept of the one-inch-tall lawn and the well-clipped garden path? Times have changed. No one today is willing to take a full day to accomplish with a scythe what a weedeater artist can accomplish in an hour—what a lawn mower can flatten in twenty minutes.

Over a hundred million Americans are said to garden. Certainly, many of them do so in a concerted effort to create a pocket paradise—a humble backyard Eden where they can walk in beauty and slow down the pace of their lives. How ironic then that they buy up a stable of hellish mechanical contrivances to help save a bit more time for feeling timeless. One might rightly wonder: do we gardeners find our timeless paradise in the garden or in our ongoing consumption of timesaving devices?

In certain respects, the American ideal of the garden seems a sterile place. We gardeners only permit special desirable plants to reside there. Our reliance on clippers for pruning, lawn mowers for mowing, and even straight-lined flower beds that don't exist anywhere in nature suggests a secret wish that these invitees would never grow beyond their bounds. Our reliance on weedeaters and herbicides amply demonstrates our intolerance for uninvited plants. If our fantasy of the ideal garden were a real place, there would be no sour sorrel sending out its roots in every direction, no thistles, none of the waist-high grass that mars every attempt to re-create pocket paradise in our own backyard. That we currently rely on timesaving devices like lawn mowers and weedeaters to such excess may offer up the best reason yet why *Utopia* is "nowhere." The ideal of a suburban paradise will probably remain nowhere so long as chickweed, dandelion, and quack grass thrive just about everywhere.

Perhaps we move one step closer to Eden by recognizing that weeds aren't the demons we always thought they were.

But I am not a Luddite. I do not bemoan the use of any and every power tool at our disposal. The impact that the weedeater and even the power lawn mower has upon the environment is mostly acoustic, and, in my case, that sonic pox upon the land lasts only for an hour or two, six times a year. Weedeater use is not, by any stretch of the imagination, a parallel problem to continued herbicide use.

If paradise now seems further away than ever, wielding the weedeater sometimes leads to a magical result suggesting that nature itself may be keeping the doors to paradise ajar. When we weedeat or mow *regularly*, the nongrasses in our path eventually wither away from lack of aboveground sustenance. The wild grasses start growing more thickly. They spread their root systems into the spaces vacated by their less-adaptive neighbors. The eventual result is a quite natural lawn.

This so-called natural lawn may never satisfy a golfer, a paradise gardener, or even an organic purist who would prefer to use a scythe. It could, however, satisfy all but the most fastidious suburban gardeners, while eliminating all need for herbicides. To nurture a natural lawn, try setting the mower blades a bit higher than convention allows—perhaps two inches off the ground. In other words, treat the grass as a living being and an ally whose needs for sunshine and respiration must be met if the lawn is to remain healthy. Call it the sentient gardener's approach to lawn maintenance: an active collaboration between human and grass. When we learn to leave the clippings in place as mulch, the lawn never needs fertilizer. The clippings eventually smooth out the surface, flattening out the lumpy quality of many natural grasses. Best of all, native grasses demand less attention than any import. They may never need watering. Nor will they ever need a weed killer. They *are* the weeds.

Every gardener encourages weeds to grow. Every time we clear land, cultivate beds, shovel dirt, or otherwise churn up the soil, we nurture the life cycle of some strong-willed, unintended plant. Although we usually do so inadvertently, we pamper the weeds as surely as we pamper any semi-real rose. Acknowledging our own complicity in this give-and-take relationship places us squarely on the path leading into the weed garden. Not acknowledging that connection leads only to chronic annoyance and wanton destruction of the ecosystem. Too many gardening books, too many county extension agents, too many agricultural and horticultural experts, would have us believe that the place that gardeners visit in the cause of inadvertently nurturing weeds is never a weed garden and always a war zone.

This is a very different sort of battlefield from the one where weedeater warriors and lawn-mower bombers join the fray every few weeks. This is chemical warfare.

It has been documented in many places that ultimately, the only winners in the chemical war against weeds are the chemical companies and their agents. There are no *local* winners because even though herbicides may raze the weeds temporarily, they corrupt the soil and the water and some of the wildlife much more thoroughly and for a much longer time. And as the humble thistle suggests, we are no match against the survival strategies of weeds. Unless we plan to pave the Earth in asphalt, weeds make invincible adversaries.

Wild plant aficionado Roger Banks describes the case of a Scottish matron who wished to eradicate the deep-rooted wild garlics from a shady garden bank as a prelude to planting primroses. Every spring she would spray the bank with whatever herbicide had been recommended that year. Each autumn, expensive varieties of primroses ordered at the Chelsea flower show were planted out to naturalize in the deep leaf mold. The following spring, just as regularly, up would come the garlic, which edged out the fragile primroses. As Banks concludes the story: "In the end this battle was only to be resolved by death; although she herself had never surrendered, she died fittingly 'on campaign.'" But the woman "had sprayed so much sodium chlorate over the years that she poisoned the roots of several large trees on the top of the bank; causing such a landslide that much of surrounding woodland eventually fell into the dell. Now, wild garlic grows even more thickly on the exposed slope to make her lasting memorial."[5]

This parable would ask us to consider the weed garden not as a war zone but as the terms of our surrender. It is the place we go to negotiate a lasting peace between uninvited plant life and gardeners, while we acknowledge our own complicity in a garden process that inevitably alters natural ecology. Agronomist Jack Harlan would ask us to be more humble still. In *Crops and Man* he seems to resurrect the metaphysical taxonomy when he writes that "if we confine the concept of weeds to species adapted to human disturbance, then man is by definition the first and primary weed under whose influence all other weeds have evolved."[6]

The discipline of land restoration seems based on this coevolutionary perception. Restoration is a crucial work that incorporates skills of agriculture, ecology, and medicine. It is, however, distinctly different from *reclamation*. While both the reclamationist and the restorationist are concerned with reintroducing vegetation to a trashed piece of land, the reclamationist pays more attention to whatever plants will thrive on bare soil and less attention to the original plant communities of the area. The restorationist remakes original ecology and is, therefore, emphatically concerned with native plants. A restoration plot might be regarded as a "living ecology museum" where communities of original vegetation are nurtured. The emergent global ecology is held at bay.

Although restoration utilizes all the skills of gardening in terms of content—in terms of encouraging the chosen plants—the objective of the restorationist often seems the reverse of a gardener's objective. Much of what gardeners refer to as cultivars, the restorationist views as weeds. Wheat, peonies, peaches, most roses—in North America, all are weeds. Meanwhile, the aboriginal plants of a specific locale are nurtured as carefully as you and I nurture tomato starts.

Restorationist William R. Jordan III describes land restoration as farming in reverse: "Traditional forms of agriculture deal with nature analytically: they dissemble a complex ecosystem like a prairie and reduce it to a simplified more easily managed form, such as a field of corn or wheat. Restoration goes just the other way. Inspired by ecological consciousness and its sense of the primacy of the whole, the restorationist deals with nature not analytically but synthetically, working to reassemble the native ecosystem in its full complexity, the natural community in its full variety."[7]

Restoration might be best understood as biocentric medicine. It is a unique form of remedy gardening; in this case, Gaia herself is the patient. In such a manner, the plants we call weeds transform into medicine—not because they contain special alkaloids, but because they are native and representative of the original ecology. They offer their cure by acting as ambassadors of place.

Jordan asks this question about healing: "How much psychological distance separates the work of healing people from the work of healing the land?"[8] In fact, that distance seems a clear function of any culture's sense of place. Okanagan elder Jeannette Armstrong may have provided an even better answer when she explained her tribe's definition of *people*: "the ones who are dream and land together . . . It means that we are part of the land."[9] In other words, curing the land can be the same thing as curing people.

The Gaia Hypothesis as originally postulated by James Lovelock and Lynn Margulis deals primarily with the way living organisms regulate the *atmosphere* in the cause of homeostasis. Many interpreters take Lovelock and Margulis at their word and view the postulated exchange of planetary gases as the only impact of Gaia. It is, however, difficult to deny that Gaia implies more than it declares outright. It is rather the philosophical implication—the metaphorical limit of the Gaian model—that has so deeply touched the public imagination and precipitated a veritable flood of speculation by environmentalists, religious leaders, and poets.

How does this relate to the weed garden? In fact, the Gaian worldview turns the human relationship to weeds on its head. When we acknowledge Gaia's role as a regulator of atmosphere, we soon discover that she makes ample use of those plants we refer to as weeds. As the thistle demonstrates, weeds germinate quickly to cover any patch of bare ground. By contrast, human food crops are predominantly fragile and unadaptable plants. To make them grow at all, farmers first work laboriously to uncover the soil and take elaborate precautions to keep it uncovered. But Gaia abhors a vacuum in the form of bare ground. It leads to erosion, which keeps plants from growing and thus respiring. Bare ground depletes atmospheric oxygen.

With all due respect to the restorationists: whether land is restored or reclaimed does not make much difference to Gaia. It was foreign weeds that saved so much of North America and Australia from the excesses of the human invasion. Those lands would be much more arid than they are today if the foreign weeds had not literally "held the ground" during a time of unprecedented native plant extinctions and agricultural expansionism. In other words, weeds are part of nature's own healing process. They are Gaia's white blood cells, her scabs, her bandages, her antibiotics. Alfred Crosby refers to the weeds as "the Red Cross of the plant world; they deal with ecological emergencies. When the emergencies are over, they give way to plants that may grow more slowly but grow taller and sturdier."[10]

The Gaian world is an upside-down world. Our own valued food crops—cabbage, corn, and monocropped banana plantations—are useless weeds because they are fragile and demand so much torn-up ground in order to succeed. Gaia employs the plants *we* call weeds to battle human food plants wherever they appear by choking them, crowding them out, and starving them of nutrients. What humans refer to as weeds are Gaia's own organic form of herbicide.

The so-called insect pests are firm Gaian allies of the plants *we* call weeds. While the weeds focus their formidable powers on covering and holding bare soil, and crowding out the most vulnerable species, the pests focus their attention on eradicating the least healthy plants within an ecosystem, paving the way, in effect, for stronger plants to root. In simple terms of the atmosphere, animal pests give off carbon dioxide through respiration and methane through flatulence. When the pests die, their carcasses decompose to create more topsoil, setting the stage for more oxygen-producing weeds.

Let it be emphasized that within the weed garden, the concept of plant *health* does not necessarily denote leafy exuberance or fleshiness or good taste. In pure ecological terms, it signifies *adaptability* to the greater needs of all the other communal processes and creatures within that same ecosystem. In Gaian terms, health signifies an ability to optimize the retention of atmospheric homeostasis. A three-foot-tall broccoli plant with huge fleshy leaves and a six-inch-wide head is hardly adaptable to any known natural ecosystem. The species is fragile. It would be extinct in a few seasons, which also means it is not the optimum plant for stabilizing anything. In Gaian terms, the broccoli is a loser.

We plant our broccoli, in effect setting the stage for the cabbage borer to arrive in the broccoli patch to mow down yet another gardener's maladaptive crop. In the upside-down world of the weed garden, we need to regard the cabbage borer as another biocentric medicine healer in the employ of Gaia. The insect pest thrives while making more room for the relatively immune chickweed, wild sorrel, nettles, and miner's lettuce to grab hold of the churned-up soil. The collaborative relationship between pests and weeds prospers only up to a certain point. Once the human food crops are crowded out, the much hardier weeds start to thrive. But these weeds have evolved formidable defenses to deal with the pests. In the biocentric worldview, the plants we call weeds sometimes act as nature's pesticide. For instance, quack grass contains a chemical that repels slugs. Thistles repel just about everything. The animals that previously thrived now have no food. They die. Yet within the Gaian web, insect populations are rarely wiped out entirely. Instead, they stabilize.

The soil garden demonstrated that the modern farm was founded upon the farmer's own sense of competition with the soil, the weeds, and the pests. Human beings are certainly among the most successful survivors in nature. We fight for our food crops and our pretty flowers in ways far more devastating to the planet than either weeds or pests do. As the weeds and pests succeed, we increasingly resort to unnatural tactics for controlling them.

The seemingly limitless abundance of the land allowed our grandparents to ignore the long-term need of developing a true land ethic. It was that same failure of organic vision—our failure as a centralized society to develop a local sense of place—that caused modern agriculture to start importing petroleum-based fertility onto the land. The human ability to destroy the land increased logarithmically. When crops were threatened by weeds and insects that adapted to the initial poisons, the farmer countered with chemical weapons that have long since tipped the balance in the farmer's favor.

Given that gloomy appraisal of modern nonorganic farming, one might well ask, What is the place of the modern farmer's unnatural tactics in this upside-down Gaian view of weeds and pests? In fact, most farming is war against the earth. It is an impediment to Gaian homeostasis, perhaps the major cause of desertification, and an obstruction to global healing everywhere it flourishes. We sometimes think of nuclear power as a kind of Pandora's box unleashing technological demons beyond any mere human's ability to control. Agriculture may be the original Pandora's box.

Only grudgingly do farm communities now acknowledge that they must relent in their efforts to dominate nature at every turn. Only grudgingly does any farm community acknowledge that *competition* with nature is a losing cause. Evidence now suggests that fifty years of chemical dependency is finally changing farm attitudes. The veritable destruction of the small farm has finally brought home the basic ecological commandment that declares that adaptability to nature offers the only long-term solution to our survival. Only renewing a sense of place can heal the deep wounds slashed into the flesh of Gaia by techno-farming.

Amid the ruins of a generation of war waged against the earth, the tragic need for a land ethic beckons.[11] A comprehension of Gaian homeostasis seems an apt (although difficult) starting point for anyone wishing to devise a viable land ethic. Such a land ethic demonstrates that the plants we call weeds are simply those un-intended plants able to thrive and *heal* broken ground; that the animals we call pests play a pivotal role in keeping Gaia healthy.

Although farming as we know it is not gardening, the best land ethic to guide farming into the next century guides the organic gardener today. The best of the modern gardeners may even regard themselves as the farming avant-garde, busy providing the ethical model on a minute scale for living at peace with nature on a larger scale. Hugh Johnson states this premise well: "If control, or attempts at it, lead to neurosis, something has gone wrong. A garden which is a battleground against the less amiable and cooperative forces of nature can scarcely be called serenity. The gardener must be a philosopher, accepting that he and his have a place in the cycle of life which nothing, or very little, can ever alter. Everything that grows is food for something else."[12]

May every farmer one day follow the path leading into the weed garden. May every farmer learn to adapt his life to the weeds.

Of all the perceptual gardens in this book, the weed garden may be the most diffi-cult one to deal with on a day-to-day level. My own example should make this perfectly clear. I garden my vegetables in raised beds and fastidiously weed out the tiny chickweed and sorrel starts that favor that richly composted soil. That is one reason why, in its most perfect form, I readily admit that the weed garden is a nowhere garden. However, like organic gardeners everywhere, I have solved the problem of bare ground by employing several complementary techniques that minimize weeding. My raised beds are never walked upon; the soil is not turned over every spring, which is, of course, a process that inevitably uncovers long-buried weed seeds in every forkful. I also mulch deeply with manure and planer shavings, both of which keep the soil surface well-covered, respiring, and alive. Since the weeds are thus kept at bay without much daily "weeding" on my part, I wonder if the process of mulching satisfies the sometimes inscrutable and always convoluted long-term strategy of Gaia.

Even the Jains, the Indian nonviolent religious sect unwilling to swat a mosquito, are vegetarians who must occasionally weed to live. Gardening is a pragmatic exercise. We all garden "somewhere," and no one ever completely attains the Utopia of his or her gardening ideals. There are many incremental variations of the weed garden, and the essential trait binding all of them together is a respectfulness for the ecology of place. I weed at the thistles on the children's play area. And yet I admire and even nurture their vigorous colonization of the clay dam. All of the variations offer a savvy lesson in local ecology.

One thing is certain about the weed garden. It fiercely refutes just about everything we have been taught to do as gardeners. Everything we have been taught as black is now seen as white. Some may conclude that it is the most difficult perception presented in this entire book. And yet only a gardener willing to explore the upside-down world known as the weed garden has any real hope of attaining the next tier of this recurring theme called a sense of place.

November

A never-ceasing drizzle of a month. A foregone conclusion of an outright down-pour of a month. Leaves fallen, grass turned brown, the first heavy frost of the year silences the peeping frogs of night. Standing on the top step of the front porch, I am startled by the unfamiliar silence. Listening more attentively now, I pick out the hollow yapping of individual neighborhood dogs barking to one an-other from every direction. The yapping verifies better than any demographic study just how much the human population has boomed in this neighborhood since the frogs were silenced this same time last year.

I step back inside, turn on the news, and watch a reporter tell me how the local rivers are overflowing their banks. Farms have been flooded out. The TV screen shows a car turned upside down with the river flowing through the driver's-side window and out the passenger's-side window. Wait a minute. I know that farm. I have driven past it many times. The news commentator rambles on and on about the federal disaster relief program and especially "the multimillion-dollar price tag" attached to yesterday's downpour. Yet never once does she point out something quite fundamental: that human beings ought to expect flooding when they build their houses on a major floodplain. The screen is suddenly filled with a talking head representing the logging companies. He is smiling, calmly denying that his industry's policy of clear-cutting the entire canyon of the upper river could have had anything to do with the increased flooding downriver. It's as if gravity and the laws of hydrodynamics cease to exist where logging occurs.

The darkness of late autumn has turned my mood jejune, even as it drives my activities indoors. I fight back, refuse to spend my days inside, cover my body with a raincoat so protective, and with so many zippers, that mountain climbers refer to it as "technical gear." I choose one of three different heights of dependable rubber boots depending on the intensity of the rain.

Over time I have collected an entire wardrobe of hats to fit the occasion: thirties' mobster homburgs, homemade knit caps, Nigerian wide-brimmed raffia, baseball caps advertising Arizona, the Boston Celtics, the Ellesmere Island National Park. I reckon that as long as my head stays dry, working up a sweat outside in the rain is any gardener's best preventative medicine against the colds and flu that overpower everyone who remains huddled up inside. Let them stare out the window, fantasizing the fair weather of next spring or last fall. Germs know that the human body was not constructed for hibernating.

Five miles from home lies a sixty-acre undeveloped pasture owned by a friend. Forty years ago, a previous owner cleared the forest and then deposited all the glacially deposited stones into two large piles on his way to making a productive hay field. The field is still productive and has long been my own main source of hay bedding for the chicken coop.

Eight or ten times each November, I drive my Ford pickup down the mucky dirt road to those significant rock piles. This has been going on for three years, and yet the rock pile still looks substantial. I originally favored small rocks, ten- to twenty-pound rocks. I cared not at all whether they were greasy slabs of shale or pockmarked basalt or white granite. By the second year I had turned far more discerning, a veritable connoisseur of rocks. I chose forty-pound granite and even gave them a name. They were the chicken-sized boulders. By the third year my preference in rocks had grown again, this time to seventy- or even hundred-pound granite boulders. Turkey sized.

I am sitting on the mossy wet ground at the edge of the sixty-acre field, sizing up a pancake-shaped treasure of a hundred-pound white granite boulder. I finally rise to my feet, start the truck, back it up as close as possible to the rock without getting mired in the mud. I open the back door, take a deep breath, and bend at the knees (always from the knees). Get a firm grip on the rock, lift it into the truck bed in one clean motion.

Back home again, the rock pile beside the driveway grows and grows until one day it reaches critical mass. It "looks" as if I now have enough rocks to start mortaring in a new terraced garden bed. November may be wet, but the temperature seldom dips below freezing, and it is a good time for doing concrete work.

I start the process by browsing my own property to locate the much larger boulders needed to lay out the bottom file of the terrace. Rolling these boulders into place—some of them well over two hundred pounds—is the greatest challenge of the entire endeavor. It is best to know in advance precisely where any specific boulder is going to end up along the drawn outline of the terrace and then dig a depression that will firmly hold the rock once it is maneuvered into place.

I have learned never to push large boulders, especially uphill. I pull them toward me, which utilizes the biceps rather than the back muscles. I have also discovered that, in general, it is easier to control an uphill journey than one downhill. I am often tempted to simply let gravity take control of a downhill roll. It's a bad tactic: the rock almost always rolls far beyond where I need it. The painful lesson of sprained fingers has taught me to resist the temptation of trying to stop the roll of a large boulder.

I take special care to plan a difficult roll. With some very large rocks I might lay my cheek right against the ground to compare the center of gravity of the rock to the incline of the slope. I determine an escape route just in case the rock takes off in midroll. The entire process sometimes seems not unlike a diamond cutter locating the precise spot to break a gemstone. Occasionally I feel like a grand master at chess planning two or three rolls in advance.

Follow these simple rules, and you too may roll, against all odds, a two-hundred-pound boulder as far as a hundred feet in one session. Without any help. But never rush it. And above all else, learn well when to walk away from a stone. Boulder rolling is best left to a specific moment in the day. I prefer late afternoons. I'm at neither my physical nor my mental peak at that time. That knowledge grants me the intuition of a conservative: the only politics worth expressing while moving boulders.

No matter how hard I try, some boulders prove too heavy or too bulky to move very far, no matter how much I may want them to roll somewhere else. I may have already completed five or ten rolls. But then the path turns steep. Or the ground itself turns to bedrock. Fearing permanent damage to my body, I know when to back off. I usually try again tomorrow.

Once in a while I simply leave the rock where it is, contented to upend it into a permanent hole. There it squats like an ungainly memorial commemorating the moment I was unwilling to hurt myself. People visit and want to know if I am designing a Japanese boulder garden. They walk around the various rocks and point out this or that subtle pattern as if it were the work of some budding rock master. I have to smile. To me the boulders convey nothing but mineral bulk wed to the limitations of my own strength. But what do I know? Perhaps that is the same limitation that motivated the builders of Japan's rock gardens.

I plant spring bulbs like galanthus and scilla around the base of these monoliths. Time passes. Delicate little flowers bloom and spread diligently every spring. Moss eventually appears on the northern flanks of my metaphorical mountains. After years, I finally learn to agree with my guests. There is a pattern here. No other garden feature is as capable of evoking a Chinese or Japanese sensibility as upended rocks. Were I to write a book about my rock-moving avocation, I'd name it *The Tao of Gravity*.

The Creative Garden

The local garden and the soil garden show the many practical ways our culture benefits from a land *ethic* founded upon a sense of place. The creative garden shows the benefits of a land *aesthetic* founded upon a sense of place. A land aesthetic may be the most significant bounty that gardening bestows upon a seeker of place. It offers us the precious gift of creativity: the passion to express our deepest feelings. Creativity and passion are manifested in the cause of beauty. When we walk in beauty outside, we walk in beauty inside.

Like all the other gardens in this book, the creative garden is a process more than an object. Consider it the procedures gardeners undertake to nurture grace and elegance in their own lives as well as in the lives of their loved ones. Most gardeners know this twice-realized sense of beauty very well. It is the main reason so many people take up gardening in the first place.

This chapter on the creative garden offers few tips about creating specific garden effects and how to feel good while pursuing them. With so much terrific literature already devoted to garden artistry, we do better to take several steps away from the typical discussion about the various color schemes, plantings, and shapes gardeners might employ inside their own garden. Instead, let's take the long view; let's search to find some basis for a land aesthetic. How do our perceptions about art and gardens in general relate to developing a sense of place in particular? By insisting on this long view, the short view will inevitably come into focus on its own—not unlike the way a landscape photographed through a small aperture setting shows both the far and the near in the same picture.

In *Parallel Botany*, fabulist Leo Lionni describes the fictitious plant called artisia whose shape transforms about every twenty-five years. Incredibly, these tranformations closely reflect similar changes in the world of human art. Two hundred yars ago the leaves and the stems of artisia looked decidedly rococo. By the middle of the twentieth century artisia had evolved to closely mirror the shape of a Calder pendant or Jean Arp collage. Lionni explains this morphogenesis by theorizing that plants represent an earlier phase in a "general artistic evolution which has reached its peak, for the moment, in the artistic products of man. The forms of nature and those which proceed from the creative impulses of humanity . . . reflect the principle that art, as a manifestation of the spirituality of man, does not have an outward and objective relationship to nature, but is, like man's body, an integral part of it."[1]

Perhaps an outrageous idea, although breeders of designer flowers coalesce fashion with evolution in ways not that far removed from the formative causation expressed by artisia. Today's Jolly Joker pansy follows the same brassy aesthetic as today's fashions. The latest tea roses produce larger flowers and far more saturated colors on a smaller bush over an extended bloom season than they did a hundred years ago. Is there any doubt that inflated flowers reflect a cultural aesthetic that regards bigger as better? Today's gardens are smaller than they once were, explaining why the plants themselves grow small even as the flowers grow large. While an ever-extending blooming period also demonstrates that more is better, it also implies something a bit more troubling. Modern people live farther away from natural processes than they did in the past. One result is that we tend to be less sensitive to and, therefore, less satisfied with plants that naturally bloom "only" once a year. Although some would interpret every one of these rose qualities to be an improvement on the species, they might just as easily be understood as a mirror on an age prone to overconsumption and distancing from nature.

The case of the fictitious artisia seems an effective springboard for describing the many ways that place affects artists, and that art likewise affects gardens. For instance, some garden historians consider Claude Monet to have been a master gardener who just happened to paint pictures as the public expression of his first creative love. They insist that the proof can be plainly seen at Monet's garden in Giverny. A hundred years after the man himself gardened there, the garden still displays the master's touch. It is an exuberant garden, an elegant garden, an impressionist masterpiece of a garden that displays to consummate perfection the studied wildness which is perhaps the most difficult gardening aesthetic to achieve. It seems self-evident why Monet considered his garden an apt subject for so many of his paintings. Or did he paint mostly to provide blueprints for his garden?

Giverny is a visual treat. The vast majority of gardeners design their gardens to favor the visual. Think of any special garden, and a pretty picture usually springs to mind: voluminous, color-matched plants of varying textures and densities growing out of crisply edged beds. Immaculately arranged collections of tiny rock-garden creepers weeping and sweeping and dripping down a hillside. We *think* of a garden and *see* a picture frozen in our memory. That is why photographs showcased in any of the hundreds of coffee-table books devoted to the creative garden are so successful at capturing their subject. It is the reason we immediately understand the terms when we hear painter and master gardener Robert Dash describe his own garden as "a constantly amended, variable essay on green—green rising into the sky, green rising through the earth, green puncturing water."[2]

We are visual creatures. Our visual sense is our most insistent sense; it rules our perception of the world and dominates our consciousness. It is the rare gardener who creates a landscape that accentuates other senses while ignoring the visual. To do so drastically alters the way we physically relate. For instance, scent in the garden comes into consciousness only fleetingly. To experience it at all, we usually need to locate our nose very close to a bloom. And when we do, we often feel a need to close our eyes in an attempt to reduce the dominance of the visual sense, if for but a brief moment.

There are fewer gardens created primarily for touching, although there is a marvelous garden in Seattle, Washington, that favors plant textures and fragrance and caters to a clientele of blind plant lovers. Perhaps rarest of all is the acoustic garden. Musical instrument maker Richard Waters has built a tuned picket fence around his yard in northern California. A song is played by taking a stick and running it along the slats. My own fondest memory of visiting a famous bamboo garden in Kamakura, Japan, is the clicking and clacking of the bamboo stems striking one another in a stiff breeze.

These nonvisual examples are rare enough to be called gardening anomalies. The overwhelming majority of the great gardeners and landscape architects throughout history were masters of the visual expression of garden aesthetics. It is an approach epitomized in our own time by the cool and elegant neoclassical garden designs of the great twentieth-century landscape designer Russell Page, or the jazzy modern-art gardens of the Brazilian Roberto Burle Marx, who mixed vibrant colors in a way suggestive of abstract expressionism.

But no matter how well the painterly metaphor serves to create brilliant visual statements, it often fails miserably as a means of establishing a sense of place. What the great landscape designers actually compose is a visual template, a one-good-look-and-then-I'm-gone approach to a sense of place. Gabrielle van Zuylen, biographer of Russell Page, expressed the essential paradox of the professional landscaping art when she wrote that any art is "an attempt at immortality. Russell Page was as acutely conscious of this as any other creator. The ephemerality of his art, and the sadness he felt for all the gardens made and lost in his lifetime, strengthened his desire to create and endure."[3]

If Russell Page was saddened by his own creative experience, it may have been because he *created* too many gardens and *lived* in none of them. He was an artist in the modern European tradition: a creator who treated each piece of land as a blank canvas and not as the personal expression of any long-term relationship to place. He came, he saw, he landscaped. And his biographer informs us that he never created a garden of his own until the very end of his life.

Not to imply that Page's landscapes are not beautiful. To the contrary, his landscapes are both stunning and unique as expressions of what trees and shrubs can do when arranged artfully in three-dimensional space. And as time passed, watching and enjoying the slow growth of the trees only added to the mystique of Page's mastery: his unerring ability to predict how things would harmonize so well over twenty or thirty years' time.

Page's talents were so formidable that, over the years, many of his clients expressed little interest in dabbling with the artist's finished layout. It would have felt a bit like doodling on a Rembrandt. In other words, amid all that beauty, Page's gardens rarely evolved through the years as the organic response between the client—the dweller of that particular piece of land—and the land itself. The garden was often bereft of process. Gardening a Russell Page landscape usually became a matter of upkeep, while keeping it intact insured a valuable real estate investment. Granted, a few of the owners transformed Page's designs in the years that followed to match their own growing sense of place. More of them never would. And for all their aesthetic excellence, Russell Page's gardens fail to satisfy the participatory criteria that define a creative garden linked to place.

Not to conclude, however, that landscape architecture necessarily denies the creative garden. Landscaping can also serve as a simple beginning, a skeleton, an object which the creative resident then transforms into a personal, never-finished process. The neophyte gardener learns, watches, listens, digs, plants, and starts to transform the space *and* himself or herself at the same pace the plants grow. As the Chinese say so well: "When the house is finished, man dies."

The creative garden turns the painterly, object-oriented metaphor inside out. If the ground is considered a canvas upon which artists compose a picture, this canvas is also capable of painting itself. More to the point: the painter is the painting. Harland Hand is a gardener living in the San Francisco Bay area who created a small garden often considered one of the most extraordinary in America. He too forgoes a painterly metaphor, preferring to express his garden design in dynamic, theatrical terms: "Nature was always the master garden designer: in nature things move, rivers flow, flowers grow where the wind scatters their seeds, rocks tumble down, the earth shifts, swells and sags, action is evident everywhere. An infinity of adventures show in every plant and time worn rock, yet nature's compositions express the most profound serenity. Could one do better than to interpret this in a garden?"[4]

Marshall Olbrich, one of the founders of the famous Western Hills Garden in California, takes the theatrical metaphor a step farther. He suggests that we cannot understand our motivation to garden until we rid ourselves of all allusions to painting and visuals. He writes, "Because of its accidental history, and the wide range of plants grown in it, our garden seems to me more like a rather disorganized novel or drama in which characters come and go, with the good pining away and the wicked sometimes flourishing."[5] As gardeners comprehend the profound dialogue that occurs between themselves and place, they start to study the aesthetic particulars of all the other gardens they visit. It is not unlike becoming the audience to one short scene of a long drama. In the process, they glean a few small bits of the conversation that occurs between another gardener and place. Like Olbrich, they do well to focus on the particulars—the choice of plants, bed siting, accoutrements—as the grammar of the conversation.

Relationship may be everything. But the tenets of the creative garden are not written in stone. A sense of place encourages other relationships besides the primary one between gardener and garden. A creative garden can be constructed in one fell swoop and still fulfill that fundamental participatory relationship to place.

Environmental artist Alan Sonfist has planted a remarkable garden he calls *Time Landscape* in a corner lot in New York City's Greenwich Village. The thousands of people who pass by it each day see little more than a tangle of shrubs and small trees set behind a cast-iron fence. Unless visitors find the explanatory plaque, they may remain puzzled why this tangle has been fenced off. The plaque informs them that the planting is an accurate re-creation of the vegetation that grew on that spot some four hundred years ago. Left to grow for a few hundred years, the small maples and beeches of *Time Landscape* will eventually grow to resemble the magnificent specimens that greeted the first European settlers.[6]

Time Landscape is an expression of land restoration taken to absurdity. The size of the plot does not come close to fulfilling the minimum plot needed for any restoration to take hold. The soil, the water, the wildlife, the air—none of it matches the original biome. Without the high fence and constant weeding, it would soon revert to the look and feel of the other vacant lots in Manhattan.

Although Sonfist's garden fails as an authentic restoration, it succeeds splendidly as an artist's metaphor. It represents the lost forest, serving as a catalyst for changing attitudes toward nature and ecology,[7] while offering an important living reminder of our responsibility to regreen the Earth. As such, it gives everyone who experiences it a small glimmer of hope that a forest could indeed grow within the community of Greenwich Village. As some gardens prioritize fragrance, touch, or sound, so this one seems to prioritize tense: a garden that reminds us of the past, the present, and the future all at the same time. Yet for all its aesthetic accomplishments, *Time Landscape* is not beautiful by any European gardening standard.

There is more to this garden than meets the eye or the standard. Gardening is the only art form that is alive, that grows. *Time Landscape* may offer a poignant metaphor about the human relationship to the land, but the maples and beeches that struggle on that harsh patch of city real estate are not art. They are living things, the descendants of a real remnant forest. The trees of *Time Landscape* have little chance of surviving as long as the human environment that surrounds them remains unlivable. Even as *Time Landscape* offers a powerful metaphor about struggling to survive, it is also not a metaphor. Those trees *are* struggling to survive. Here lies the central paradox of this particular creative garden. Even as it expresses the Utopian hope of a nowhere garden, so it is growing, putting down roots, throwing its seed to wind. Even as it exists as a powerful work of art, so it is not art.

Alan Sonfist has designed other projects that are on display in art museums. Society regards him as an artist and his *Time Landscape* as "a work of art." That kind of recognition has been more problematic for Mel Chin's design for an experimental planting in a toxic landfill in Minnesota. It took several tries before the National Endowment for the Arts relented to fund it. The Endowment's concern was that the project was not "a work of art."

But just like *Time Landscape*, it is. And it isn't. Not only is Chin's *Revival Field* inconvenient to visit, it's hazardous to human health. It is located in the middle of a 307-acre landfill that had recently burned for two months. In the middle of the plot, Chin arranged ninety-six plants within a circular chain-link fence. This was, in turn, enclosed inside a square chain-link fence. The plantings inside the circle included dwarf corn, lettuce, and pennythrift. Each species was recommended by Chin's collaborator, toxic-waste specialist Rufus Chaney, for its ability to absorb toxic metals through the roots. The space between the two fences is planted with nonabsorbent plants and serves as a scientific control.

The plantings in the present work of art will eventually be harvested and the metals recovered, leaving purified soil as the future work of art. Scientist Chaney admits that artist Chin's geometry is scientifically superfluous but that as art, "it brings attention to the problem, not just the solution." Chin adds that "as an art form it extends the notion of art beyond a familiar object/commodity status into the realm of process and public service."[8]

Mel Chin's experience with the National Endowment demonstrates that our society upholds a distinction between artists and nonartists. We are taught to believe that artists like Monet, Russell Page, and Alan Sonfist possess mysterious God-given talents beyond the pale of "nonartists." In *Drawing on the Right Side of the Brain*, art teacher Betty Edwards comments that artists themselves often do little to dispel the mystery of their gifts. Ask an artist how he or she draws so well, and the reply might be, "Well, I just have a gift for it, I guess," or "I really don't know; I just start in and work things out as I go along."

Edwards concludes that this kind of answer doesn't explain the process at all, and "a sense that the skill of an artist is a vaguely magical ability persists. People even feel that they shouldn't take a drawing course because they don't know already how to draw. But this is like deciding that you shouldn't take a French class because you don't already speak French."[9]

Society makes the attainment of an art career such a daunting task that even the artists themselves start to suspect that getting beyond "paying one's dues" is a state of grace that awaits only the verifiably gifted. The rewards that accompany success only enhance that feeling. But money tends to devalue that which it cannot truly possess. Because it can never truly possess a "gift," the marketplace demands that artists turn their gift into products. Increasingly, those products are available only to the wealthy. Art—the gift of creative genius—quickly degenerates into art the investment. Art the investment spawns art the status symbol.

Our art is a profane art. Even as it has transmuted itself into the product of an elite corps of artists, so it has set adrift from the heart of culture—the center of our lives. Art has lost its sacred spark. A spiral is set a-spin. The sense of an artist being gifted and of art being separate from common life creates the climate that generates the riches. Nonartists of the world learn to regard this so-called high art as something for which they are audience. Fewer of them are buyers. Nonprofessional expressions of art are categorized as hobby or recreation. Recreation (re-creation) seems a key symptom of a profane culture. It is what we do with our time when we are not busy making a living.

The Wodaabe of Niger are a nomadic people who live on the fringes of the western Sahara. They possess no word for *museum*, no concept of art separate from life, no idea of hobby. Like most traditional people, the Wodaabe do not limit the creative expression of their culture to an elite, and therefore they do not think of art as the relationship between artist and audience. Art is, instead, the creative interaction between a people, their culture, and the Earth. It is a way of life lived. When the concept of art is explained in their language, the people retranslate that concept back into English as a paraphrase of one of the statements that opened this chapter: "Art seeks grace and elegance in all things."[10]

Half a world away, the Navajo of the American Southwest coined another of the sayings that opened this chapter: when we walk in beauty outside, we walk in beauty inside. It is an aesthetic statement rich in respect for the natural environment, a spiritual one-liner suggesting every reason ever set forth to develop a sense of place.

Though the Navajo grow corn and beans, they do not utilize their gardens in the Western sense of a primary aesthetic expression of nature. Sand painting serves that function instead. That we, in turn, do not regard sand painting as a form of gardening is probably another result of our English aristocratic gardening roots. Yet sand painting strongly reflects the raked-gravel gardens found in Japanese monasteries. Sand paintings are created as a kind of "power spot" on the Earth. Because sick people lie down on the design in the hope of being cured of what ails them, the form seems to merge the sacred garden, the creative garden, and the remedy garden. That the spirit of the sand is said to speak directly to those who chant over it recommends a sentient garden. But sand painting is hardly a familiar form of gardening. It is, rather, an artistic expression of place that we know as a garden only by first expanding our definition of gardening to include the many expressions of earth aesthetics manifested by the indigenes who live outside our own culture.

David Mabry-Lewis has written that unlike the Navajos and the Wodaabe, "we moderns think of *living* as: what we do for a . . ." It is this definition of life itself that turns some of us into artists and the rest of us into either audience for these professionals or hobbyists for ourselves. Either way, "what we do for a . . ." keeps our profane art from ever becoming what the Wodaabe insist it is: "a way of life lived."

What course might we take to better integrate a sacred sense of art into our own lives? This question seems especially provocative when viewed in relation to the National Gardening Association's statistic that there are seventy million gardening households in the United States and that the majority of these practitioners consider their avocation to be the primary artistic expression in their lives. The potential is obvious. Gardening may already offer us the bridge across the gap that separates art from the rest of life.

In most cases, this is an opportunity not yet taken. The vast majority of gardeners cannot tread the integrative path so long as they relate to gardening anthropocentrically, as the control of nature for aesthetic purposes. Unfortunately, this is our gardening legacy. Nor will it truly become integrative so long as we perceive it as a *leisure* activity. It is not, however, the things we may do for leisure that cause the problem but rather the perception of leisure as one-half of a compartmentalization of activities into work and play. Let's face it. Most people view gardening as a hobby—a much-loved hobby but a hobby nonetheless. The word *hobby* insinuates that we rank our art forms. Although most people (including most art critics) would consider gardening to be a genuine form of artistic expression, they give it a lower "rank" than the so-called high arts of painting, dance, music composition, drama, literature, and even landscape architecture.

A lower rank may be due to the fact that gardening is universally regarded to be a feminine art form. By this, I do not mean that only women do it—or that women do it best—but rather that gardening is inherently nurturing, domestic, unprofessional, and especially, noncompetitive. When we think of gardening in artistic terms, we tend to place it on just about the same rung as cooking, quilting, and all the other homely arts. The homely arts accrue a lower ranking *because* they are nurturing and noncompetitive in a society that exalts professionalism and competition.

On the positive side, pressures that confront painters, composers, dancers, and writers to produce "works" do not nag gardeners. The pressure is off, which goes far to explain why practitioners multiply. The vast majority of gardeners have no wish to turn their hobby into a career—into high art. They only want to garden.

Rules governing the aesthetic particulars should never be taken too seriously. As the local garden earlier demonstrated, aesthetics might be understood as a set of articulated opinions expressing a person's or a society's sense of beauty and feelings. Beauty *is* in the eyes of the beholder. Composer of unorthodox music John Cage seemed to expand on this idea when he wrote that "art is anything you can get away with." Cage's dictum has since developed into one of the conceptual cornerstones of late-twentieth-century art.

In practice, "anything you can get away with" implies that the "high" artists of the world are a slightly belligerent bunch of intellectuals who calculate the effect of their work by setting both feet parallel to the ground like a character out of some Hong Kong karate movie. Art isn't exactly what makes you feel good. It isn't even about beauty. Cage's dictum is rather about the *politics* of art, about artists doing whatever it is they need to do to push the envelope of the acceptable. Cage suggests that it is the responsibility of artists to exploit the cracks in society's defenses. And anyone who impedes that momentum deserves to be cast as an aesthetic KGB operative.

Even as Cage's laissez-faire aesthetic is meant to break down fences, it actually fortifies the fence that currently separates the masculine high arts from the homely feminine arts. Cage cheers on creative combativeness in the cause of individual creativity. By doing so, he offers little support for the organic, cooperative, earth-centered, aesthetic pursuits—those humble, traditional, and usually domestic expressions of the artistic temperament that are meant to nurture a sense of place—pursuits like cooking, making a home, designing a landscape, growing a garden. In such a light, this aesthetic founded on "anything" is now seen to be a very specific sort of aesthetic. It helps aspiring "high artists" to proceed in, and perhaps cope with, a profane society. If Cage's highly competitive version of a social contract between profane artists and a profane society seems troubling, there is reason to be distressed. His dictum reflects, in microcosm, the philosophy that guides our profane civilization's relationship to the Earth itself. Indeed, our society's relationship to nature is, and has been for a very long time, anything we can get away with.

The creative garden would serve instead as an intersection, a locus, where a land aesthetic meets a sacred sense of place. In such a manner it offers one antidote to the creative ailment that lies at the heart of our profane dilemma. Look at it this way: Gardeners are like mask makers because a garden is not unlike a mask upon the Earth. In our own culture we make masks for theatrical entertainment. Or we hang them on walls as objects. But these are profane uses of a mask—serving either as pure decoration or as an externalized covering meant only to conceal the true identity of its wearer. But remember, in this case, the wearer is the Earth itself.

The creative garden offers a different sort of mask because, in this case, the gardener is an integral part of the whole. This mask is not decoration but rather, like totem masks carved by aboriginal peoples all over the world, a vessel containing its own spirit. The wearer, the Earth, takes on the spirit of the mask, even as the mask—the gardener and the plants—takes on the spirit of the wearer. In such a manner, creative gardeners make masks upon the land primarily as a means of linking themselves more directly to the spirit of place.

Despite that lofty description, attaining the creative garden need not be a difficult task. As with so many other concepts in this book, the gap that separates the prevailing mode of gardening from the proposed ideal is not very great. Gardening already provides a breath of sunshine offering people relief from a profane society. The garden has always been a retreat, a place for recovering one's bearings. Locating the path leading into the creative garden demands just a few pointed nudges in a new direction.

Embracing a new gardening aesthetic is a twofold process. First, we must honor all the natural processes of the Earth as sacred. This includes developing a respect for all beings, an idea described in the chapter on the sentient garden. And second, a simple recognition: we need to acknowledge the garden as a process we personally undertake to develop our hands, our hearts, and our minds to better create a sense of place. For this reason, Russell Page's gardens fail the test.

This new gardening aesthetic is completely perceptual. It offers no tips about complementary colors, varied leaf textures, the structure of garden beds, the verticality of trees, or any of the other subjects that usually accompany a discussion about gardening aesthetics. Perhaps paradoxically, all the particulars of the creative garden follow John Cage's dictum to the letter. Color, texture, shape, what have you—all of them are anything you can get away with. The aforementioned Japanese raked-gravel garden contains no plants whatsoever. Its ephemeral Navajo complement, the sand painting, disappears within hours or days of completion.

Neither raked-gravel gardens nor sand paintings wage chemical war upon the soil. They use little or no water resources. Because they focus gardener and visitor into a deep—some might say, Gaian—appreciation of nature, both uphold the criteria set for the creative garden. By contrast, regard the suburban lawn. With its chemical dependency on fertilizers and herbicides, with its immense abuse of water resources, the lawn displays no sense of place. It grows where there is no mindfulness of its implications or its greater linkage to the Earth.

Those who agree that a lawn may be environmentally reprehensible, but that it is not displeasing to look at, miss the point. A holistic sense of beauty synthesizes ethics with aesthetics to enhance a sense of place. A green lawn maintained by herbicides is ugly in the same way that any act of violence to place is ugly. No matter how luxurious it appears, it exists as an unheeding act against the Earth.

Despite the fervency of these crusading ideas, the garden always finds a gentle way of its own to transform consciousness. It speaks softly on its own behalf. When we learn to listen, it guides our hand to action, providing its own aesthetic particulars of place. As we have seen, Harland Hand writes that "nature's compositions express the most profound serenity. Could one do better than to interpret this in a garden?" The most beautiful gardens exhibit the process and the result of gardeners who know how to listen to place.

Given the sharp angles of my own land, anything else but a garden accentuating the up-and-down tumble and flow would be simply too difficult to produce. As a dweller on this land, I have developed aesthetic preferences that clearly reflect the exigencies of land and climate. What works here is what I have learned to admire most. A sense of place and a land aesthetic are unified. They are synonymous.

The flow from one season to the next is never so crisply defined here as it is in Minneapolis or New England. Last year, the combination of wet and dark and cold that locals usually refer to as fall lasted from mid-November through February, with just two weeks of winter sandwiched in around the new year. A newly planted viburnum (*Tinus lucidum*) bush planted along the front walk kept a grip on its thick shiny leaves all through that nonwinter. Yet I had planted this variety of viburnum only because that particular spot seemed perfect for a deciduous shrub possessing superb fall color, fragrant spring flowers, and wonderful iridescent blue berries. That it failed to produce color proved a disappointment.

I have never been a proponent of the traditional landscaping school that rips shrubs and trees out of the ground when they fail to produce the desired effect.

When a hole in the garden cries out for a new shrub or tree, I choose the species and the representative plant very carefully. Once its roots are covered with garden soil, a plant acquires certain inalienable rights to life and prosperity; I would no more rip it out of the ground than I would bring a cat to the pound for displeasing me. Call it destiny. Better yet, call it coevolution.

In the case of the viburnum, I had never given any thought to planting an evergreen shrub in that space. Evergreens like box or laurel (or certain other Laurestinus cultivars) seemed too much like opaque walls utilized to hide something. All during that winter, I observed as this deciduous-shrub-turned-evergreen set out to reinvent the front walk as a winter canyon rising from the driveway to the front door between opaque walls of shiny green. But I came around. That spring, inspired by this fresh view of the walk, I purchased several conifers to meet the creative potential evinced by that viburnum. They were soon planted all along the walkway. The canyon seemed complete. Summer passed. Fall arrived. But this time the season took a very different route on its journey toward winter. Fall lasted four weeks. By mid-October, frost was appearing on the ground every morning. Winter was fast upon us.

The viburnum tricked me a second time. By the middle of October its leaves started turning red and yellow. They hung on the bush for weeks and weeks, appearing more colorful with each passing day. At first, it was difficult for me to reconcile the fact that this plant was not going to be evergreen after all. My desire to create an evergreen front walk was voided by the same plant that had taught it to me in the first place.

Reexamining the facts about the viburnum family in a plant ID book, I realized the fault was my own. Unlike certain other Laurestinus cultivars that are, indeed, fully evergreen, the Lucidum variety is neither deciduous nor evergreen. It is "semi-evergreen." Coevolution or not, I considered getting out the garden fork and moving the shrub to another part of the property. I began perusing the pages of plant catalogs: searching for a "true" evergreen viburnum, such as the very shiny (and hard-to-find) *Viburnum pragense*. I studied camellias, star jasmines, euonymus. I visited my mother-in-law's large rhododendron garden.

The yellows and reds of the virburnum intensified. During a particularly momentous storm that occurred in the second week of December, the leaves blew off the shrub and scattered all over the walk. For days afterward, it was the walk's turn to draw in the eye, transforming itself into a glorious yellow-and-red carpet. Over the next month the striking colors slowly metamorphosed into a rotten brown. By February, the leaves had disappeared into the gravel.

I was getting the best of two worlds. The viburnum would sometimes grant the gift of fall color, and sometimes it would remain evergreen. The plant had also tripled in size over those two years. Meanwhile, the addition of all the conifers had started to fulfill my dream of a green canyon. Sedums planted on the edge of the various rock walls spilled over into the terraces directly below. Trailing campanulas, lithodoras, phlox, kinnikinnick, wintergreen, and lamiums completed the effect of gray rock melding into silver or green leaves. They all mixed together to make a continuous hundred-foot rise of tumbling rocks and plants from driveway to front door.

Over time, I have come to regard the viburnum as an aesthetic mentor. The way it communicates its own colorful and rather unpredictable relationship with place seems to mirror my own unpredictable relationship with place. This young shrub has shaken up my aesthetic sense even as it fulfills the climatic requirements of its genes. It keeps me guessing. Another summer. Another fall. This past winter was cold but not very wet. The viburnum dropped half its leaves in November and retained the other half until spring, when new leaves appeared. Flower buds, which in the past had always swollen in March and bloomed in April, this year made their appearance in November. The first fragrant cluster of white flowers appeared just before Christmas. A few more bloomed sporadically during January, February, and March. The greatest show occurred in early April when the entire bush was covered in lacy flower clusters. As always, the viburnum's fragrance remains unsurpassed.

In a profane culture, gardeners tend to take far too much credit for the beauty found in their own gardens. It is as if the choices that gardeners make, and the beauty they create, are accomplished in a vacuum, in spite of nature and in spite of the plants themselves. For instance, listen to artist and gardener Robert Dash: "In creating a garden one must often run counter to nature, the true spirit of the place being the perspicacity and wisdom and spiritual strength of the gardener, rather than the place itself or the earth on which he works that is no more than a blank canvas."[11]

How might we answer this statement? In *Mind and Nature*, Gregory Bateson tells the story of bringing a cooked crab into an art class and asking the students "to produce arguments which will convince [Bateson] that this object is the remains of a living thing."[12] The artists note that the object's shape is symmetrical, that the subject is "composed, like a painting." Someone points out that one claw is larger than the other, which means it may not always be symmetrical. Someone else observes that although one claw is definitely larger than the other, both claws are bilaterally symmetrical, meaning that they are composed of the same parts. And in all comparable objects the large claw is almost always on the same side. Furthermore, these parts are similar to the claws of a known living thing, the lobster. The relationship between crab and lobster claws is also analogous to the relationship between a human hand and horse's hoof. Bateson comments that nature is a creative maker of patterns. The *pattern that connects* the lifeless crab to other living beings is shape, form, and relationship. And finally, poetically, "the anatomy of the crab is repetitive and rhythmical. It is like music."[13]

Many biologists have taught us to regard evolution as a creative pattern that connects people to nature. Theoretical botanist Rupert Sheldrake refers to evolution as "the affirmation of a continuing creativity in the universe, in life, and in humanity."[14] Charles Darwin himself spent his professional life fighting the nineteenth-century religious dogma that perceived God, and not nature, as the artist and designer of the universe. We might regard Darwin's essential achievement as shifting Western culture's identity of the so-called creator (the first and last artist) from God to nature.

In that light, what seems missing from Robert Dash's description of gardening creativity is a sense of sacred participation with nature—a perception that gardening may serve as one of our best sources for manifesting creative evolution. If so, then there is no blank canvas here. And if so, Dash's point of view emerges as just another dull statement about control. The pattern that connects people to gardens has "run counter to nature" for far too long. The pattern that needs to emerge is, instead, coevolution.

The parable of the agenda-setting viburnum suggests that it is sometimes very difficult for us to welcome the intuitive linkage of coevolution into our own lives. In fact, our rationalist culture has been particularly heavy-handed and therefore quite successful at teaching us to reject intuition wherever it shows its face. We all know the differences between intellect and intuition and spirit, which seems another way of saying that we all know the differences between art and science and religion. When reason stands at odds with intuition or spirit, more often than not, reason wins. Contrarily, the society—almost always preindustrial—that honors intuition also tends to blur those same distinctions we prefer to keep so well honed. It is this blurred place I choose to call the creative garden. It is the place where science is art is religion.

Within the creative garden the agenda-setting viburnum emerges as a kind of horticultural shaman, whispering incantations into my ear that detail a sense of place. I listen attentively. The message changes over time. Recently, it taught me a wonderful theorem revealing information about the evolution of place. This theorem is also a prayer to the guardian of the front walk. I sometimes think of the prayer as a magic spell. Other times I regard it as a formula and even a recipe. The formula, no I mean the prayer, no I mean the magic spell, no I mean the recipe, no I mean the theorem has transformed the walk between the driveway and the front door into a creative study in draping blue leaves and evergreen shininess. This walkway remains a two-way street.

December

A few years ago we had a storm that blew down so many large trees that a few of the region's newspapers saluted it as "the storm of the century." It's true. That was some storm.

Except a year later, a storm moved through here one night that blew down ten times as many trees. Thirty-two trees blown down on my own six acres. The scorekeepers in the neighborhood accounted me to be one of the lucky ones. Another neighbor lost two hundred and fifty trees on fifteen acres. This time the regional journalists must have learned their lesson. There was nary a peep about any "storm of the century."

Those two storms caused people all over this region to start looking at the sky in a new way. Just plain folks, old-timers, conservative folks—folks who never before gave it a thought that our industrial success might possibly be sowing the seeds to our own failure—all of them started holding court about the greenhouse effect. And most of them seemed in agreement. Whatever the reason, the weather *is* changing. It *has* mucked up any remote chance of long-term prediction. No one seemed imaginative enough to predict what damage a *real* storm of the century might look like.

Those two storms were frightening. I lay in bed, listened to the wind come close to tearing the roof off my house, and wondered how life would change if these storms became common. Within ten years there might not be any fir, alder, or pine trees left in the entire Northwest. It's a disorienting thought, mostly because it's suddenly too easy to imagine it happening. It causes me to join my neighbors in reading up on everything having to do with the upcoming greenhouse effect. Funny, but not one of the projections even mentions that the winds might blow hard enough to blow down enough trees to transmute the lush Northwest into a grassy plain.

I took some time off from work after the second storm, ventured out into the woods with a chain saw to start cleaning up the mess. It took me several months to buck the windfall into fourteen-inch lengths and then split them by hand into a three- or four-year firewood supply.

I observed that the majority of the trees in these parts have a center of gravity tipped toward the southwest, buttressed over time against the prevailing southwestern winds. Because these fierce storms blew from out of the northeast, they attacked the trees where they were weakest.

During the weeks preceding the storm, it rained and rained, causing the soil to loosen up, making it even more difficult for the trees to withstand ninety-mile-an-hour winds no matter what direction they originated. Too bad the temperature was so balmy. A frozen ground would have held the roots far better than a soggy ground. Too bad the northern winds hit the southwestern-balanced trees sitting in wet clay. It mowed them flat in a matter of minutes.

I knew the original forest had been clear-cut back in the mid-1940s. The forest that grew up on its own over the last fifty years was much more thickly spaced than any established forest. Now, with the forest floor partially cleared of debris, I noticed that the distances between the still-standing trees seemed to approximate the spacing of an old-growth forest. Did the winds serve as nature's tool for weeding the forest?

In a dense forest, when one tree falls it often takes its closely spaced neighbors down with it. One result is that the trees that remain are able to spread their roots over a much-extended area and will be better braced against the next wind that comes along. In those few locations where the trees had, for one reason or another, already attained old-growth spacing on their own, fewer trees fell. Staring into the dark jumble of this dramatically altered fifty-year-old forest, I recognized the spacing of a two-hundred-year-old forest. It was evident that the wild winds had done much to ensure the restoration of old growth.

Realizing that ten thousand trees blew down overnight within four miles of home, I no longer have an inkling of what plants might survive here over the next century. All I know is that the weather affects the forest, the forest affects the tent caterpillars, the tent caterpillars affect the orchards, the orchards affect the deer, the deer affect the soil,

and the greenhouse effect's all around, all around,
the greenhouse effect's all around.

The Political Garden

Has it been nearly two years? Has that much time passed since I first walked down the hill to plant a tiny sequoia tree, sat down beside it for an hour to ponder the deeper meaning of the act, and then bolted back up the hill to jot down some ideas about the passage of time that eventually resulted in this book about garden-ing? Despite two years of growing, and two years of writing, the changes in the tree's height and girth would hardly seem any different if no more time had passed than it takes a reader to advance from the earlier chapter on the one-tree garden to this late point in the narrative. What's a few years to a giant sequoia tree? It stands precisely where we all left it so many months (or chapters) ago. I suppose it's utilized the time fortuitously, easing itself into place, roots kept busy exploring the depths even if the boughs haven't started exploring the heights.

The relationship between that little tree and this gardener has altered much over those months. I stopped visiting the one-tree garden a year ago—last June when the trail down to it became nearly impassable with tall grasses, elders, brambles, and seedling alders. Then five months passed, during which I paid my respects to the tree no more than four times. I only started visiting routinely again when the rains came in earnest last October. Although the real reason for my ex-cursion down the hill was turning on the water pump, I always managed at least a brief interlude by the side of the tree. Over time my one-tree garden has transformed itself into a garden of other sentiments as well. It is a secret garden, a seasonal garden, an unexperienced garden, and thus a garden unadmired by human senses.

Something occurred a year ago that would briefly alter the mood of solitude that always accompanies a visit to the one-tree garden. Last spring, my elder daughter brought home a baby sequoia tree as part of a school reforestation program. This one was bare-root, just four inches tall, a veritable infant of a tree no more than a single season out of its seed case. The two of us, father and daughter, potted up the seedling that same afternoon. Then, as things sometimes happen, we both forgot about it.

One day last October, I was clearing up odds and ends in the garden storage and noticed the little stick of a sequoia seedling perched on the far corner of the potting table. Its roots peeked out the bottom of the pot and wandered an inch across the tabletop. Its needle tips had started to turn the bright hue of a grocery store orange. I shook my head in dismay, realized that if the tree was to live, it needed to be planted in the ground immediately. Then and there I made a decision that in less dire circumstances would have seemed inconceivable: to plant it across the pond from the other sequoia. I balked. Could I willingly destroy my shrine of a one-tree garden?

Perhaps I could. The distance between the two trees would be quite substantial. And a body of water lay between them. Both trees were so small that, with the dense alder canopy severely limiting the vision of any garden wanderer, it would take five years or more before a person standing next to one of the trees would even be able to spot the other one in the gloom of the alder bottom. I assured myself that gardens depend on change more than gardeners need stand on ceremony.

I strode down the hill with the potted tree perched on the blade of my shovel. The pond was full, its surface oily and black—a result of the tannin exuded from the leaf drop that occurred a few weeks earlier. I chose an open spot directly across the pond from the one-tree garden, dug a hole in the clay, added some loam from the nearby apple orchard, and dropped the tree inside. I could feel the presence of the other sequoia, although, from this distance, I could not locate it visually amid the tall, beige grasses of autumn. For the next fifty years or more, any visitor to this place would perceive the greater area of the pond encompassing two distinct one-tree gardens. Sometime after that, my own great-grandchildren might start to view the area as a two-tree garden.

I didn't visit the pond at all during the next three months.

One morning in late January I traipse down the hill with the water pump balanced on one shoulder and a can of gasoline hanging from my opposite hand. The creek is running hard. The pond is full and in fact overflowing its spillway. I fill the pump with gasoline, set it on a piece of plywood, first screw in its heavy inflow hose, next attach the more pliable outflow hose, and finally yank on the ignition rope. The noisy two-cycle engine throbs to attention. A minute passes, during which the suction grows strong enough to turn the outflow hose hard as a rock, signifying that the water is pumping two hundred feet all the way around the hill to exit at the much larger goldfish pond we use for summer irrigation.

I leave the pump whining and jump across the creek to search for the new-comer sequoia. It takes me a long moment to locate the tiny sapling in the tall brown grass. When I find it, I am saddened to discover that the tree's needles have turned completely orange. It is obviously dead. I am not surprised; the orange tips had hinted that the tree was dying when I planted it here three months earlier. I pull it out of the ground without ceremony and then examine the soggy roots a moment, hoping to find some some sign of life. Nothing. I snap the dry brittle wood of the matchstick trunk just to be certain and then throw the two pieces over my shoulder like salt spilled at table.

I walk around the pond, noticing along the way that the tall grass has recently been bent back. Either a deer or, less likely, a dog has browsed through here within the past twenty-four hours. Two sets of fresh deer tracks jump out at me from the icy clay of the shoreline. When I walk to the back of the rise, my face drops as I spot two green limbs ripped off the trunk of the sequoia tree. They have been neatly deposited on the flattened grass. Not a bit of it has been consumed. Stooping down to examine the damage more closely, I notice that the deer's an-noying experiment in sequoia palatability has left the main trunk unscathed. The breakage occurred on the branches themselves. Although the deer has certainly bruised the tree, these are not fatal wounds. A gardener with a mind for pruning might have likewise chosen to clip off the same lower branches, if not more neatly.

Far more worrisome, the needles on the four remaining branches are starting to turn orange. Only the main leader remains pure light green, as if offering a glimmer of hope that the tree retains a fragile hold on life. The deer predation occurred much too recently to have caused the discolored needles. It is more likely the result of this tender sapling spending the winter in a ground that has frozen and heaved, then melted and flooded, then frozen and heaved and melted again over these past few weeks. Now it's frozen again. But easing into place seems any tree's version of learning. If this ailing student survives this winter, I imagine it will have learned something quite essential about thriving on this spot and should then be able to handle any future winter.

The whine of the pump irritates me. I walk across the crumbly frozen ground to turn it off and then shuffle back to the disaster scene to take a seat on the same propped-up alder log I deposited here so many months earlier. It was cold last night. Everything is frosted this morning. Despite the bad news of one dead sequoia tree and another sick one, the scene is so tingly beautiful this morning that it causes me to recognize the impenetrable underbrush of summer as a kind of wise old gatekeeper whose job it is to ensure that the special vista of this place remains accessible only when the garden is at its most frosty. I am not upset by the dead tree. Despite my seemingly cavalier planting attitude, the place feels much more becoming as a one-tree garden.

The sequoia's gray-green needles with the ominous orange tips are covered in rime this morning. They reflect the gray winter sky better than anything else in this secret landscape. The bright orange tips make the tree look lit up from inside. I wonder about the wisdom of finding too much luminescent beauty in what is actually a symptom of the tree's sickness.

Peering closer to better examine the glow of the individual needles, I smile, as always, to observe just how little the sequoia's needles resemble those of its California cousin, the coast redwood. I make a mental note to find an ID book and compare the sequoia needles with those of the taxonomically unrelated cypress. I sigh, seriously consider turning on the pump again and leaving the area. Yet I do not move from the log. I stare at the ground awhile, stare at the jaggedness of the ice forming along the pond's edges, stare at the glistening rime starting to melt off the tree. I stare at the black water of the pond, then at the heavy clay-mud sticking to my lug-soled boots. My mind slowly vanishes. When I relocate it, I find myself contemplating a recent piece of community news.

A wealthy neighbor drained a twenty-acre reservoir on his sprawling ranch last fall in preparation for repairing a broken gate valve in the dam. The local planning department duly informed him after the fact that he had their permission to drain the pond and make the repairs to his dam without applying for any special permit. But then, with the reservoir empty, the landowner realized that his reservoir had become clogged with weeds as a result of the bottom silting up to a depth of several feet. He decided to take the next logical step of scraping the pond down to its original blue clay bottom. Heavy machinery was brought in. The rather large hole was well along the process of being deepened when officials of the planning department came to call once again.

This time they informed the man that several parts of his shoreline had silted up enough over the years to be designated as wetlands. Those wetland portions of the ecosystem had also transformed into a seasonal habitat for threatened trumpeter swans. Federal and state regulations demand permits for dredging, for altering wetlands, and for tampering with a swan habitat. The landowner was incensed. He argued that he wasn't *digging* a pond but was simply renovating an existent reservoir he desperately needed to feed his cattle. He accused county officials of meddling in what he considered to be a private matter.

Had that been the extent of the incident, I am quite certain I would have sided with the landowner. I tend to take the long view about such matters. His landscaping scheme is hardly commensurate with anything dire like clear-cutting a forest. The damage, if any at all, is only temporary. The substantial creek that feeds the reservoir will fill it to the brim in just one winter. And no matter how much reclamation the man decides to do, nature is likewise going to start reclaiming his reclamation the moment that dredged-out acreage starts filling back up again with water.

Although the body of water is deeper and wider than before, the landowner had the good sense to leave much of the shoreline shallow as prime trumpeter swan habitat. No doubt the swans will be back within the year. Over time—three years, maybe five—the wetlands spreading out from its shallow banks should grow larger than they were before. The cattails, sedge, and willows that formerly crowded its shoreline will already be well along at reestablishing themselves along the edges. This will make a superb habitat for the buffleheads, wood ducks, mallards, Canada geese, and all the other waterfowl that favor this area at different times of the year. It should take a much longer period of time, twenty or thirty years, before the gate valve starts to display signs of resilting. It may be a hundred and fifty years before the reservoir's transformation into a wetland is complete.

In other words, all the evidence suggests that the landowner's plans were always nature-friendly. Just as the bulldozer work guarantees his own water needs for a long time to come, so it also ensures the long-term vitality of the pond and the wetlands. But I also sympathize with the regulators who demanded the landowner cease and desist. State and federal legislators deserve praise whenever they draft laws to curtail a growing problem of too many wetland-draining desperadoes on bulldozers.

But the bureaucracy sometimes errs by applying blind justice without also weighing intent. In this case, the officials might have done far better to balance the result of the dredging with their own unheeded regulations. When they didn't consider intent, the man got angry. That anger caused the bureaucrats to dig in their heels. It seems just as well that the planning department's investigation of purported foul play inevitably drags on for months and sometimes years. As the issue stood, I empathized with my neighbor's frustration to be left alone to do the right thing. Unfortunately, the issue didn't stand still. Something else arose that soon demoralized the entire neighborhood. It relates directly to a sense of place.

The account of the incident reported in the local newspaper left the impression that the landowner must have turned petulant when openly confronted by the planning department. He later spoke candidly to the news reporter, wishing to remind all his neighbors of certain inalienable rights we all possess as American property owners. If the government wouldn't let him do to his property what he wanted to do, then the hell with the pond. The hell with the land. He would subdivide the square-mile ranch into its hundred or so prezoned five-acre plots. Then he'd sell off the pieces one by one. Such a development would, of course, alter the extended neighborhood for miles around. It would transmute a sizable chunk of forest lands, pastures, and wildlife habitat into a suburb larger than anything ever seen in this island county, necessitating extensive additions to existing county services. Police, health care, schools, and ultimately taxes—all boosted a notch to cope with the influx of so many new homeowners descending on the landscape. Imagine, an entire rural ecosystem leveled because one man got irritated by a government process warranted to protect threatened swan habitat! The swans would never return to the lake. They might flee all the other lakes in the area as well.

It has been two weeks since I read the interview with the landowner in the local newspaper and came away feeling violated by the man's threat to uphold his "rights" by destroying this place I call home. My own house lies about a mile through a forest from the reservoir. It would change things here irrevocably. I am more dismayed over mounting evidence that this expression of property rights seems to be a trend. It is the third case in a year in which a local landowner has responded to the newly stiffened permit process—instituted, by the way, only as a measure to keep track of runaway growth and the destruction of natural habitat—by leveling an open threat, not precisely against the government which easily rolls over resentment, but rather against his own neighbors and against the fragile land itself. Each of these three landowners has asserted the same thing. The new regulations governing the preservation of land are immoral because they violate a principle deemed more inviolate than the Earth itself: the fundamental human right to do to one's own land what one pleases to do. Staring at the sick tree for a long time, I can find no cure for my melancholy and no handle on this bizarre concept of ensuring a right to place by destroying that place.

The tree wishes to inform me not about rights or even melancholy but about something less straightforward although perhaps more fundamental than either. Animals move about while plants grow in place. By this process of moving about, animals alter natural habitat quickly while plants do so far more slowly. We animal movers—whether we fly like a swan, crawl like an aphid, swim like a salmon, bound about like a deer, or walk on two feet like a human—seek our livelihood, the survival of our progeny, our very sustenance off the face of an immovable land.

Perhaps true, although it also seems grossly unfair to lump all the animals together, as if every species' movement purveyed an equal effect. To compare a wild animal's capability to alter habitat to a human being's much-increased capability to do the same lacks all sense of proportion. Aphids, swans, deer, even locusts and gypsy moths—they might as well all be legless and growing in place in comparison with the much greater swath left by the human species moving across the width and breadth of the planet during this late twentieth century.

We human beings are acutely aware of our own predominance. It is the main reason we find so little necessity to strike any balance with the other creatures. In that sense we relate to the Earth as if we are gods. Our own modern system of perceiving land, that which we refer to as *ownership*, mirrors this sentiment by drastically skewing the scale toward the human right to control land while ignoring a sacrosanct view of nature. For instance, the landowner weighed what he regarded to be the quite massive asset of his own property rights against what he also believed to be the subordinate rights of the ecosystem. There was such a discrepancy between the two weights sitting at opposite ends of the scale that it seemed a moot point to even comprehend the issue in terms of balance. The result is one more profane expression of our profane culture. Few landowners possess a sense of place that would let land exert any political or ethical right on its own behalf.

The little sequoia tree prods me to remember something it alluded to long ago concerning time out of balance. While the landowner takes five or ten minutes to issue his threat against the land, so the trees on that same land grow less tall than any human eye will ever be able to perceive. I try it for myself: stare into the half-dead boughs of a disheveled sequoia sapling for several minutes but notice no change. Yet during such a short moment, all the creatures of this place have grown more vulnerable to the whims and desires of fast-moving human culture.

I conclude that, at least from a tree's point of view, many of our own most precious social ideals—liberty and property ownership among them—exert a metabolism disconnected from the land itself. What are our laws and our rights? From a tree's point of view they are nothing but intellectual abstractions formulated to anchor the fast-changing quirks of the human personality. No matter how we choose to govern it, the land remains constant and slow. And yet the land is also far more democratic than any human society. It is governed by a rhythm created by all the species moving and rooting in concord.

Unlike the human mind, land is quite incapable of acting abstractly—even as the human relationship to land seems to become more abstract than ever. Wetland legislation drafted to nurture place possesses an abstract rigidity that does not permit it to bend to the exigencies of real situations. Likewise, a local planning department wanting only to protect land is unable to perceive the signs of a healthy ecosystem through the lens of fixed, abstract strictures that always take precedence over the land itself. On the other side of this abstract ledger, any regulation, good or bad, gets shouted down by people who insist that their abstract right to control land expresses something more profound than the land itself: the cherished sense of independence so promoted by the American dream. And the result? When the independent human mind is asked to cease and desist, to hold back awhile, to root, to be less "free" in simple regard for the much slower rhythms of nature, it reacts by threatening to destroy the cause of that stricture. I stare into the black oily mirror of the winter pond and realize with some irony that Thomas Jefferson, our own prime architect of American liberty, was a fierce champion of developing a sense of place. Ultimately, the inalienable rights he championed too often encourage human rootlessness as if it were an entitlement.

I stare at the tree and apprehend a hard lesson about moving and staying still. How might the affairs of human culture be different if we were as relatively static as a tree? If we were as bound to a specific habitat as a trumpeter swan? Were human beings modulated primarily by the long-term rhythms of the land, how different would be all our lives? And how moot would be any discussion about developing a sense of place. For a swan and a sequoia tree both, a sense of place is built into the genetic code.

The questions I invite, and the answers I imagine, turn me despondent. I have, here, regurgitated a brief tale concerning a reservoir, a land bureaucracy, and a property owner. Furthermore, I have alluded to a pattern in property-rights advocacy spearheaded by wealthy men, each of whom owns several large parcels of land that causes none of the men to actually reside upon those contested parcels year round.

But is it fair to conclude that the holders of vast tracts of land lose contact with the soles of their feet more often than do the rest of us? I have no answer to that, although it doesn't matter anyway. The deeper issue of protecting place is no longer in the hands of a few wealthy individuals who may or may not have forgotten how to plant their feet. The potential for destruction has trickled down to the masses. What was once the power of a few aristocratic individuals to dominate land and global resources has now become—at least in our own culture—the power of the majority to do the same. Too many people have the opportunity to reach for the consumerist lifestyle we call "the good life." The ability to aspire to the good life has become endemic. It may turn out to be our great undoing. The good life seems just another abstract construct, in this case a lifestyle model based on constant economic expansion. This model declares that the health and even the security of our economy is dependent not on a respectful stewardship for this place we call home but on a resource network that grows forever as the result of human consumption of natural resources.

But the emperor has no clothes. Growth is not sustainable because resources are limited. They always will be limited, which, in its own way, causes the dream of the consumerist good life to transmute into an eating disorder. At some recent moment in history—perhaps as recently as the last ten years—the moment finally arrived when the planet could no longer keep pace with human consumption. But the moment was largely imperceptible. The event made no news broadcast because the sea change it bodes barely affects our own lives. It is future generations who must deal with the consequences.

My heavy thoughts abruptly vanish as a lone raven in a tree farther down in the alder grove starts to cluck out a sharp sound like two woodblocks struck together. I listen intently to discover some rhythm to the clicking. There is no discernible pattern to it. I laugh out loud, although I'm not sure why I do so. I soon hear the gusty wingbeats of the raven flying toward me to investigate the source of the raucous laughter. I click my tongue to emulate its woodblock call. The raven spots me, circles once overhead, and then in the aloof manner of its race flies off without answering. Nor does the tree answer my silent rave about human consumption. It wishes to remind me of nothing else besides rooting. But how does rooting equate with notions about human freedom? Can we be free and also be rooted to place? In fact, whether we recognize it or not, even human beings, the consummate moving species, are utterly bound to the natural world. As long as we inhabit the Earth, we can never be free.

My property-rights neighbor obviously disagrees. His threat to the neighborhood asserts, instead, that true freedom includes a freedom from ecology. Nature itself can be sacrificed as easily as anything else when it interferes with *rights*. But if this tactic were even possible, is it freedom? What is this freedom? Is it something more than just a noble idea hatched in the minds of human beings? In fact, this view of freedom seems moot at best and pathological at worst. It insists that human beings live attached to "inalienable rights" that would disattach them from the Earth.

What my neighbor (and others of his ilk) might refer to as ecological indenture, others just as fervently refer to as a cause for some rejoicing. Rooting—acquiring a sense of place—offers a clear path for all who are now seeking directions about living harmoniously with nature. Whether it is the food we eat for breakfast, the wilderness that brings us tranquillity, the manner we dispose of our garbage, or the garden that grants us the gift of creativity, we thrive even as we acknowledge fealty to all that nurtures us.

But who is ready to change their lifestyle? And even if we wanted to, who can show us the best way to do so? Perhaps ironically, most environmental groups don't have much to offer us over the long run. Despite what every environmental brochure in the world tells us about saving this vista or saving that species, such a strategy juggles and reorders the *symptoms* of this deep crisis without producing any lasting change. Change will not occur until we all acknowledge that the only permanent solution is prevention. Prevention resides not externally but within ourselves.

Succeeding at this venture demands much humility on our part. Our striving for the good life causes men and women to feel as if they are gods. There are many among us who still clamor to be late-twentieth-century gods. They are easily intoxicated by their own continued success. They have little desire to relinquish their transient spell over the land's own diminishing resources. To do so means that, ultimately, human beings are not gods. We are as bound and chained to this fair land as is any trumpeter swan.

Who hears that conclusion and still rejoices? In fact, this is a hard medicine to swallow, perhaps as disruptive to our dream of ourselves as the problem itself is disruptive to the planet. Let Thomas Berry declare once again what he stated at the start of this book. It is "not simply the physical loss of resources in an economic sense. It is even more devastating to us inwardly than it is to the planet outwardly."[1] In fact, Berry's prognosis is shared by a growing group of thinkers who agree that the only real solution to the so-called global crisis is a tranformation in human consciousness. We begin by wringing out our consumptive assumptions as if we were wringing water out of a sponge. The deep healing begins when we honor the genuine healing relationship that exists between a person and the place he or she inhabits.

What else can we do to insure that transformation succeeds? Philosopher Terence McKenna proposes that "we adopt the plant as the organizational model for life in the twenty-first century, just as the computer seems to be the dominant mental/social model for the late twentieth century, and the steam engine was the guiding image of the nineteenth century."[2] We, the increasingly rootless species, must learn to root. We, the taking, the utilizing, species, must learn to nurture the ground that sustains us. Root and nurture. This is the sequoia tree's fundamental message. It is, in fact, every plant's message. In that sense, the one-tree garden is a garden espousing a political point of view. I, for one, am converted. I wish to spread the news, which is the reason I have given this fundamental message a name. I call it a sense of place.

Gardening is one rooting regimen with the potential to cure the human neurosis of always peering outward to find satisfaction and to discover challenge. Let us look to the cultivated plants, the roses and the yews; to the weeds, the thistles and the clover; to the wild plants, the mosses and the birches. A closer regard for all these immovable plants enhances our own ability to root. Like the plants themselves, gardeners thrive when they realize that everything on Earth, plant and animal alike, deserves to live in a garden. You and I deserve to live in a garden.

Plants also offer an organic vitality once referred to as *veriditas* by the twelfth-century mystic Hildegard of Bingen. *Veriditas* links us more directly to the Earth goddess Gaia: she who must supervise any relationship between people and place that develops in the coming years. The goddess is referenced here in the sense of the Chinese yin—the nurturing, female aspect of a two-pronged apprehension of the universe, a cosmic principle in balance with the yang, or male principle. It is the female principle yin that invokes nurturing and receptivity. So it is easy to understand why a goddess, Flora (and not a god), oversees gardeners. It is the same reason that Gaia had to be female; the same reason that Earth is generally regarded to be a mother and not a father.

Norman Gras writes in his *History of Agriculture* that throughout history "plant cultivation was primarily a woman's occupation." Archaeologist Joseph Caldwell adds that "most of the earlier agricultural innovations have been made by women." William Strachey observed that within the Indian cultures of the seventeenth-century Virgina colony "the women, as the weaker sort, be put to the easier workes, to sow their corne, to seed and cleanse the same of the orabauke, doder, and choak weed." Jennifer Bennett points out in her book *Lilies of the Hearth* that just as the ancient clay goddess images were stuck into the soil to be worshiped, so women, too, were always rooted, which is precisely the reason the feminine gender is so often compared to plants. It foreshadows the fact that most plants are today given feminine Latin names.[3] The linkage runs deep. Everything we learn inside the garden about nurturing, slowing down, linking up with and respecting all species, is absolutely crucial to the founding of a less violent and aggressive hierarchical society outside the garden.

Because the garden is yin, it also offers a very specific political lesson for men. Many books have been written recently that connect some of the most basic problems of our society with a deeply seated gender bias. For instance, our own society's lack of respect for the Earth, as well as our lack of equality with each other, may be the inevitable result of any society that utilizes competition as its organizing principle. Historian Riane Eisler points out that competition has always been a key trait of societies governed by men. She calls this the *dominator model.*[4]

Quite opposed to the dominator model is another, perhaps more ancient model Eisler refers to as the *partnership model.* This model emphasizes such principles as conciliation, a sacred respect for the Earth, and a minimization of competition which, on its own, results in a marked decrease in warfare. Eisler's two models have been drawn here a bit more black and white than does them credit. No matter; it should still be evident that our own society draws more of its traits from the dominator model than from the partnership model. Our own profane relationship to the Earth offers a striking example of the dominator model in action. The present state of the Earth implies that this model is now failing us.

Obviously, we have much to learn from a model that emphasizes cooperation and promotes a sense of place. The partnership model does so by invoking nurturance as one of its fundamental organizing principles. Nurture one another. Nurture the Earth. But how do we learn to do so? Once again, the value of the garden turns politically constructive. Gardens were the traditional province of women because nurturance lay at the heart of the endeavor. Gardening exists only a few steps below parenting at making nurturance accessible to men, and in a nonthreatening manner as well. Let us all look upon this classroom of the soil as a training ground for teaching men a quality our own culture often fails to teach them: how to nurture.

Syndicated columnist William Raspberry seems to reach much the same conclusion when, writing for the *Washington Post,* he describes the deep schizophrenic trauma confronting our civilization. He argues that many political tenets, whether they represent the Right or the Left, are mostly irrelevent in a world where resources are sorely depleted, ecosystems are crashing, and human population growth is out of control. He makes the radical point that nation-states are themselves antiquated because they mostly serve to protect borders that no longer have much meaning in a global macrosociety. If we are to survive, nations need to be replaced by shifting "the power down to the community level." Raspberry concludes that "the future of the globe—may depend on our willingness to embrace a set of values that rank gardens ahead of gold." But he does not deny the obvious. Such a shift in our value system would signal catastrophic change given the importance of our current "mythology of dreams about achieving wealth."[5]

Ranking gardens ahead of gold does not mean that when enough people start enough gardens the global crisis will be solved. Better to regard it, instead, as a step in the right direction: the kind of activity that enhances our relationship to environment, community, and home. The gardening connection is capable of helping us alter the context of our own perceptions—away from all the externalized studies and debates and toward a direct bonding between individuals and the Earth as the only true source of community and home.

I hang my head, stare at my boots, trace a semicircle where the ground has heaved around the base of the alder log. My little sequoia seems to have taken me to the brink of a rather large political revelation. But it stops me there; now guides me away from my head and brings me back down to the soles of my feet. Even though my worst suspicions about the demise of the dominant culture seem plausible, and even though I sometimes seem to hear future generations pleading with my own generation to reconnect to place, these connections feel askew whenever anyone trumpets them too stridently.

I am no analyst, no pundit, no social planner, no politician. I am in no position to offer up ten-point schemes, five-year plans. I do not sit on blue-ribbon panels. Nor do I write a syndicated column read by people who do. Moreover, I believe that political ideals tend to fall apart like a house of cards when asked to guide the overworked administrators trying to solve real social problems while operating within the constraints of limited budgets. The connections I intuit are just that, intuitive. A sense of place remains a sense, a perception, a feeling.

Nor am I a political iconoclast or a Luddite demanding that society devolve back to the solitude and the wild spaces of Thoreau or John Muir. The places they cherished, the places that lent them their own richness of vision, were much larger and wilder than anything my little garden evokes. Their own expressed dream to live close to nature was more accessible to them than is the dream of any late-twentieth-century man. But the Walden of Thoreau is now a study in parking lots. The Yosemite of Muir caters to millions of vacationers who gain access by passing through a toll booth. To discover the deep connection to nature that these visionaries described in such glorious detail, we need to set off on a more difficult journey—at least perceptually—than Thoreau or Muir could have ever imagined. Our journey takes us into a far more humble ground. The task is clear: we need to be awed not only by the magnificence of Yosemite's half dome, or even by the described wildness of the mid-nineteenth-century Maine woods, but by the place we inhabit. Still, the work started by Thoreau and Muir remains much the same: to regreen a planet that needs regreening.

I am not a master regreener—a master gardener in the manner of Gertrude Jekyll, Roger Swain, or Binda Colebrook. I am a self-proclaimed tree gazer: a one-tree gardener who relates to the great issues of our time from within the spirit of the land I call home. My own broadside to the garden is rather a song to place. My mentor in this endeavor is Walt Whitman. As with Whitman, my foremost credential is a wild heart that is full to overflow with a love of Earth and home. Earth and home define my thinking even as they clarify my center. It is here, staring contentedly into one or another of my many garden beds, feet planted flat on the ground, that I willingly spend the rest of my days.

Two weeks pass before I visit the sequoia tree again. Not much has changed. Same orange tips. I fret that the tree appears even more sickly than last time. Two more weeks pass. This time I am distressed to discover that every branch of the tree except for the central leader has turned that same solid orange color.

I run up the hill and return with a hand pruner. I carefully snip off the dead branches, snip off a few hanging shards of bark, and then stand back to take a look. The ambience of the tree is totally altered. What had previously looked like a full and bushy sapling as wide as it was tall now looks like a three-foot-tall bark-covered stick with only the slightest semblance of green sprouting from the tallest tip.

Another month passes. The tip of the leader turns a lighter green. It seems to have grown a half inch—as if the tree itself is finally making a tentative exploration of the world around it. To be honest about it, I am not certain if this observation is actually true, or if I just want it to be true.

Another month passes. Early May. There has not been another peep in the local papers about my neighbor's threat to subdivide his land. Driving past it every day, I notice that the reservoir itself is full to the brim. It looks better than ever. And full of water birds. I conclude that the landowner's warning to his neighbors was actually an idle threat, shouted out to the world in an act of sheer exasperation. The land is off the hook until next time.

It has been an exceedingly wet and cold spring. Resorting to tall rubber boots to keep my legs dry, I poke my way down the hill through a veritable fairyland of fir and alder seedlings, then through some tall purply grass and taller ferns, pulling aside the branches of ocean spray and elder that droop full over the trail with the weight of each morning's dew. The clover around the pond is six inches tall. Elderberries have seeded themselves along the outer edges of the dam and are already a foot tall. They look inconsequential next to a grove of self-seeded foxgloves that have sprouted from the crater left by the torn-up roots of a storm-toppled fir. Foxgloves are as luxuriant as a jungle plant with their huge, veiny leaves and stalks topping out at nearly four feet tall. How could all that growth start from a seed barely visible to the human eye? I estimate that the foxglove's pink-and-cream flower spikes will bloom in three more weeks. Sword ferns have started popping up everywhere on the hard clay banks of the pond. Amanita mushrooms with warty white caps peek through the clover. Within another few weeks this place will be so overgrown as to be inaccessible without a machine.

Pulling apart some four-foot-tall ferns, and then stooping down where I expect the tree to be, I am elated to notice that its central leader has grown a full four inches since the last visit. Surrounding the leader is a halo of several new sprouting branches spreading out symmetrically from the center.

The tree lives.

I sit down on the wet grass and grin from ear to ear. No thoughts. Nothing at all comes to mind. Moments pass. I jump to my feet, touch my toes, kick my heels, and quickly run up the hill to share the good news with the world.

Acknowledgments

My debt includes all the gardeners who ever showed me how to do it. It includes all the garden writers whose books consistently set a high standard for accuracy and passion. It was they who assured me that neither gardens nor plants always act as any expert predicts. My debt is deeper still to the nature writers whose insights and images constantly inspire me to better hone my own literary clarity.

Several locals assisted me. I thank former San Juan County Agent Lee Campbell for answering many specific questions about the various interactions that occur between plants and this place we both call home. I thank the ever-helpful women of the local library for locating so many of the books noted in this text; and Sandra Wilson, whose own wonderful library of gardening books set many of my ideas to bubbling. I thank the Reverend Paul Hayden for explaining the difference between the Christian and Jewish Sabbaths; and Hart's Nursery in Mount Vernon, Washington, for providing so many of the rare and unusual plants I seek out, including the little sequoia tree that plays such a large part in this book. I thank Marian Richey for her incorrigible enthusiasm about my changing garden. And Rich Osborn for bringing the writings of Gregory Bateson and D'Arcy Thompson to my attention. I thank Amity Gardens and Island Green for providing so many of the perennials that adorn my garden. Thanks go to Rick King at the local gravel pit for supplying my garden with rocks, and to False Bay Farm for providing my garden with a bottomless supply of composted manure.

I thank people farther afield: authors Paul Hawken and Thomas Moore, for reading and commenting on an earlier draft of this manuscript, and Forest Shomer, who also read an earlier draft and wrote so many sharp comments in the margins that helped clarify several of my most high-flying ideas. I thank editor Ginny Merdes of the *Seattle Sunday Times Pacific Magazine* for encouraging me to write several short garden columns. These include the essays on slugs, nurseries, and rose fragrance, as well as the kernel of the chapter "The Semi-Real Garden."

I thank the man who sent in a fierce letter to *Pacific* commenting that my essay on nurseries got his vote as the rudest garden piece ever to see the light of day. I was genuinely surprised that any garden writing could elicit such a heated response. I thank the professional nursery people who came to my defense—commenting that the nursery essay was certainly incisive but that it was also correct. That dispute made me understand for the first time that I was not writing just another gardening book.

I acknowledge with deep gratitude Alan Slifka, Brad Stanback, and Elizabeth Jones, for generously providing the support that permits my work to change, grow, and flourish. I thank my literary agent, Felicia Eth, for knowing how the professional book world functions when I still don't have much of a clue.

I acknowledge my wife, Katy, and my daughters, Claire and Sasha, each of whom adds her own unique eye and hand to a garden we all love so much.

$\mathcal{N}otes$

Introduction: The Local Garden

1. Jim Nollman, *Spiritual Ecology* (New York: Bantam, 1990), p. 4.
2. An interview with Thomas Berry by Bernard Cunningham and Jo Roberts, in *Macrocosm USA*, ed. Sandi Brockway (Cambria, Calif.: Macrocosm USA, 1991), p. 172.
3. Jack Turner, "In Wildness is the Preservation of the World," *Northern Lights*, vol. 7, no. 4 (Fall 1991), p. 8.
4. Michael Pollan, *Second Nature* (New York: Atlantic Monthly Press, 1991).
5. Peter Berg, *The Planet Drum Review*, no. 18/19 (1992), p. 6.
6. Kirkpatrick Sale, from a brochure included in the Patagonia catalog entitled *Economy and Environment*, Fall/Winter 1992, p. 72.
7. Hugh Johnson, *The Principles of Gardening* (New York: Fireside/Simon & Schuster, 1979). This may be my own all-time favorite gardening book. Johnson puts it this way: "The essence is control. Without constant watchful care a garden—any garden—rapidly returns to the state of the country all around it" (p. 8).
8. Terry Tempest Williams, *Refuge* (New York: Pantheon, 1991), p. 49.

January: The One-Tree Garden

1. Forest Shomer, personal note to the author.
2. Percy Bysshe Shelley, quoted in *Introduction to Literature*, ed. Lynn Altenbernd and Leslie L. Lewis (New York: Macmillan, 1963), p. 283.

3. Steve Wall and Harvey Arden, *Wisdomkeepers* (Portland, Oreg.: Beyond Words Publishing, 1990), p. 68.

February: The Nowhere Garden

1. Ian Todd and Michael Wheeler, *Utopia* (London: Orbis Publishing, 1978), p. 7.
2. Ibid.
3. Theodore Roszak, *The Cult of Information* (New York: Pantheon, 1986), p. 146.
4. Jerry Mander, *In the Absence of the Sacred* (San Francisco: Sierra Club Books, 1991), p. 62.
5. Witold Rybczynski, *Home* (New York: Penguin, 1987).
6. William Morris, quoted in Todd and Wheeler, p. 112.
7. Stanley Crawford, *The Garlic Testament* (New York: HarperCollins, 1992), p. 57.
8. Nancy Paddock et al., *Soil and Survival* (San Francisco: Sierra Club Books, 1986), p. 93.
9. Genesis 3 (King James Version).
10. Joe Hollis, "Paradise Gardening," *Katuah Journal* (Spring 1992), p. 3.
11. Ibid.
12. Ibid.

March: The Soil Garden

1. Nancy Paddock et al., *Soil and Survival* (San Francisco: Sierra Club Books, 1986), p. 6.
2. Ibid., p. 35.
3. Dan Jason, *Greening the Garden* (Philadelphia: New Society Publishers, 1991), p. 2.
4. William Bryant Logan, "Hans Jenny at the Pygmy Forest," *Orion* (Spring 1992), p. 18.
5. Ibid.
6. Reported in *Clearinghouse Bulletin of the Carrying Capacity Network*, October 1992, Washington, D.C.
7. Quoted in Christopher Bird and Peter Tompkins, *Secrets of the Soil* (New York: Harper and Row, 1989), p. 2.
8. John Lust, *The Herb Book* (New York: Bantam, 1983), p. 105.

April: The Sentient Garden

1. Peter Tompkins and Christopher Bird, *The Secret Life of Plants* (New York: Harper and Row, 1973).
2. Leo Lionni, *Parallel Botany* (New York: Knopf, 1977) p. 11.
3. Michael J. Cohen, "Is the Earth a Living Organism?" National Audubon Society Expeditions, Sharon, Conn., 1985, p. 1-1.

4. Keith Thomas, *Man and the Natural World* (New York: Pantheon, 1983), p. 20.
5. David Suzuki, from an interview with Michael Toms, *New Dimensions Journal* (April-June 1993), p. 3.
6. Hugh Johnson, *The Principles of Gardening* (New York: Fireside/Simon & Schuster, 1979), p. 8.
7. Lewis Hyde, "The Gift Must Always Move," *CoEvolution Quarterly* (Fall 1982), p. 15.
8. Jim Nollman, "In Search of Beluga," *NewAge Journal* (June 1992), p. 71.
9. Ken Wilber, *Grace and Grit* (Boston: Shambhala Press, 1991), p. 109.
10. W. H. Hudson, Far Away and Long Ago (Everyman's Library, 1918), quoted in Thomas, p. 192.

May: The How-To Garden

1. Leo Lionni, *Parallel Botany* (New York: Knopf, 1977), p. 52.
2. Michael Pollan, *Second Nature* (New York: Atlantic Monthly Press, 1991), p. 52.
3. Anthony Paul and Yvonne Rees, *Designing with Trees* (Topsfield, Mass: Salem House, 1989), p. 82.
4. Forest Shomer, personal note to the author.

June: The Semi-Real Garden

1. Graham Stuart Thomas, *The Art of Gardening with Roses* (New York: Henry Holt, 1991), p. 141.
2. Peter Beales, *Classic Roses* (New York: Henry Holt, 1985), p. 199.
3. Jon Singer, *Heirloom of Old Garden Roses* catalog, St. Paul, Oreg., 1992–93.
4. Terence McKenna, *The Archaic Revival* (San Francisco: HarperCollins, 1991).
5. Richard Goldschmidt, quoted in Rupert Sheldrake, *The Presence of the Past* (New York: Vintage, 1989), p. 275.
6. Allen Lacy, *Home Ground* (New York: Farrar, Straus and Giroux, 1984), p. 57.
7. Vita Sackville-West, *The Illustrated Garden Book: A New Anthology by Robin Lane Fox* (New York: Atheneum, 1986), p. 19.
8. Katherine S. White, *Onward and Upward in the Garden?* (New York: Farrar, Straus and Giroux, 1981), p. 71.
9. David E. Clark, ed., The Sunset New Western Garden Book (Menlo Park, Calif.: Lane, 1984).
10. Stephen Lacey, *The Startling Jungle* (Boston: David R. Godine, 1990), p. 136.
11. Beth Chatto, *Plant Portraits* (Boston: David R. Godine, 1986), p. 66.
12. Forest Shomer, personal note to the author.

July: The Remedy Garden

1. David Hoffmann, *The Holistic Herbal* (Longmead, Eng.: Element Books, 1986), p. 16.
2. James Lovelock, *Gaia, a New Look at Life on Earth* (Oxford: Oxford University Press, 1982), p. 9.
3. Edward S. Ayensu et al., *Our Green and Living World* (Washington, D.C.: Smithsonian Books, 1984), p. 30.
4. Ibid.
5. Claire Kowalchik and William Hylton, eds., *Rodale's Illustrated Encyclopedia of Herbs* (Emmaus, Pa.: Rodale Press, 1987), p. 62.
6. John Lust, *The Herb Book* (New York: Bantam, 1982), p. 143.
7. Kowalchik and Hylton, p. 295.
8. Ibid.
9. Henry Beston, *Herbs and the Earth* (New York: Doubleday, 1935), p. 21.
10. Kowalchik and Hylton, p. 336.
11. These two ideas were suggested by herbal historian Kathleen Harrison McKenna.
12. Kathleen Harrison McKenna, personal communication to the author.
13. J. G. Frazer, *The Golden Bough* (London: St. Martin's Library, 1963), p. 81.
14. Kowalchik and Hylton, p. 438.
15. Ayensu et al., p. 184.
16. Ibid., p. 185.
17. Kowalchik and Hylton, p. iv.
18. Lust, p. 210.
19. Ibid.
20. Kowalchik and Hylton, p. 438.

August: The Predator's Garden

1. Laura C. Martin, *Garden Flower Folklore* (Chester, Conn.: Globe Pequot Press, 1987), p. 24.
2. Binda Colebrook, *Winter Gardening* (Everson, Wash.: Maritime Pub., 1984), p. 96.
3. Jerry Klieger, "In Celebration of Worms," in *The Whole Earth Catalog* (Sausalito, Calif.: Point Foundation, 1970), p. 79.
4. Tom Parker, *In One Day* (Boston: Houghton Mifflin, 1984), p. 12.
5. John Robbins, *Diet for a New America* (Felton, Calif.: Earthsave Foundation, 1989), p. 190.
6. Ibid.
7. Wendell Berry, "The Reactor and the Garden," *The Cultivator*, vol. 14, no. 3.
8. Joan Halifax, *Shaman the Wounded Healer* (New York: Crossroads Publishing, 1982), p. 82.

September: The Sacred Garden

1. Witold Rybczynski, *Waiting for the Weekend* (New York: Viking, 1991), p. 71.
2. Ibid.
3. James Swan, *Sacred Places* (Santa Fe: Bear and Company, 1990), p. 127.
4. "The Hau de no sau nee Address to the Western World," quoted in Jerry Mander, *In the Absence of the Sacred* (San Francisco: Sierra Club Books, 1991), p. 42.
5. Swan, p. 100.
6. "The Hau de no sau nee Address to the Western World," p. 42.
7. Winona LaDuke, Patagonia catalog, Fall/Winter 1992, p. 73.
8. Ibid.
9. From a speech by Jeannette Armstrong delivered at Elmwood Institute in Berkeley, California, quoted from the Summer 1992 catalog of courses for Omega Institute, Rhinebeck, New York.
10. Dolores LaChapelle, personal correspondence to the author.
11. Paul Devereux, *Earthmind* (New York: Harper and Row, 1992), p. 21.
12. Ibid., p. 192.
13. Michael Pollan, *Second Nature* (New York: Atlantic Monthly Press, 1991), p. 57.
14. Thomas Christopher, *In Search of Lost Roses* (New York: Summit Books, 1989), p. 109.
15. Keith Thomas, *Man and the Natural World* (New York: Pantheon, 1983), p. 238.
16. Swan, p. 50.
17. Dorothy Maclean, *To Honor the Earth* (San Francisco: Harper, 1991), p. 76.
18. Rabbi David E. Stein, *A Garden of Choice Fruits* (Wyncote, Pa.: Shomrei Adamah, 1991), p. 55.
19. All three quotes from ibid.
20. Lao Tzu, *Tao Te Ching*, trans. D. C. Lau (New York: Penguin, 1963), p. 59.

October: The Weed Garden

1. Claire Shaver Haughton, *Green Immigrants* (New York: Harcourt Brace Jovanovich, 1978), p. 176.
2. Alfred W. Crosby, *Ecological Imperialism: The Biological Expansion of Europe, 900–1900* (New York: Cambridge University Press, 1986), p. 162.
3. Ibid.
4. Susan J. Wernert, ed., *The Reader's Digest Book of North American Wildlife* (Pleasantville, N.Y.: Reader's Digest, 1982), p. 463.
5. Roger Banks, *Living in a Wild Garden* (New York: St. Martin's Press, 1980), p. 62.

6. Crosby, p. 168.
7. William R. Jordan III, "Restoration and Reentry in Nature," in *Finding Home*, ed. Peter Sauer (Boston: Beacon Press, 1992), p. 106.
8. Ibid., p. 107.
9. From a speech by Jeannette Armstrong delivered at Elmwood Institute in Berkeley, California, quoted from the Summer 1992 catalog of courses for Omega Institute, Rhinebeck, New York.
10. Crosby, p. 168.
11. Nancy Paddock et al., *Soil and Survival* (San Francisco: Sierra Club Books, 1986), p. 40.
12. Hugh Johnson, *The Principles of Gardening* (New York: Fireside/Simon & Schuster, 1979), p. 30.

November: The Creative Garden

1. Leo Lionni, *Parallel Botany* (New York: Knopf, 1977), p. 103.
2. Robert Dash, quoted in *The American Man's Garden,* ed. Rosemary Verey (Boston: Bulfinch Press, 1990), p. 137.
3. Gabrielle van Zuylen, *The Gardens of Russell Page* (New York: Stewart, Tabori, and Chang, 1991), p. 101.
4. Harlan Hand, quoted in Verey, p. 132.
5. Marshall Olbrich, quoted in ibid., p. 50.
6. Jory Johnson and Douglas Johnston, "Nature Reconstructed: Ecological Design and Public Understanding," *Orion* (Winter 1993), p. 19.
7. Ibid., p. 24.
8. Ibid.
9. Betty Edwards, *Drawing on the Right Side of the Brain* (Los Angeles: Tarcher, 1979), p. 3.
10. Quote from David Mabry-Lewis, the narrator and primary writer of the TV series "Millennium," which discusses the culture and arts of both the Wodaabe and Navajo.
11. Dash, quoted in Verey, p. 137.
12. Gregory Bateson, *Mind and Nature* (New York: Dutton, 1979), p. 28.
13. Ibid.
14. Rupert Sheldrake, *The Presence of the Past* (New York: Vintage, 1989), p. 272.

December: The Political Garden

1. An interview with Thomas Berry by Bernard Cunningham and Jo Roberts, in *Macrocosm USA*, ed. Sandi Brockway (Cambria, Calif.: Macrocosm USA, 1992), p. 172.

2. Terence McKenna, *The Archaic Revival* (San Francisco: Harper, 1991), p. 218.
3. All quotes here are from Jennifer Bennett, *Lilies of the Hearth* (Camden, Ont.: Camden House, 1991), p. 28.
4. Riane Eisler, *The Chalice and the Blade* (San Francisco: Harper, 1987), p. 45.
5. William Raspberry, quoted in the *Seattle Times*, November 27, 1992.

Index